NEURODEVELOPMENTAL DIFFERENTIATION

OPTIMIZING BRAIN SYSTEMS TO MAXIMIZE LEARNING

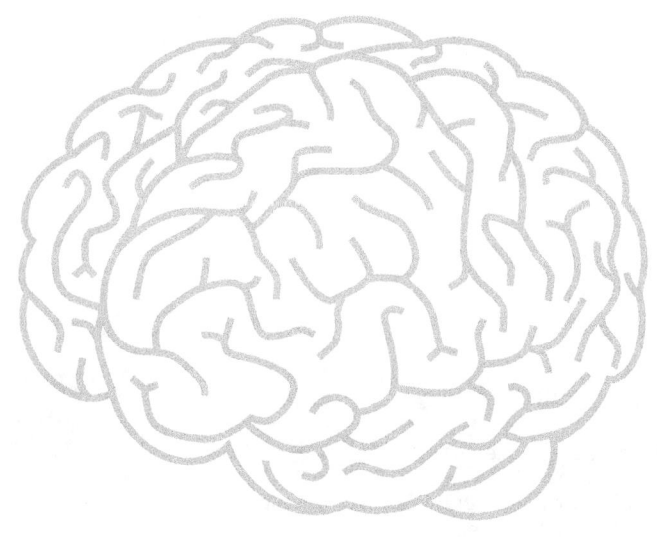

ANDREW FULLER & LUCY FULLER

© Andrew Fuller and Lucy Fuller 2024

First published in 2020 by Hawker Brownlow Education
Published in 2021 by Solution Tree
This edition was published in 2024 by Amba Press

All rights reserved. No part of this book may be reproduced or transmitted in any form or by any means, electronic or mechanical, including photocopying, recording or by any information storage and retrieval system, without prior permission in writing from the publisher.

Published by Amba Press
Melbourne, Australia
www.ambapress.com.au

ISBN: 9781923116696 (pbk)
ISBN: 9781923116702 (ebk)

A catalogue record for this book is available from the National Library of Australia.

ACKNOWLEDGMENTS

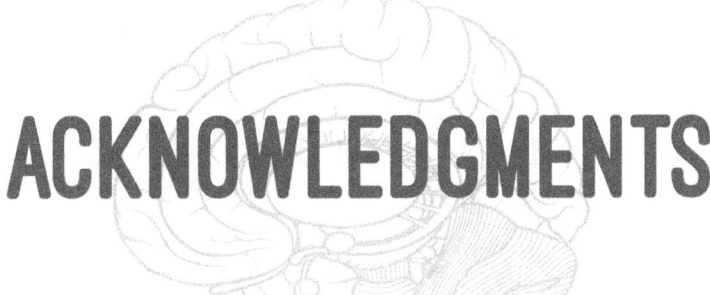

We would like to offer great thanks to Dianne Beardall, Sue Bell, Rebecca Cody, Daniel Cohen, Hazel Day, Lorraine Day, Anne Doody, Rod Dungan, Vicki Forbes, Vicki Hartley, Faye Hauwai, John Levin, Charles Lovitt, Dorne Lonergan, Georgie Nutton, Yanying Lu, Christine Payard, Meredith Shears, David Tyson, Charuni Weerasooriya, and the Victorian Association of State Secondary Principals.

We would also like to acknowledge the generous, good-spirited sharing of ideas that we have experienced from more teachers than we can name or count—thank you to you all.

TABLE OF CONTENTS

About the Authors vii

Foreword ix

Introduction. 1

Chapter 1 Spatial Reasoning 21

Chapter 2 Perceptual and Motor Skills 39

Chapter 3 Concentration and Memory 63

Chapter 4 Planning and Sequencing 91

Chapter 5 Thinking and Logic 109

Chapter 6 People Smarts 127

Chapter 7 Language and Word Smarts. 149

Chapter 8 Number Smarts .171

Chapter 9 Implementing Neurodevelopmental Differentiation 195

References and Resources. 205

Index 217

ABOUT THE AUTHORS

Andrew Fuller is a clinical psychologist who specializes in neuroscience, learning, and resilience. He works with schools around the globe to help increase the well-being and success of young people. Andrew's early career began in psychiatric crisis teams, where he often worked with people who were contemplating suicide. This led him to discover his passion for working with people to help them create futures they can fall in love with. Andrew is the author of many books, including *Unlocking Your Child's Genius: How to Discover and Encourage Your Child's Natural Talents* (2015), *Tricky Kids: Transforming Conflict and Freeing Their Potential* (2013a), *Tricky Teens: How to Create a Great Relationship With Your Teen . . . Without Going Crazy!* (2014), *Tricky People: How to Deal With Horrible Types Before They Ruin Your Life* (2013b), *The Revolutionary Art of Changing Your Heart: The Essential Guide to Recharging Your Relationship* (2019a), *Your Best Life at Any Age: How to Acknowledge Your Past, Revive Your Present, and Realise Your Future* (2019b), and *Feelings: How to Stay Sane in a Crazy World* (in press).

Lucy Fuller is a passionate educator who practices the Montessori framework. Her work integrates this framework with her ongoing development of every student's learning strengths and success.

FOREWORD

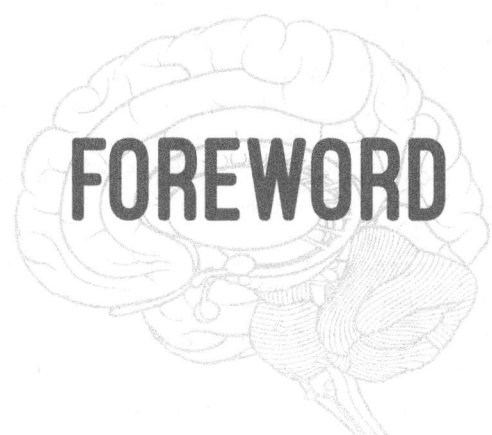

At first meeting, you would be forgiven for assuming Andrew Fuller is more qualified to speak about surfing than psychology. His sunburst locks and casual wardrobe may initially mislead a crowd of people who are poised to have their problems solved through a keynote or two. There is something quite disarming about his rascal-like appearance—accentuated by a mischievous grin—and his contagious laughter. But all these outer indicators speak to how grounded Andrew is, as well as his distaste for anything pretentious and his deep commitment to joy.

I first encountered Andrew's expertise in 2005 in New Zealand, when I watched him address more than two hundred educators with clarity and levity in equal measure. While lines forming at the end of sessions are not unique, I watched how many people wanted to step forward and enjoy a more intimate dialogue with Andrew. The attraction was possibly as much about his manner as about his knowledge. Approachable, articulate, and witty, Andrew is authentic and very engaging, so much so that it has a mirroring effect.

My first opportunity to actively share with Andrew was as an educator. Based on his performance in New Zealand, I started booking him to engage with students, parents, and teachers at my school. With groups of multiage students, he would ride the waves of energy and emotion like a master teacher. I would watch students absorb and note down his strategies with an intensity usually only reserved for those they felt were *on their side.*

Not long after Andrew's relationship with our school was established, I found myself recommending his books to parents and referencing them at various times myself. Again, the accessibility of his writing was reassuring. As our friendship emerged across the years, I was struck by how readily I would offer Andrew my latest parenting indiscretions, but it was no surprise to him that as a parent I am deeply flawed yet purposeful.

NEURODEVELOPMENTAL DIFFERENTIATION

As I have often mentioned to Andrew, dinnertime rants articulating my top-three responsibilities as a parent are always accompanied by an extravaganza of eye rolls from my children and husband. But the intention in outlining my parenting duties is to manage expectations transparently, usually as protesting erupts about us not being "like every other family" and me being described as "the worst mother ever"! In case you're wondering, my eminently judicious list of priorities as a parent is (1) to keep my children safe, (2) to educate them brilliantly, and (3) to embarrass them wildly.

As an educator, it is my optimism and aspiration that initiated my partnership with Andrew. Again, assembly rants articulating my top three responsibilities as an educator are often met with applause from students. In case you are curious, my self-declared, equally sensible list of priorities as a principal is (1) to keep students safe, (2) to optimize learning conditions for them to thrive, and (3) to enable the growth of their virtues and wisdom.

Underpinning both of these lists is a commitment to making my belief in others visible. Our children and adolescents need to know that we, the adults in their world, have a wholehearted belief that they are uniquely capable individuals, especially in their formative years. Across twenty-five years working with learners and their families, I have also formed enduring understandings about the identification and optimization of learning strengths as a pathway to motivating positive attitudes and expanding skills and virtues. And it is in this space that Andrew's insights and my own experiences as a parent and educator seamlessly align. Learning can absolutely be improved through a strengths-based approach that connects learners to new ways of being and to new discoveries.

If you are seeking a hopeful companion on the quest to championing young people and their potential, *Neurodevelopmental Differentiation* is an uplifting choice. Utilizing both scientific and educational research, this resource's advantage is that it outlines the *what* and the *how* of implementing brain-based differentiation, culminating in student-led individualized learning plans. Schools, parents, and students can utilize the associated learning-strengths analysis to map plans for each semester, prioritizing what strengths to build on and what next to boost. This is a resource to support open conversations and forethought; it is a reminder, too, that while the complexity of students and their brains can be daunting, it is also fathomable.

As a parent and educator, I value neurodevelopmental differentiation as a proactive, research-informed approach that is learner centered and pragmatic.

Yours in unearthing strengths,

Rebecca Cody
Principal
Geelong Grammar School
Toorak, Victoria, Australia

INTRODUCTION

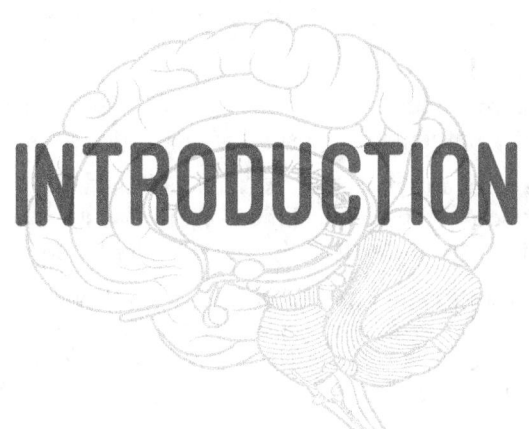

Imagine a school where the motto is "Here, everyone gets smart." Not just some students. Every student.

Imagine a school where all students know their learning strengths and how to use them to develop other areas of learning.

Imagine a school where all teachers know their own learning strengths, as well as how to utilize their students' learning strengths to differentiate learning in their classes.

Imagine a school where teachers, psychologists, and support staff share a common understanding of how to identify and develop collaborative approaches to overcome blockages to learning.

Imagine a school where parent-teacher-student meetings focus on forward planning to identify learning strengths and develop strategies that use this knowledge to prioritize and develop a learning area over the following semester.

This book aims to create these schools through the power of neurodevelopmental differentiation. In this book, we use neurodevelopmental differentiation to assess and build students' inherent strengths in eight major information-processing circuits in the human brain to increase their outcomes.

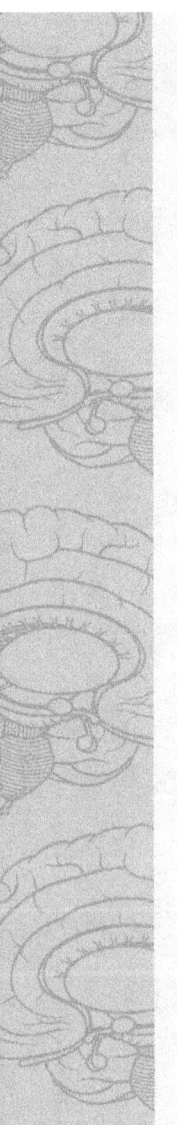

The Eight Information-Processing Circuits of the Human Brain

1. **Spatial reasoning:** Thinking in pictures enhances our capacities in science, mathematics, design, engineering, art, and construction.
2. **Perceptual and motor skills:** We learn as much with our bodies as with our brains. Muscle memory, motor skills, and physical coordination relate strongly to our ability to learn.
3. **Concentration and memory:** To learn well, we need to focus to take ideas in, and then process and link those ideas to other aspects of our knowledge in order to retrieve and communicate them.
4. **Planning and sequencing:** All the knowledge in the world will count for little if we can't make plans of action and order the steps needed to implement them into workable sequences.
5. **Thinking and logic:** In a complex world, weighing the pros and cons of issues, questioning and evaluating the validity of information and ideas, and developing and testing hypotheses are vital life skills.
6. **People smarts:** You could possess learning strengths in all these other areas, but if you lack the ability to understand both yourself and other people, your attempts to become successful could be thwarted.
7. **Language and word smarts:** In a world brimming with words and opinions, distilling the main ideas and knowing how to communicate your own ideas succinctly and articulately are major life advantages.
8. **Number smarts:** Too often, traditional schools limit thinking about numbers to mathematics classrooms, even though everyday life and all careers require numeracy to succeed.

Every teacher has some students who struggle in some of the preceding areas and others who have great learning strengths in one or two but can't broaden their successes to other areas. Every teacher also has some students who, while incredibly adept at one of the preceding areas, remain unfairly self-disparaging about their capacities in other learning areas and avoid them, sabotaging their own success.

When we encounter these students each year, we remind ourselves—as all good teachers do—that every student progresses at a different rate, has different strengths, and comes to school with a wide range of life experiences and strengths. So we try different approaches.

Introduction

We revise the work with the student individually; we teach concepts in three other ways; we adjust the requirements of the task; we develop rubrics to try to cater to interests; we make links with other learning; we use relevant digital tools; and we create visual reminders and stick them to desks, to the walls, and sometimes to the students themselves.

In the afternoons, we stare at the inspirational quotes adorning our desks, which remind us that no two flowers bloom in exactly the same way, and struggle with the fact that something is just not working for these students, but we do not know what it is or how to help. At these times, it is important to remember that when a flower doesn't bloom, we must look to fixing the environment in which it grows before fixing the flower.

Education is about the development of individual minds. Effective teachers help each of their students to achieve his or her potential. For those schools already using character strengths (Peterson & Seligman, 2004), learning strengths and neurodevelopmental differentiation bring this type of thinking directly into classrooms to enhance learning (see figure I.1).

1. Assess students' learning strengths using the reports at the website My Learning Strengths (www.mylearningstrengths.com).

2. Plan with students and parents how to build on existing learning strengths.

3. Use cross-fertilization tables (in each chapter of this book) to build and broaden strengths.

4. Access the full report on learning strengths that includes strengths, areas to develop, and potential career paths available (www.mylearningstrengths.com).

5. Regularly refer to students' learning strengths to build engagement in learning.

6. Provide coaching and feedback as learning strengths develop.

7. Reassess students' learning strengths each semester.

Figure I.1: How to use learning strengths to build success.

What Learning Strengths Are *Not*

Before we begin to examine how to implement neurodevelopmental differentiation in the classroom, we must be clear from the outset about what learning strengths and neurodevelopmental differentiation are *not*.

We do not claim learning strengths are a form of intelligence. This is not a replication of Howard Gardner's (2011) work on multiple intelligences, and learning strengths are not fixed styles of learning as proposed in the learning style theory of auditory, visual, and kinesthetic learners (Fleming & Bonwell, 2019).

Learning strengths are not end points used to categorize people or fit them into fixed or set typologies. They are starting points to engage students and parents in planning how to use and leverage these strengths to improve other areas of learning. Neurodevelopmental differentiation is not about boxing students in but about opening up possibilities and cross-fertilizing strengths into other areas.

The purpose of identifying learning strengths is not to help people find their learning strengths and then limit them to those areas. It is intended to help students, parents, and teachers know which of the eight information circuits it is easiest to begin from to build success in other learning areas.

Learning Strengths and How Brains Process Information

Since 2016, research on neuroscience has created an explosion of new awareness about how brains input, process, and output knowledge (Barrett, 2017; Buzsáki, 2019; Collins, 2019; Howard-Jones et al., 2018; Sapolsky, 2017a; Sterling & Laughlin, 2015; Thompson et al., 2019). This research has the capacity to make learning more successful and enjoyable for students and to help parents and teachers make more positive impacts.

This new area of research originated when the focus on the location of specific brain functions shifted to how the brain becomes aware of itself, or consciousness (Dehaene, 2014), and how it develops pathways or circuits to process information through myelination (Yeo et al., 2011).

Myelination involves white brain matter forming a sheath over pathways in the brain. This process makes some of the axons, the brain's connective transmission lines, function faster and communicate more quickly than others. These myelinated tracts form functional networks that occupy up to 40 percent of brain volume and increase the speed of information transmission (Dehaene, 2014; Sterling & Laughlin, 2015). While this process takes place throughout life, it occurs rapidly in the frontal lobes during late childhood and the early teenage years. Learning usually arises from relationships between these networks, rather than from activity in isolated areas of the brain (Buzsáki, 2019).

The body and the brain form an interconnected information system. Research on emotions and the brain shows us how physiological responses directly affect our thinking and feeling (Barrett, 2017). We know that 80 percent of the fibers of the vagus nerve (derived from the Greek and Latin words for wanderer, or traveler) transmit information from the body to the brain. The vagus nerve connects the brain stem with major organs, including the heart, lungs, and stomach and intestines (Porges, 2017; Sapolsky, 2004). In fact, the vast bulk of our neurochemicals are created, and most of our serotonin is stored, in our stomachs (Doidge, 2007). In terms of learning and functioning, the body and the brain are intrinsically linked (Collins, 2019).

Practice changes us. When we engage in specific learning tasks over an extended period, it physically changes our brains and makes a difference to our performance (Gogtay et al., 2004; Just & Varma, 2007; Keller & Just, 2009). We can see this most vividly in studies of the brains of taxi drivers and piano tuners (Colvin, 2018), but it is likely this is true of us all. We are all neurodiverse because our brains are unique. This is best demonstrated by the Enhancing Neuro Imaging Genetics Through Meta-Analysis (ENIGMA) Consortium findings based on scans provided from 1,400 scientists from forty-three countries (as cited in Thompson et al., 2019).

We Are Getting Smarter

There is clear evidence that not only are people getting smarter but also the increase is occurring exponentially. Research by psychologist James R. Flynn (2012) shows intelligence scores since 1960 have lifted dramatically at about three IQ points every decade.

This increase in potential is well researched and profound. And while it has implications for the world as well as for students personally, the problem is many of the teachers we work with see no evidence of this increased human potential in their classrooms.

Consider for a moment how this increase in potential is achieved. Our brains are enclosed in skulls that can't get any bigger. If we look at human skulls from long ago, we will notice they are about the same size as our own today. So the increase in capacity has had to occur without an increase in size. There is no evidence that brains have altered structurally in thousands of years (Eccles, 1989)—if anything, they have reduced in size (Hawks, 2013).

Brain density also changes as we develop and mature (Giedd, 2015; Thompson et al., 2019), with synaptic density peaking by six to seven years of age for most brain regions before thinning slightly. The brain thins as we become more specialized in processing information.

So how do you increase the power of the brain without increasing its size? The answer is in how the brain processes information. This is how you develop ideas, thoughts, and memories, as well as how the brain communicates with and within itself.

The brain has different ways to process information. The first is the three hundred trillion connections in the brain. Basically, the wiring in your brain consists of brain cells (neurons), axons and dendrites (connectors), and synapses (the gaps that allow information to be transferred). The amount of wiring in your brain changes through neuroplasticity. While the macrostructures of the brain are predetermined, the wiring of the brain is more a product of your life experiences. The difficulty with wiring is that it takes up lots of space.

To accumulate more capacity in a limited space, your brain uses other ways that take up less space to process and transmit information both within and between cells. These four main information-processing methods include (1) allostery, (2) electrical, (3) chemical, and (4) protein molecules.

1. Allostery involves macromolecules, often protein molecules, binding to one another in different combinations to transmit information over relatively long distances in the brain.
2. Electrical signaling is known as *conduction*. Neurons have developed special abilities for sending electrical signals (known as *action potentials*) along axons. Electrical transmission of information involves ions, or electrically charged particles, across neuronal membranes.
3. Chemical transmission of information involves neurotransmitters (dopamine, serotonin, glutamate, acetylcholine, norepinephrine) transferring messages between the gaps, or clefts, in synapses to receptor cells.
4. Protein molecules also transmit information within themselves as they construct the inner workings of the brain and the connections between them (Sterling & Laughlin, 2015).

Together, these four methods allow the brain to function in higher gear without taking up more space.

Increasingly, it appears these information-processing methods are all interlinked, and each has regulatory function over the others (Buzsáki, 2019; Sterling & Laughlin, 2015; Yeo et al., 2011). But not all information pathways communicate at the same speeds or with the same efficiency (Yeo et al., 2011). You have experienced this. Your realization that someone is not responsive to your jokes and lovely conversation after a long, tiring week is a lot slower than your reaction to stepping barefoot on plastic toy bricks in the dark. In that case, your foot sensors have contracted before you've even had time to think *ouch*.

After a while, these ways of processing information form into networks (Giedd, 2015; Thompson et al., 2019; Yeo et al., 2011). This accelerates some forms of thinking and makes cognition easier. Even concepts that initially challenge us become easier with successful repetition, practice, and time. These are our learning strengths.

Our brains process more information in a day than ever before. Estimates range from a fivefold increase since 1985 to a 40 percent increase since 1950 (Flynn, 2012; Restak & Kim, 2010). The speed at which we make decisions is also increasing (Ridderinkhof & van der Stelt, 2000). The obvious question is, How do we harness that thinking and decision-making power? That is the point of this book.

Neurodiversity

Your brain is as distinctive as your fingerprints. Your genes, thoughts, memories, and experiences have all combined to create a uniquely patterned piece of intricate neural architecture. No one thinks in exactly the same way as you, and that means you are smart in your own way.

You don't have to observe people for very long to realize that some people are better at some things than others. Some people almost froth at the mouth with excitement when they get a chance to think about numbers, while others would run a mile and then keep running. Some people's fingers nimbly caress musical instruments while others can barely squeak out a note.

We all have different brains. We are *neurodiverse*. This means we all have different learning strengths and we all have areas that will be challenging for us. Few of us are jacks-of-all-trades. While we could neurodiversify education and set up specific schools for people with mechanical aptitude, mathematics prodigies, future novelists, and budding musicians, that would only limit people.

Success and enthusiasm are contagious. If you know what your brain learns easily (your learning strengths) and apply this to other areas that challenge you, it broadens you as a person and expands your capacity for success in life. But information doesn't just stay in one head. It jumps from brain to brain as we share ideas. In a classroom, this means everyone can get smart when he or she has the support of others.

This book aims to create schools that value all sorts of brains and are open minded enough to embrace and celebrate all types of success—from the highly gifted, exceptional student who panics when faced with an area that does not come easily, to the struggling reader who stumbles painfully over each syllable.

The Ten Most Important Things Teachers Need to Know About Neurodevelopmental Differentiation

It's critical to keep in mind the following ten items about neurodevelopmental differentiation.

1. The brain has some information pathways that are more effective than others.
2. These information pathways can be thought of as learning strengths.
3. Engaging students where they are already strong and using those strengths to build other areas increase motivation.
4. Students are getting smarter even though we may not always see this in schools.
5. The brain and the body are one system. When the body is out of sorts, the brain doesn't learn as well.
6. Explicitly teaching students specific activities with clear learning intentions and success criteria changes their brains by consolidating and refining new information pathways.
7. We need to think differently about how we teach if we are to utilize the increased learning capacity of our students.
8. When we develop expertise in a skill, we use less information-processing power to achieve the same result. What is initially hard to do becomes easier.
9. When one student's ability to process information improves, the entire class benefits. Ideas jump from head to head as learning becomes more enjoyable.
10. Being aware of learning strengths can develop a contagion of success in schools.

Brain-Based Differentiation

Traditionally, we have thought about differentiation as the way teachers individualize:

- The content (what is being taught)
- The process (how it is taught)
- The product (how students demonstrate their learning) and the environment in which they learn, to meet the needs of individual students (Sousa & Tomlinson, 2018; Tomlinson, 2017)

Neurodevelopmental differentiation takes these concepts and applies them to the different systems in the brain. Processes that develop naturally for some students have to be taught explicitly to others. To treat all students and their brains the same way is to treat them unequally. We need to tailor our interventions to the brains we are teaching. This requires us, as teachers, to make small but significant changes to our teaching practice. It also involves teaching students about their brains and how they learn so they can use their strengths to overcome obstacles in learning. Unlike a box of tricks, these practices will help to identify and overcome the blockages causing students' learning challenges.

Often, we can recognize when a student is not progressing but are not sure what to do about it. We know something is not right and so refer the student for testing. But if he or she doesn't have a diagnosable disability, we are left with few strategies. So a conclusion is sometimes made that if the student doesn't have a learning disability, then he or she must be *stupid*, *unmotivated*, or *hopelessly lazy*.

Not all learning blockages are detected by traditional psychological and other testing. To help students become adept and resilient learners, we need to become knowledgeable about how to develop their relevant brain systems and overcome their vulnerabilities.

Identifying Learning Strengths

In his therapy room, Andrew had the privilege to work with thousands of students who were disenchanted with school. Some were fearful. Others were nonchalant. They had all given up.

The puzzling thing is that these students were clever. Almost always, their discussions revealed an area of passion where they felt capable and interested in learning, but in most cases this area was invisible to their teachers, their parents, and sometimes even themselves.

Even students who had been identified as exceptional or gifted were prone to this malaise. For example, students who had been identified as highly number smart were often self-denigrating about their abilities in other areas. They couldn't see how they could apply their learning strengths in one area to others.

If this was happening for our highest-performing students, we despaired for those students who hadn't identified any learning strengths at all.

All these students had the capacity to be successful but had lost both the belief in themselves and their desire to try. Some of them lacked knowledge about how to succeed in school, and almost all of them had no idea where to begin their journey toward success.

In Andrew's professional development workshops, teachers expressed frustration that while they knew some of their students weren't progressing as they should, they felt they lacked ways to work out exactly what was blocking students' progress, as well as guidelines about how to help them. This applied to their clearly capable students as well as those who were struggling.

From all these discussions came the inspiration for neurodevelopmental differentiation and learning strengths. At the same time, our good friend and educational colleague Vicki Hartley, an experienced senior educator who has worked with gifted but troubled students in Queensland and New South Wales, Australia, made the point that so many students she had taught seemed to have many pieces of the educational puzzle in place but that they struggled repeatedly with some areas of learning. She suggested writing a book to help those students and their teachers.

After analyzing the research on brains and learning, Andrew wrote *Unlocking Your Child's Genius* (2015), which outlines the main strategies for school success. While parents and teachers responded well to it, there was one problem: the students whose lives would be changed by the information in the book weren't terribly interested in reading it. Their loss of self-belief and desire to try extended to a disinterest in reading books about these types of issues. This led to the development of a research-based learning-strengths analysis anyone can use for free at My Learning Strengths (www.mylearningstrengths.com). A complete analysis that outlines an individualized learning plan based on each person's learning strengths, strategies, and potential career paths, as well as ways to develop inputs, processing, and outputs, is also available.

This free analysis provides users with a letter outlining their two most prevalent learning strengths as well as an area to develop (see a sample letter in figure I.2). Thousands of students worldwide completed the learning-strengths analysis in the first month of it going live in early 2019, and its use has grown exponentially since. It seems it is rare for students to hear about something they are good at from someone who is neither their teacher nor their parent.

Many students, parents, and teachers have taken the time to communicate just how valuable they have found the analysis, but what surprised us was that even the students Andrew saw in his therapy room valued the letter over some of the things he was saying to them. There is value in receiving information from a website, it seems.

Success Is Based on Leveraging Strengths

As we all know, one way of creating success in life is to discover what you are good at and do more of it. But for the types of tasks you are not as good at, there are three main options to address them.

1. Cross-fertilize skills from areas you are good at into areas you are not as good at.
2. Do less of that type of task.
3. Eventually get someone else to do them for you.

This is a level of strategic thinking that is hard to do when you are young unless you are guided to it. So identifying learning strengths serves as a catalyst for success by informing students they are smart, the ways in which they are smart, and how they can use those smarts to lift their performance in other areas.

Introduction

Name: Robin Hood   Grade Level: 8

Dear Robin,

Congratulations! **Spatial reasoning** is one of your learning strengths. Not all of your best thinking is done using words. Being able to move, link, and sequence objects in space in our heads relates to design, art, and high-level sporting achievements. You can use spatial reasoning to outline a flowchart, choose your clothes for the day, complete a jigsaw puzzle, or construct a model. Visualizing increases mathematics, imagination, creativity, and understanding. You can also develop great fashion sense. Being able to reason spatially is a major advantage in the world.

Your **people smarts** and skills are another one of your learning strengths. Your most sophisticated people smarts include emotional intelligence, people reading, emotional regulation, knowing how to calm yourself and others, rapid de-escalation methods, stress management, constructive feedback, motivational skills, compassion, relationship building and maintenance, and clear communication. Being able to relate well to people is a major advantage in the world.

You could use your learning strengths to develop in other learning areas by:

- **Perceptual and motor coordination:** Drawing or moving your body as you solve problems
- **Concentration and memory:** Remembering a series of movements to help you recall how to do something
- **Planning and sequencing:** Walking through the steps of a problem
- **Thinking and logic:** Drawing flowcharts
- **Language and word smarts:** Talking yourself through an issue and relating it to people you know
- **Number smarts:** Using shapes and different objects to represent the different parts of a mathematical calculation

You might consider sharing this letter with someone you trust, such as a parent or teacher, so that he or she can understand your learning strengths and the area in which you are still developing.

The full report provides you a complete list of your learning strengths, some areas to work on with more strategies, and potential career paths.

I hope the information you gain by doing this will help you to fulfill your potential.

Never lose sight of your dreams!

Andrew Fuller
Clinical Psychologist

Source: Adapted from My Learning Strengths, n.d. Used with permission.

Figure I.2: Sample learning-strengths-analysis letter.

By opening a door to experiencing success, neurodevelopmental differentiation aims to re-energize all students, but especially those who are disheartened or feel anxious and sometimes worthless. For those who have already identified a learning strength in one area, it helps them expand those skills to other learning areas.

Learning strengths are also not a substitute for a full psychometric assessment of a student, but understanding these strengths and using the strategies discussed in this book may help teachers and parents to more accurately assess when a full assessment is needed.

The Neurodevelopmental Differentiation Approach

Neurodevelopmental differentiation capitalizes on the neuroplasticity of brains and involves teachers:

- Understanding the role of each of the eight brain information-processing systems
- Acknowledging that all students may have learning strengths as well as blockages in one or more of the systems
- Understanding that brains develop individually and recognizing that blockages are also part of development but that their significance can vary
- Identifying the current pattern of learning strengths
- Giving students opportunities to develop their skill level in brain systems and tracking their progress
- Determining the next priority areas for development

The eight brain information-processing systems—(1) spatial reasoning, (2) perceptual and motor skills, (3) concentration and memory, (4) planning and sequencing, (5) thinking and logic, (6) people smarts, (7) language and word smarts, and (8) number smarts—represent the way most humans learn. They also reflect key dimensions of learning and mirror the curricula of most educational systems across the world. The order in which they are presented is also significant.

When we are babies, we live in a visual world and use our spatial reasoning to make sense of those shapes and images. We begin to use our bodies in increasingly coordinated ways and use our perceptions to make sense of the world as we play with toys and begin to crawl (Gopnik, Meltzoff, & Kuhl, 1999; Mustard, 2010).

Focusing our attention and remembering where things are placed allows us to become purposeful and to act in sequenced ways. This becomes the basis of thinking and logic as we act as young scientists conducting experiments in our world. Some of these experiments involve people, as we begin to work out what others will do if we perform specific actions.

As we develop, we learn to use language and words as ways of interacting with the world. Our number sense begins early in life and continues to develop throughout our childhood and teen years.

Inputs, Processing, and Outputs

Each of the eight information-processing systems has inputs, processes, and outputs (see figure I.3).

- **Inputs** relate to the ability to perceive and absorb new information.
- **Processing** relates the organization and links information to create knowledge.
- **Outputs** relate to the retrieval, expression, and communication of knowledge. These include signals to the spinal cord to move the body, to the autonomic nervous system to affect internal organs and glands, and to release hormones from the pituitary gland into the body.

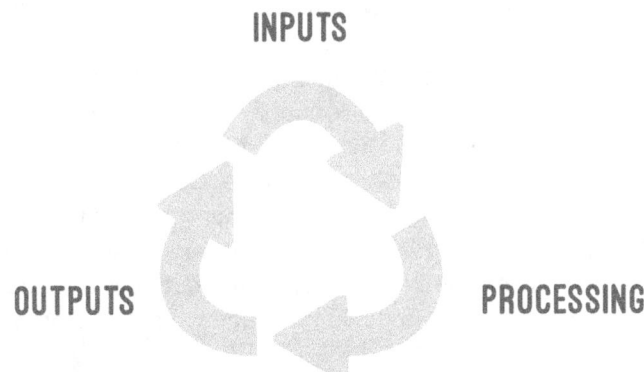

Figure I.3: Inputs, processing, and outputs model.

An improvement in any one of these three areas will often lift the others. For example, if you improve your processing of information by making better notes or developing a way of organizing your ideas, your outputs—or retrieval, expression, and communication—usually improve. This is due to the better organization of ideas, as well as the work you have put into transforming those ideas. If retrieval improves, you will often experience greater success, not only due to improved memory but also through greater transfer and application of ideas. In turn, this helps inputs by priming you to focus on, prioritize, and absorb or encode new, relevant information.

But just as we can develop skills in each of these areas, there can also be blockages to learning in the inputs, processes, and outputs of each system.

Inputs

Our inputs are our ability to absorb new information into our brains. We often think about inputs from the external world into the brain, but it is also the case that the brain has its own internal inputs. In this way, the brain is an anticipatory system that makes predictions (Buzsáki, 2019). You might think about students who appear distracted by their own internal thoughts, such as daydreamers. Other students may maintain high levels of agitation or anger unrelated to the current circumstances. Students who have blockages in inputs often:

- Can't select the most important thing to focus on
- Can't keep up with new information or can't maintain concentration
- Gloss over details
- Can't follow instructions
- Repeatedly ask, "What are we doing?"

Processing

When we process information, we organize it for later use. Processing also involves thinking, evaluating, classifying, linking, prioritizing, and discriminating. Using thinking structures (such as "What is this similar to?" and "What is this different from?") allows us to process information more quickly and consider issues more thoroughly. But just as we do not want blockages in processing, we also do not want processing to become too concrete. Otherwise we risk missing the unique aspects of information, objects, and events (for example, if the only processing tool we have is a hammer, every problem looks like a nail). Processing often has to do with having routines and systems that help us organize what we do and how we do it. Students who have blockages in processing often:

- Can't organize themselves
- Manage their time poorly
- Rarely make notes or find main ideas
- Do not discern patterns
- Have messy or disorganized workbooks and lockers
- Show no signs of systematic planning

Outputs

Outputs refers to our retrieval, expression, or communication of ideas. Outputs often relate to the fluidity of movements and actions, the retrieval of ideas, and the use of learning from past actions to increase current levels of performance. Students who have blockages in outputs often:

Introduction

- Are unable to transfer knowledge from one class to another
- Struggle with recall unless cued (indicating the knowledge is present but that the students struggle to communicate it)
- Have poor follow-through
- Panic in tests
- Demonstrate little linkage of ideas

A summary of inputs, processing, and outputs present in each of the eight brain information-processing systems is outlined in table I.1.

Table I.1: Summary of the Eight Brain Information-Processing Systems

Learning-Strength Area	Main Brain Area	Inputs	Processing	Outputs
Spatial reasoning	Nondominant hemisphere	Visual awareness	Linking images	Design, number smarts, art, sports
Perceptual and motor skills	Motor cortex, cerebellum	Perceptual sensitivity	Muscle memory	Coordinated actions
Concentration and memory	Anterior cingulate gyrus, hippocampus, cerebellum	Focus	Organization of information (encoding and decoding)	Attentiveness, sustained learning, creativity, retrieval
Planning and sequencing	Frontal lobes (especially the left side)	Goal setting	Prioritization	Implementation of actions
Thinking and logic	Frontal lobes	Consideration, evaluation	Similarities and differences	Reasoning
People smarts	Limbic system	Emotional intelligence	Emotional regulation	Compassion, social skills
Language and word smarts	Broca's area, Wernicke's area, the "letter box" area	Letter-sound combinations, listening, reading	Comprehension	Expression, story creation, communication
Number smarts	Intraparietal sulci	Number sense	Manipulating numbers	Reasoning, problem solving

How to Use This Book

This book aims to make teachers' working lives easier and more effective by helping to detect what might be stopping students from achieving more success. Neurodevelopmental differentiation equips students, teachers, and parents to identify learning strengths and apply them to the development of other learning areas. The emphasis on developing the learning strengths of all students is designed to increase engagement, mastery, and, ultimately, success.

It can be used to determine a student's learning strengths and needs, or this can be done by completing the learning-strengths analysis (www.mylearningstrengths.com). We recommend you complete the analysis for yourself first to consider which approach your students will find most helpful.

Each chapter in this book is designed to help teachers and parents identify students' learning-strength areas as well as ways to improve functioning in each area. Each chapter also contains strategies teachers can use in classrooms to detect blockages in each area as well as methods to overcome them. This culminates in the development of an individualized learning plan for each student, ideally developed in collaboration with parents and students.

The purpose of neurodevelopmental differentiation is threefold.

1. When we build from our learning strengths, engagement increases and success becomes more likely.

2. Teachers can use this information to differentiate learning in classrooms, as outlined in figure I.4 and table I.2.

3. With the help of teachers, students and parents can use this information to develop an individualized learning plan (see page 204). This enables teachers, parents, and students to identify some strength areas to develop further over the next semester as well as an area to work on that has yet to be developed.

Introduction

① All students complete their analysis of their learning strengths (www.mylearningstrengths.com).

② Teachers complete their own learning-strengths analysis.

③ Teachers build a grid of the learning strengths of the class (see table I.1, page 15).

④ Teachers use specific groupings and tasks to build on students' strengths.

⑤ Teachers demonstrate how different learning-strengths areas can be used in the topic or subject being taught.

⑥ Teachers look for opportunities to cross-fertilize strengths areas into other learning areas that are not as developed.

⑦ Teachers reassess the learning strengths each semester.

Figure I.4: How teachers can use learning strengths to differentiate classrooms.

Table I.2: Sample Learning-Strengths Grid

Student Name	Spatial Reasoning	Perceptual and Motor Skills	Concentration and Memory	Planning and Sequencing	Thinking and Logic	People Smarts	Language and Word Smarts	Number Smarts
Minh T.	High		High		Low			
Sarah H.		High			High			Low
Nitika I.	Low			High			High	
Jackson Z.		Low	High					High
Coen B.	High	Low					High	
Tyler T.	High	Low						High

NEURODEVELOPMENTAL DIFFERENTIATION

Each chapter introduces one of the eight brain information-processing systems and follows a similar format.

- **Brain Systems Involved** identifies the biological parts and areas involved in making the specific brain area function.
- **Links to Other Brain Systems** outlines the biological parts and areas involved in making the specific brain system function, as well as how the system relates to and intersects with the other seven brain information-processing systems.
- **Inputs** explains how information relating to the brain system is taken in by the brain.
- **Processing** explains how information relating to the brain system is processed by the brain.
- **Outputs** explains how information relating to the brain system is expressed mentally and physically.
- **Key Signs** outlines both positive and negative signs of the brain system in students, to determine whether they have a learning strength in that area that has yet to develop.
- **Ways to Assess in the Classroom** suggests informal tests and activities that can be used to gain a picture of a student's strengths or blockages in each area. This will, in some instances, indicate a need for referral for more specialist assessment.
- **List of Issues** provides a template to record how well the student can accomplish or undertake actions related to the inputs, processing, and outputs of the brain system.
- **Evidence That This Can Be Improved** presents the research-based support that the brain system, including its inputs, processing, and outputs, can be improved.
- **Improving Inputs** introduces ways to improve how the brain takes in information.
- **Improving Processing** introduces ways to improve how the brain processes information.
- **Improving Outputs** introduces ways to improve how the brain expresses information both mentally and physically.
- **Cross-Fertilization Strategies** presents a list of strategies and activities to help teachers and parents identify how to build learning strengths in the brain system being discussed by utilizing the student's learning strengths in other brain systems.
- **In Summary** provides a brief outline of the information presented in the chapter and presents a set of reflective questions to guide your thinking on how this brain area is or could be represented in your classroom.

The aim of differentiation is to individualize learning to meet the needs of each student. To help parents, teachers, and students develop individualized learning plans, an outline is presented in the section beginning on page 198.

Summary

Research on how brains learn and process information has the potential to change the way we think about schools and learning. We are entering an exciting time in which parents and teachers are the neuroarchitects involved in designing and constructing students' brains.

By designing interventions based on what students can already do well (their learning strengths) and applying these skills to areas they have yet to develop, we can increase motivation and excitement about learning.

Chapter 1
SPATIAL REASONING

When we read what someone else has written, we usually discover what the author thinks. When we think in pictures, we often discover what *we* think. Thinking in pictures is not only a powerful tool in problem solving; it also contributes to knowing oneself. Thinking is linking, but not all thinking is best done using words.

Spatial thinking concerns the locations of objects, their shapes, their relation to one another, and the trajectories they take as they move (Newcombe, 2017). Our most sophisticated spatial reasoning skills involve the abilities to think in several planes and rotations, move, mentally link and sequence objects in space, design, create art, apply geometry and trigonometry, and accomplish high-level sporting achievements. How we come to acquire skills in this area is an interesting journey of brain development.

When we think in pictures or symbols rather than words, we are reasoning spatially. We use this skill when we outline a flowchart, choose our clothes for the day, complete a jigsaw puzzle, or construct a model. Visualizing increases imagination, creativity, and understanding.

Spatial reasoning has been the basis of important scientific discoveries. Famously, Albert Einstein used spatial reasoning to imagine his formula of mass-energy equation (or $E = mc^2$). James Watson and Francis Crick also used Rosalind Franklin's flat x-rays of diffraction images to complete the spatial reasoning and envision the double helix shape of DNA (as cited in Sapolsky, 2017b).

Spatial reasoning has also been the basis of artistic and architectural creations. Filippo Brunelleschi used it to design the dome of the Santa Maria del Fiore cathedral in Florence, Italy. Zaha Hadid used it to design her award-winning buildings, including the Riverside Museum in Glasgow, Scotland, and Michelangelo certainly used it to create the mural on the ceiling of the Sistine Chapel in Vatican City.

Career Areas That Utilize Learning Strengths in Spatial Reasoning

Astrophysics, mathematics, fashion design, geology, chemistry, engineering, air traffic control, police and detective work, epidemiology, construction, surgery, art, mechanics, chess, choreography, set design, sports, aviation, sculpture, geology, interior design, plumbing, sailing, teaching, hairdressing, navigation, ballistics, architecture, and rocket science are career areas that utilize learning strengths in spatial reasoning. Helping students consider career paths that call on their learning strengths may ease their way into a successful professional life.

The highest-level spatial-reasoning skills enable people to visualize how component parts combine to form a whole object, match similar shapes, and consider how different parts interact, such as cogs in a mechanical sequence or different dyes composing a pattern on clothing. Both pattern matching and pattern detection are components of spatial reasoning (Newcombe, 2010).

The ability to anticipate is a lesser-known attribute of spatial reasoning that involves seeing what is *not* there (Herman, 2016)—for example, what is missing in a work of art or a design or what shape might logically come next in a series. This aspect of spatial reasoning is linked to imagery and imagination (Newcombe & Frick, 2010).

All these skills are called on in the sciences (especially in physics), the arts (especially in drama), mathematics (especially in geometry and trigonometry), design, navigation, metalworking, and carpentry courses.

Whether students have learning strengths in spatial reasoning, we aim to have all students develop skills in this area, as it is a foundational skill.

Brain Systems Involved in Spatial Reasoning

Different tasks require different learning skills and use distinct parts of the brain. In addition to the aims of the lesson, let all your students know what brain systems they'll be using in each lesson or activity to familiarize them with their brains. Spatial reasoning occurs on the nondominant side of the brain (usually the right side; Butterworth, 2019). The main parts of the brain involved in spatial reasoning are outlined in figure 1.1.

While it might be expected that the retina, the optic nerve, and the occipital lobes would be mentioned here, spatial reasoning is not dependent on visual processing. People who have been blind from birth can reason spatially—in fact, they rely on it to navigate around their homes and neighborhoods.

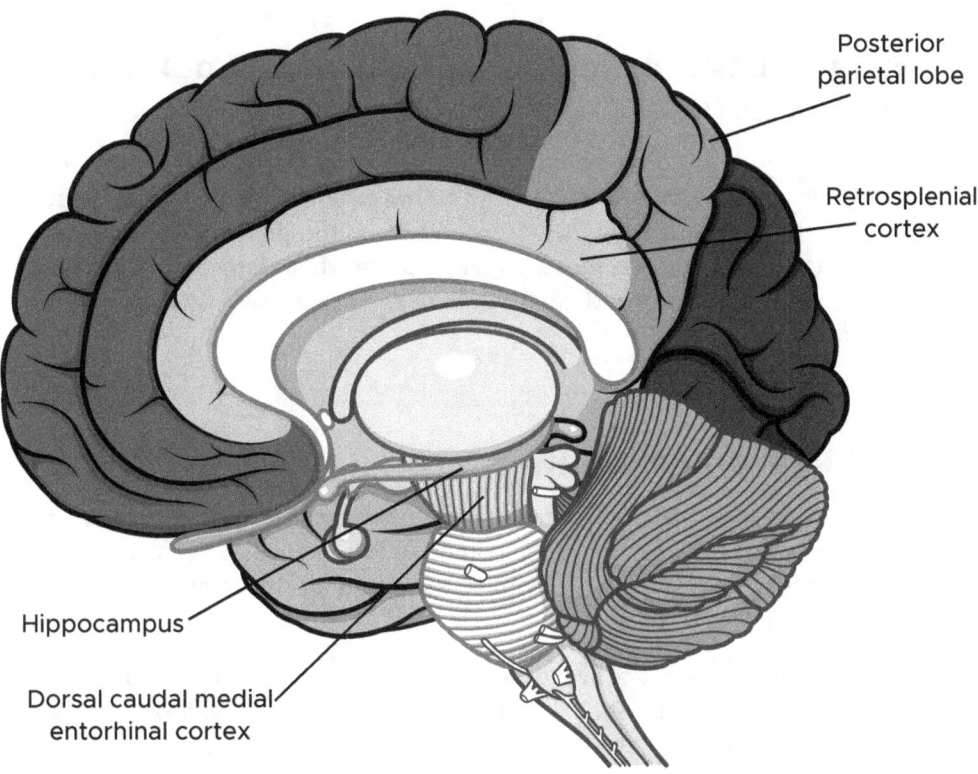

Note: The illustrations in this book are indicative only. While we have tried to be as accurate as possible, the diagrams in this book do not attempt to replicate the precision of a text on neuroanatomy.

Figure 1.1: Parts of the brain involved in spatial reasoning.

Links Between Spatial Reasoning and Other Brain Systems

The posterior (rear) parietal lobes link with the nondominant side of the brain to create spatial images. This links with the premotor cortex to create actions (Sapolsky, 2017a; Sterling & Laughlin, 2015).

Spatial reasoning links to various other learning areas and brain areas, including perceptual and motor skills (in playing sports, catching a ball, and making gestures), thinking and logic (in the sciences and mathematics), planning and sequencing (in perspective taking and map and graph reading), people smarts (in facial recognition, communication, and interpreting emotions and body postures), and arts and design.

Spatial reasoning also requires an understanding of symbolic language and words (Newcombe & Frick, 2010), such as *under*, *over*, *beside*, *left*, *right*, *curve*, *straight*, *triangle*, *rectangle*, and *bending at twenty degrees* or *at a ninety-degree angle*.

What Blockages in Spatial Reasoning Look Like in Adulthood

When we don't develop our spatial-reasoning learning strengths, there can be long-term consequences. Adults with blockages in spatial reasoning often find it hard to follow directions, find little enjoyment of art, can't read maps, can't picture success, can't visualize what mathematics problems are asking them to do, and can't visualize the steps involved in mathematical problems.

Spatial-Reasoning Inputs

From playing with building blocks, knitting, sewing, playing badminton, and fixing bicycle chains to considering the configuration of chess pieces on a board, spatial reasoning begins with tactile learning (Gopnik et al., 1999; Inhelder & Piaget, 1999; Platas, 2017).

Some concepts are best conveyed spatially, such as proportion, velocity, planetary orbits, and molecules. Spatial tools such as concept maps, flowcharts, and graphic organizers can help students gain an overview of ideas and processes.

Students with blockages in spatial reasoning are often seen by others as clumsy or disorganized. They may stand too close or too far away from the people or objects they are interacting with, so they may be thought of as lacking a sense of personal space. These students may also find it hard to tell their left from their right and can confuse positional language, such as *over* or *under*, *in* or *out*, and *left* or *right*, making it hard for them to follow directions.

Spatial-Reasoning Processing

There is overlap among spatial reasoning, imagery, and creative imagination. To reason well spatially requires thinking about what might happen next or what might be missing in a sequence. It is as much about imagining what is *not* there as it is about what *is* there.

Students with strengths in spatial reasoning are often accomplished at more practical learning areas with hands-on, material-based activities.

Students with spatial-reasoning blockages often find mathematics difficult (Butterworth, 2019). Unless they are taught explicitly through the use of blocks, dice, dominoes, and playing cards, mathematics eludes them. This is due to the abstract concepts of the learning area, especially where shape, area, dimensions, volume, and space are involved. These students will often also have problems reproducing patterns, sequences, and shapes. Spatial-reasoning blockages may also result in poor hand-eye coordination.

Our senses differ in terms of how sensitive they are to information inputs, and we don't process all the inputs our senses give us. Table 1.1 shows us the information processed by senses. The physical tools of spatial reasoning, sight and touch, account for more than half of the information being consciously processed.

Table 1.1: Information Processed by the Senses

	Bits of Information Input per Second*	Bits of Information Processed Consciously per Second
Eyes	10,000,000	40
Ears	100,000	30
Skin	1,000,000	5
Taste	1,000	1
Smell	100,000	1

*A *bit* is the smallest piece of information.

Source: Adapted from Nørretranders, 1999.

Only 77 of the 11,201,000 bits of information our senses input every second are consciously processed (Nørretranders, 1999), which tells us that we do a lot of filtering of reality in order to function effectively. Our awareness and consciousness are very compressed forms of reality. While it is tempting to consider what might happen if we increased our conscious awareness, we could become so overwhelmed with incoming information that effective action would become impossible.

By improving students' learning strengths in spatial reasoning, we enhance their ability to utilize the information they consciously process.

Spatial-Reasoning Outputs

Students often excel when provided with opportunities for multisensory learning (see table 1.2, page 26). Hands-on activities improve pattern detection, sequencing, creativity, and organization. Creating art, dancing, orienteering, completing block or picture puzzles, surveying, mapping, model building, and sculpting are some examples of spatial-reasoning activities.

Many students who struggle in other areas possess learning strengths in spatial reasoning.

Table 1.2: Key Signs—Spatial Reasoning

	Positive Signs	Concerning Signs
Inputs	The student: • Uses mental imagery to relieve the need to put every idea into words • Thinks visually	The student: • Has a misguided sense of direction • Does not know left from right
Processing	The student: • Thinks about scientific and mathematical concepts spatially	The student: • Can't complete simple mazes or follow a straightforward trail • Can't copy a drawing reasonably well for his or her age • Finds jigsaw puzzles almost impossible
Outputs	The student: • Can develop diagrams, flowcharts, mind maps, graphic organizers, and concept maps	The student: • Is unable to sequence pictures, images, or shapes • Can't reorder a series of images to make a logical story

Ways to Assess Spatial Reasoning in the Classroom

The following ideas will not replace a full psychological or pediatric assessment, but they may give teachers and parents an idea if further investigations are merited.

Students' ability to complete some of the following tasks will give you an idea of their capacities or difficulties in using spatial reasoning to learn well. Most of these can be used to make an assessment of specific students, but they will also benefit the entire class. Students can do the following.

- Lay out pieces of work. You can observe how ordered and organized it is.
- Arrange pictures in sequences. This is a gauge of how clearly a student can think spatially and pictorially: Does it make a logical sequence? Can the student explain it to you? Students with blockages will often make an arrangement with little logical sense.
- Develop a model of the planetary system. Is there some system regarding relative distance, order, and size? Students with blockages may make all the planets the same size or have them equidistant.
- Develop chemical models of atoms and electrons or compounds. How ordered and organized are they? Students with blockages will often have random sequences.

- Act out stories. Can students understand and mimic the correct movements (for example, going over, under, or through something)? Students with blockages will often not know what to do.
- Combine shapes to create an image.
- Match two-dimensional shapes. Present students with a set of shapes or objects and ask them to confirm which two are identical.
- Read a map. Can students follow a route?
- Draw what they would see if they were standing in the middle of an avenue of trees. Look for a sense of perspective—this will often be lacking in students with blockages.
- Produce a drawing of what they would see if they were a bird flying over their home.
- Draw a familiar local building. Do students include all the features?
- Complete trail-making tests. Using a grid like the one shown in figure 1.2, ask students to find *E4*, then draw a line to *A2*, then to *G6*, then to *B7*.

A	B	C	D	E	F	G
1						
2						
3						
4						
5						
6						
7						

Figure 1.2: A trail-making test.

You can also try the following.

- Display a series of shapes, as well as a shape that will be presented in pieces or with a different orientation. Ask the student to choose which shapes would form the full picture if you put them together, and vice versa. Students with blockages usually find these types of tasks extremely difficult.
- Draw a series of cogs turning in different directions, and ask the student to predict which way the last cog will turn. Students with spatial blockages will often guess and can't explain their answers.

Whether a student successfully completes or struggles to finish a series of the preceding activities will not necessarily indicate a problem, but these tasks will serve as a guide to his or her current level of learning strengths in spatial reasoning (see figure 1.3, page 28).

Use this list to rate the spatial-reasoning strengths of the student. Assign a score out of ten (with one being "can't do this" and ten being "great at this") for each of the statements that follow. (A student at the average level of his or her class would score a five.)

Issue	Rating
Inputs	
The student:	
• Can identify similarities and differences	
• Can follow a trail or a map	
• Is able to use directions to find something	
• Can arrange pictures in a sequence to tell a story	
• Can complete a jigsaw puzzle at an age-appropriate level	
Processing	
The student:	
• Can complete age-appropriate mazes	
• Can arrange images into a logical sequence	
• Can combine shapes to create an image	
• Can see what a missing element of an object might look like	
• Can use dice, dominoes, or blocks to think about numbers	
Outputs	
The student:	
• Can develop mind maps, graphic organizers, flowcharts, and concept maps to expand and link ideas	
• Is able to manipulate different objects in his or her head and imagine how they might combine	
• Can copy a drawing at an age-appropriate level	
• Can draw objects from different perspectives or consider how they might look from different angles	
• Can communicate ideas spatially or visually	

Figure 1.3: List of issues with spatial reasoning.

Discuss your concerns and compare these results with other teachers who are familiar with this student to confirm your observations.

Evidence That Spatial Reasoning Can Be Improved

There is considerable research indicating that durable improvements in spatial reasoning occur after playing Tetris and practicing mental rotation, task-specific practices, origami, and dance (Newcombe, 2010).

As with every other information-processing and learning area in this book, practice improves performance. The more often students are allowed short spans of time to hone their skills, the better. As a general rule of thumb, you should expect to see some improvements after six weeks of fairly regular practice, but be patient—it takes time to develop skills. If no improvement is evident after six weeks, you may need to consider either different activities or further assessment to identify blockages that haven't yet been identified.

Identifying the areas one needs to improve on and targeting them as areas to practice is defined as *deliberate practice* (Colvin, 2018). Most of us fall into the easy trap of practicing the things we are already good at because it feels good when we gain an easy sense of accomplishment. But if we want to improve at something, we need to find the areas in which we are not as competent and focus on developing them.

Very few people like practicing things they find difficult. Deliberate practice (repeatedly doing the things we find challenging) is hard work, and students can often become disheartened and disinterested, eventually finding ways to avoid practicing.

This is why the cross-fertilization strategies in each chapter of this book are so important. If we can identify students' learning strengths and find ways to use them to lift other areas they find challenging, the amount of practice, and eventually their level of performance, increases.

As the pressure to perform well can inhibit some students from trying new things, teachers may want to label these deliberate practice sessions as *tryouts*, where students try hard things without feeling they have to succeed every time.

Enhancing Spatial Reasoning

Familiarizing students with spatial tasks and related language or terms will help build their spatial reasoning (Newcombe & Frick, 2010). Ask students questions like the following.

- "How many animals are hidden in the picture?"
- "Which of these shapes has a right angle in it?"
- "Can you touch your right shoulder with your left hand?"
- "Can you find the route on a map from home to school?"

All these questions trigger our perceptions of objects in space. They teach students to not just see things but observe them, because spatial reasoning is not just about seeing things. It involves thinking about what you see. Tell students it is like being a detective who uses all the visual and spatial clues available at a crime scene to work out what happened. Research by Nora S. Newcombe (2010) and Newcombe and Andrea Frick (2010) shows that repeated exposure to these type of questions increases students' spatial reasoning.

Improving Spatial-Reasoning Inputs

Improve spatial-reasoning inputs by encouraging students to notice variables such as the relative sizes and locations of component parts, an awareness of what is in the foreground and what is in the background of images, three-dimensionality, symmetry versus asymmetry, and left versus right (Levine, 2002). Teachers will often need to prompt students to do this by asking questions that require students to reason about and explain what they are seeing.

Another important aspect of spatial-reasoning inputs is the relationship between parts and the whole. Encourage these links by asking students questions like "What goes with what?" and "How does the whole relate to its constituent pieces?" While looking at a picture or scanning a map, we use spatial reasoning to link different parts.

Improving Spatial-Reasoning Processing

Processing puts the reasoning into spatial awareness. While it is lovely to look at a beautiful painting, it is quite a different thing to consider its meaning, why the artist has used this medium to portray the scene, and the story of what you are seeing.

In improving spatial-reasoning processing, we often need to give students the words they can use to think with. Increase the use of spatial language as students progress: *up*, *down*, *left*, *right*, *diagonal*, *over*, *under*, *proximal*, *trajectory*, *adjacent*, *angle*, *rotation*, and *projection*, to *sine*, *cosine*, *tangent*, *secant*, and *cosecant*. The more familiar students become with these terms, the more able they will be to use them in their own spatial reasoning.

To help increase spatial awareness and reasoning, Amy E. Herman (2016) proposes the acronym *COBRA*.

- **Concentrate on the camouflaged:** Look for inconspicuous objects.
- **One thing at a time:** Discover hidden images and connections; don't multitask.
- **Break:** Take a brief mental break every twenty minutes by switching to a task that uses a different set of skills.
- **Realign your expectations:** Given that we only consciously process seventy-seven of the more than eleven million bits of information our senses perceive every second, we need to remain curious and rid ourselves of preconceptions.
- **Ask someone else to look with you:** As we all perceive the world differently, others will see things you cannot.

Many students need help with time management, setting itineraries and timelines. Teachers can help students develop this skill by asking students to devise schedules, complete projects in stages, and demonstrate work in progress.

Some students become disoriented or inattentive when given multistep instructions, which may indicate they are battling inadequate sequential memory. Breaking down the steps involved in a task or project into ladders of understanding as outlined in chapter 4 (page 103) may be helpful for these students.

Students who have difficulties with spatial reasoning (or concentration and memory) should be encouraged to verbalize their ideas. Talking through where they left something—whispering under their breath, "I put it in the bottom left drawer"—and then visualizing it in that place can help to address these difficulties.

Improving Spatial-Reasoning Outputs

Spatial reasoning relies on the ability to use your imagination to visualize concepts, and it forms the basis of abstract reasoning (Herman, 2016).

To be able to do this, students need to have a strong understanding of the concrete world around them. To support students in developing their spatial-reasoning strengths, we need to provide them with opportunities to build on and transition from hands-on experiences to abstract concepts. As students' understanding becomes more developed, we can begin to remove the concrete materials gradually and empower them to think conceptually and abstractly.

One method for doing this is to ask students to translate geometric shapes into words. For example, instead of picturing an octagon, students can understand that *octo-* usually means "eight" (for example, use octopus and its eight legs), so an octagon must have eight sides.

Spatial Reasoning and STEM

The emergence of STEM (science, technology, engineering, and mathematics) provides a great opportunity for developing spatial reasoning in students. A review of fifty years of research finds clear overlaps between the two areas (Wai, Lubinski, & Benbow, 2009), although Danielle Harris and Tom Lowrie (2018) find there remains some confusion about the differentiation of mathematics and spatial tasks among teaching professionals.

A comprehensive review conducted on behalf of the Organisation for Economic Co-operation and Development (as cited in Newcombe, 2017) studies research that shows successful STEM students have good spatial skills, students with higher scores on spatial ability are more likely to enter careers in science and mathematics, and strong spatial skills are predictive of mathematics achievement from kindergarten to the end of elementary school. Importantly, the review demonstrates that spatial-reasoning skills can be improved through training.

The types of STEM activities that promote spatial reasoning include learning about shapes in early childhood, working puzzles, identifying parts of shapes that would make a whole object, practicing origami, carrying out mental-rotation tasks, using number lines, zooming in and out on scales of representations, reading maps and graphs, navigating, and sketching or drawing.

One example of a spatial-reasoning training program has been designed by Sheryl A. Sorby (as cited in Sorby, Wysocki, & Baartmans, 2003). This includes a ten-week series of hundreds of activities in folding, rotations, cross-sections, and orthographic projections and has been shown to increase scores on spatial-ability tests and a small but significant increase in scores in calculus.

Spatial-Reasoning Cross-Fertilization Strategies

If a student has a learning strength in spatial reasoning, table 1.3 suggests some strategies that could be used to help extend learning in other areas. These are some key suggestions to stimulate your thinking and can be adapted to your classroom or time frame as you see fit.

Table 1.3: Extending Learning From Spatial Reasoning

Learning-Strength Area	Sample Strategy
Perceptual and Motor Skills	**Students can:** • Use images or objects to represent different aspects of an issue or problem by writing their ideas on paper • Build models of key concepts they are learning about • Link images of information they want to learn with specific movements to increase retention **Teachers can:** • Embed movement into learning (for example, estimation followed by measurement) • Introduce matching games (for example, multiplication games in which half the class has the questions and the other half has the answers and students need to match them up) • Use puzzles and art (mathematics as art) to link concepts such as perspective and angles with spatial thinking • Use drama to physically demonstrate concepts • Place objects representing different aspects on a table representing their relationships to one another • Build models of the planetary system • Explore robotics—construction and coding of robots involve both spatial reasoning and perceptual and motor skills • Use mathematics to calculate where a thrown ball, paper plane, or javelin will land **At home, families can:** • Organize a cupboard or a closet or pack a suitcase • Learn specific skills, like catching and throwing a ball, snapping fingers, playing a musical instrument, building with blocks, juggling, sculpting, playing a sport, knitting, and cooking
Concentration and Memory	**Students can:** • Use different-colored pieces of paper for different tasks • Recall information by placing it on an imaginary pathway **Teachers can:** • Make visual, as well as verbal, explanations of ideas • Recall patterns, trails, and sequences • Create maps from memory • Draw from memory **At home, families can:** • Play memory, or matching, card games • Play Pictionary • Play spot-the-difference games

continued →

NEURODEVELOPMENTAL DIFFERENTIATION

Learning-Strength Area	Sample Strategy
Planning and Sequencing	**Students can:** • Arrange images or pictures into a logical sequence • Use graphic organizers (for example, mind maps) • Create visual, pictorial notes **Teachers can:** • Ask students to follow instructions to build or make something • Identify the steps involved in a physical skill (for example, the steps involved in kicking a soccer goal) • Physically map out the linkages and steps between students' current positions and their goals, or where they want to be • Teach students to dream forward and plan backward • Use sticky notes, counters, markers, or objects to sequence the stages or steps in solving a problem • Try perspective taking—if you were planning a house, imagine you were doing so from the perspective of a builder, an interior decorator, a plumber, or a homeowner **At home, families can:** • Encourage children to learn to dress themselves • Cook (the child plans it all, from going shopping to completing the meal) • Encourage children to make their own lunches for school • Plan homework and study times • Explore kite construction and flying • Learn map reading • Play pickup sticks • Play checkers • Play dominoes • Draw
Thinking and Logic	**Students can:** • Create flowcharts, posters, and mind maps • Use physical materials, such as pictures, to map out ideas **Teachers can:** • Use visual representations of complex issues, especially ethical dilemmas involving values and conflicting interests or demands • Play join-the-dots • Break codes and ciphers • Identify causes and effects **At home, families can:** • Create trails around the house with clues so children can solve problems or riddles and follow a path • Play chess • Play backgammon • Play Battleship

Spatial Reasoning

Learning-Strength Area	Sample Strategy
People Smarts	**Students can:** • Watch video or film clips with the sound down and try to guess what's going on (watch them again with the sound on; over time, astuteness in reading people will improve) **Teachers can:** • Use pictures of faces to develop emotional detection • Discuss different types of communication, including texting, talking, emotional signaling, posture and body language, semaphore, and Morse code • Watch how people move and consider what emotions different movements convey • Use drama to act out different emotions • Use images and texts to infer how characters might be feeling and what their motives might be **At home, families can:** • Mix with a variety of people • Attend family functions and practice reading emotions • Ask children to speculate how specific people might be feeling
Language and Word Smarts	**Students can:** • Learn that words are to authors as paints are to artists—one can create images through words (for example, write a vivid account so the reader can almost *feel* the sensation of peeling an orange) **Teachers can:** • Introduce estimation activities and thinking about the upper and lower levels of a range • Use graphic novels • Ask students to produce their own picture books and explain their understanding through a combination of writing and drawing • Provide students with the opportunity to create storyboards, comic strips, and drama performances • Use resources that combine written information with visual information • Introduce stories involving symbols, codes, and ciphers • Read and write action stories • Write a story using as many symbols as possible **At home, families can:** • Help children become familiar with spatial language—*over*, *under*, *left*, *right*, *top*, *bottom*, *middle*, *near*, *far*, and so on • Help children become familiar with spatial concepts such as *bent*, *curvy*, *square*, *rectangle*, *circle*, and *cube* • Help children become familiar with higher-order spatial concepts such as *eclipse*, *projectile*, *trajectory*, *exponential*, and *circumnavigation*

continued →

Learning-Strength Area	Sample Strategy
Number Smarts	**Students can:** • Picture number problems through pie charts, pizzas, flowcharts, or percentages of people **Teachers can:** • Introduce the Singapore bar model method for mathematics • Illustrate problems • Include movement-based mathematics activities • Write calculations vertically rather than horizontally **At home, families can:** • Use the language of numbers in relation to shopping, saving, and people's heights • Encourage visualization of numbers (for example, How far do you think it is from here to the store? How tall is that building? How long have we been driving?)

In Summary

Learning strengths in spatial reasoning enable people to design exquisite structures, complete beautiful art pieces, visualize intricate scientific and mathematical models, and construct wonderful buildings. A world deficient in spatial reasoning would be a world lacking in design, functionality, and beauty.

Once developed, learning strengths in spatial reasoning can be applied to enhance success in other areas. They can be used to:

- Choreograph dance and movement (perceptual and motor skills)
- Pick out the main idea or concept (concentration and memory)
- Identify a series of steps that need to be taken to achieve an outcome (planning and sequencing)
- Visualize the processes in solving a problem (thinking and logic)
- Recognize emotions in ourselves and others (people smarts)
- Link images and sounds and emotions (language and word smarts)
- Think abstractly and theoretically about mathematics (number smarts)

Spatial reasoning is the foundation for building success in school and in life. This positive effect on success is especially enhanced when it is linked to perceptual and motor skills.

Reflection Questions

- What strategies will be most valuable in strengthening the spatial reasoning of your students?
- Which other members of staff need to be involved in this discussion?
- Should any student's parents or guardians be involved in this discussion?
- What opportunities are there in your learning-area activities for students to strengthen their spatial reasoning?
- How can you orchestrate more of these opportunities?
- Self-audit:
    - How many learning activities in your classroom this week have incorporated spatial reasoning?
    - How many learning activities in your classroom this week have incorporated spatial-reasoning practice and development?

Chapter 2
PERCEPTUAL AND MOTOR SKILLS

Our brains develop from perceptual and motor skills upward. These are our earliest skills and the foundation of almost everything we do.

Every time you cross a busy street, you are protected by your perceptual and motor skills. Your ability to assess the speed of oncoming traffic, the distance across the road and the time it will take you to get to the other side, and your muscle memory of looking left and right before you cross the road all help keep you safe and stem from this brain system.

At the highest levels, perceptual and motor skills are the embodiment of gracefulness. To observe the artistry of ballet dancers, sculptors, and athletes is to watch perceptual and motor skills that have been honed over years of practice.

Career Areas That Utilize Learning Strengths in Perceptual and Motor Skills

Dance, coaching, engineering, horse riding, radar operation, heavy machinery operation, mimicry, juggling, magic, crafting, clowning, fashion design, construction, pottery, carpentry, law enforcement, music, physiotherapy, osteopathy, speech pathology, occupational therapy, teaching, athletics, crane operation, mechanics, and the arts are some of the career areas that utilize learning strengths in perceptual and motor skills. Helping students consider career paths that call on their learning strengths may ease their way into a successful professional life.

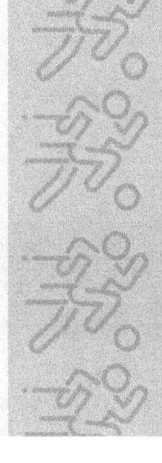

Our most sophisticated perceptual and motor skills involve accurate perception, the integration of our senses, and the coordination of our bodies. These factors directly determine our ability to learn, as new learning begins with sensory perception. How we acquire skills in this area is an interesting journey of brain development. The main types of motor function are as follows.

1. **Gross motor function** (using large muscles such as in bending, balancing, crawling, walking, and jumping)
2. **Fine motor function** (using smaller muscles, particularly the muscles in the hand, for drawing, painting, tapping, and constructing)
3. **Graphomotor function** (used in writing)
4. **Oromotor function** (used in speech and language for communication)

When functioning well, motor actions reinforce memory and learning. But if they do not, we almost invariably have learning blockages (Blythe, 2017).

Art, physical education, and music teachers are among the most astute diagnosticians of students' perceptual and motor skills.

Brain Systems Involved in Perceptual and Motor Skills

Different tasks require different learning skills and use distinct parts of the brain. In addition to the aims of the lesson, let all your students know what brain systems they'll be using in each lesson or activity to familiarize them with their brains. The main parts of the brain involved in perceptual and motor skills are shown in figure 2.1.

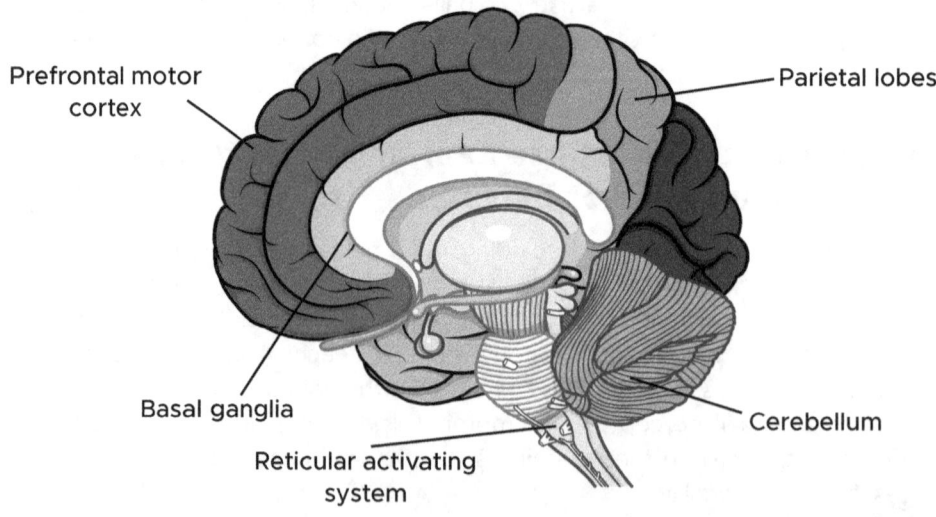

Figure 2.1: Parts of the brain involved in perceptual and motor skills.

The entire body is an information-processing system. There is a two-way dialogue constantly transferring between the brain and the body. The brain tells the body, "Let's go and do this now," while the body feeds the brain information about temperature changes, balance issues, memory, emotions, pain and stress, and energy levels.

This relationship is so powerful that if two of your fingers were sewn together so that their surfaces functioned as one, your brain would reorder the sensory map of the hand from five fingers to four (Sterling & Laughlin, 2015).

Links Between Perceptual and Motor Skills and Other Brain Systems

As our perceptual and motor systems are essential services, impairments in these areas show up in almost all areas of learning.

There are links with language and word smarts (dyslexia and reading problems), people smarts (behavioral issues), spatial reasoning (dysgraphia and eye wobble), number smarts (dyscalculia), and concentration and memory (distractibility and poor muscle memory; Sterling & Laughlin, 2015).

What Blockages in Perceptual and Motor Skills Look Like in Adulthood

When we don't develop our perceptual and motor skills learning strengths, there are long-term consequences. Adults with blockages in perceptual and motor skills often are poorly coordinated, are clumsy and break things, experience small scrapes and injuries, have poor sensory awareness, can't dance, find it difficult to balance on one foot, and avoid sports.

Perceptual and Motor Skills Inputs

Many of our motor movements become automatic and habitual after a time of initial experimentation.

Perception is the use of all our senses to gain information. Our senses of touch, vision, hearing, taste, and the haptic (where our bodies are in space) provide inputs faster than our conscious thoughts. When you are going to sneeze, you probably notice the tickling feeling in your nose before you ever think, "I am going to sneeze"—and certainly before the sneeze occurs.

Perceptual and Motor Skills Processing

Neuromotor functions make things like cursive writing, playing the violin, assembling models, and cutting with scissors possible. The sequencing of bodily movements enables dance, sports, music, and art, as well as relating to and understanding other people through body language.

The intricacy of processing even minor body movements is extraordinary. In order to create even a small shift in posture, the body has to alter its pattern of muscle contractions. This requires a change in the distribution of oxygen and an altered vasomotor pattern to redistribute blood. While this is happening, the active muscle needs to take up glucose, triggering insulin secretion from pancreatic cells (Buzsáki, 2019). Once you appreciate the amount of processing that brings about even a minor change in your stance, you realize that the capacity of people to play sports or practice musical instruments is astonishing.

Perceptual and Motor Skills Outputs

From our observations, demonstrating proficiency in games and sports is an important factor in students' self-esteem and confidence.

Some active students have high levels of outputs in this area. They need to be busy and on the move almost all the time. These students may study best by reading notes or books resting on the handlebars of an exercise bike as they pedal.

If a student is struggling in this area, many teachers we work with find that placing a pool noodle under the student's feet as he or she sits or seating the student on an inflatable exercise ball can help improve the student's outputs (see table 2.1).

Ways to Assess Perceptual and Motor Skills in the Classroom

The following ideas will not replace a full psychological or pediatric assessment, but they may give teachers and parents an idea if further investigations are merited.

The fluidity and coordination of the body and the functioning of the vestibular system, which controls balance, play a powerful role in one's ability to learn. Identifying and correcting blockages in these areas enhances learning outcomes (Blythe, 2014).

Students' ability to complete some of the following tasks will give you an idea of their capacities or difficulties in using perceptual and motor skills to learn well.

Table 2.1: Key Signs—Perceptual and Motor Skills

	Positive Signs	Concerning Signs
Inputs	The student: • Perceives sights, sounds, and smells accurately and acutely	The student: • Has poor hand-eye coordination • Can't balance on one leg • Is clumsy
Processing	The student: • Can catch and throw a ball • Writes fluidly	The student: • Struggles to write • Displays jerky and asymmetrical movement
Outputs	The student: • Is able to follow a rhythm • Demonstrates fluidity of movement or dances • Is able to read body language	The student: • Has a poor sense of personal space • Is unable to read body language • Demonstrates poor coordination of movement

Most of these can be used to conduct an assessment of specific students, but they will also benefit the entire class.

- Coloring in, tracing, and pasting activities can reveal motor preferences and abilities.
- Drawing, running, and handwriting are all essential motor skills, as are tying shoelaces, typing on a computer, playing an instrument, and kicking and catching a ball.
- Mimicking hand-movement series can show how long it takes for students to remember and demonstrate a sequence. Explain to students that you are going to demonstrate a series of hand movements. Without verbal prompts, clasp your hands together and then separate them and make a fist. Tap the top of your fist with the other hand, then tap the bottom of your fist, and then tap the top again. Ask students to repeat the sequence. If they cannot mimic the sequence, repeat it until they can.

Visual Tracking

Similarly, a student's ability to scan and visually track movements relates to his or her capacity to learn. Identifying blockages in this area should prompt a referral to a specialist.

- Can the student follow the movement of your index finger across his or her visual field (side to side, up and down, diagonally)?

- Can the student move his or her eyes toward the source of a sound (such as you snapping your fingers on either side of the student)?
- Can the student visually track the movement of a ball or a piece of crumpled-up paper as it is thrown?

Gross Motor Skills

Activities such as climbing on playground equipment, jumping on trampolines, and playing ball games demonstrate gross motor function.

Determine whether the student can:

- Move forward and backward
- Jump in one spot with both feet
- Hop on one foot and stand on the same foot for up to five seconds
- Kick a ball forward
- Catch a bounced ball using two hands most of the time
- Throw a ball overhand
- Go up and down stairs without assistance
- Ride a bicycle or tricycle using the pedals

Fine Motor Skills

Determine whether the student can:

- Hold a crayon between thumb and fingers firmly
- Draw squares and circles
- Draw a person with between two and four body parts
- Copy square shapes
- Copy some capital letters
- Use a pair of scissors to cut a piece of paper in half
- Make a bridge out of three blocks
- Complete an interlocking puzzle with five to seven pieces
- Tie his or her shoelaces
- Tie a knot

Oromotor Skills

Determine whether the student:

- Has difficulty chewing food or chokes easily

- Drools excessively
- Displays poor closure of his or her lips when using a spoon or fork
- Has a speech impediment

General Perceptual and Motor Skills

Determine whether the student:

- Responds to visual, auditory, or tactile input with basic movements of body parts (for example, a high five or handshake)
- Reaches for or moves toward people or objects by moving his or her body or limbs
- Controls his or her body by using sensory information to explore or react to changes in the physical environment
- Demonstrates awareness of his or her major body parts or limbs by testing their potential movements
- Coordinates the movement of his or her large and small body parts or limbs in different ways
- Changes aspects of his or her effort and spatial or directional movement in relation to people and objects around him or her, with adult guidance
- Prepares for and changes aspects of his or her effort and spatial or directional movement in relation to people and objects in familiar spaces around him or her, on his or her own
- Prepares for and changes aspects of his or her effort and spatial or directional movement during unfamiliar activities, in altered environments, or on different surfaces

Whether a student successfully completes or struggles to finish a series of the preceding activities will not necessarily indicate a problem, but these tasks will serve as a guide to his or her current level of learning strengths in perceptual and motor skills (see figure 2.2, page 46).

Discuss your concerns and compare these results with other teachers who are familiar with this student to confirm your observations.

Primitive Reflexes

Our brains are not blank slates when we are born. Some patterns are preconfigured to help us survive infancy, including a series of primitive reflexes.

As we develop and mature, these primitive reflexes are inhibited and replaced by postural reflexes that help us to function, learn, and control our bodies. This

Use this list to rate the perceptual and motor skills strengths of the student. Assign a score out of ten (with one being "can't do this" and ten being "great at this") for each of the statements that follow. (A student at the average level of his or her class would score a five.)

Issue	Rating
Inputs	
The student:	
• Is aware of right and left	
• Spins, paces, lunges, twirls, rocks, or flicks fingers	
• Can grip a pen	
• Demonstrates balance	
• Is able to avoid bumping into things, or is neither clumsy nor accident prone	
Processing	
The student:	
• Demonstrates finger dexterity	
• Demonstrates eye tracking	
• Is able to refrain from jumping, kicking, bouncing, throwing him- or herself, or bumping into objects or people	
• Is not overly sensitive to sound	
• Is not averse to touching certain textures (sticky, sandy, and so on)	
Outputs	
The student:	
• Is not perturbed by specific odors	
• Plays games and sports	
• Can recall and follow a sequence of movements	
• Displays smoothness and coordination of movements	
• Can write by hand	

Figure 2.2: List of issues with perceptual and motor skills.

usually occurs by three years of age, but not all children achieve this by that stage (Taylor, Houghton, & Chapman, 2004).

The continued presence of primitive reflexes is associated with learning difficulties and may be seen in students with dyslexia, attention deficit hyperactivity disorder (ADHD), dyspraxia, and autism spectrum disorder. For example, nine-month-old babies who are unable to sit unaided, crawl, stand, and take their first step often lag in terms of learning at five years of age. The presence of some primitive reflexes has been found in 45 percent of fifth- and sixth-grade students (Blythe, 2014).

A study by the North Eastern Education and Library Board in 2004 (as cited in Blythe, 2017) of seven mainstream schools in Northern Ireland finds that 48 percent of five- to six-year-olds and 35 percent of eight- to nine-year-olds have some residual primitive reflexes and that this relates to poor educational attainment and reading levels. But if the ongoing presence of primitive reflexes is accurately assessed and then addressed, the student often finds it easier to access higher-cognitive tasks and learning in academic settings.

Problems with muscle tone, balance, and coordination (signs of immature reflex systems) can impede learning irrespective of intelligence. Poor control of eye movements can delay reading, writing, copying, number smarts, and spatial reasoning (Blythe, 2014; Taylor et al., 2004).

Three particular primitive reflexes to be aware of are:

1. The asymmetrical tonic neck reflex (ATNR)
2. The symmetrical tonic neck reflex (STNR)
3. The tonic labyrinthine reflex (TLR)

The Asymmetrical Tonic Neck Reflex (ATNR): The Archer or Fencing Position

The ATNR is usually present in babies from two to six months of age. This reflex is discernible when movement of the head to one side causes the arm on that side to extend and the other arm to bend.

Vision problems can occur if this reflex is uninhibited, including difficulty in focusing from far to near, visual tracking across the midline (the middle of the body, between right and left vertically), differentiating left from right, keeping balance, skipping, marching, and undertaking activities that involve crossing the midline. This can also interfere with writing control (leading to poor handwriting) and eye control for reading. Students with a persistent ATNR will often place their books on an angle when writing (Blythe, 2017).

The Symmetrical Tonic Neck Reflex (STNR)

The STNR is usually present between six months and one year of age. This reflex is discernible when a crawling child looks up—as the neck extends, his or her arms straighten and legs bend, causing the child's bottom to lower and the child to sit on his or her heels.

While this reflex helps us with hand-eye coordination and crawling as babies, if it is uninhibited, students might display poor posture (slumping in chairs or sometimes sitting on their feet), walk on their knuckles, or sit in a *W* position on the ground. Such students may be messy eaters and have poor hand-eye coordination (particularly displaying as the inability to catch a ball). They may also not be able to sit still when looking up at the board and then down at their page in the classroom (Blythe, 2017).

They may struggle to shift between visual fields (from far to near and back again), which is essential for copying tasks, and can have problems focusing close up, making it difficult to see words on a page. They may also have problems with paying attention and learning to swim. Unsurprisingly, people often pass off the retention of this reflex as simply being clumsy.

Teachers may observe the STNR when students look down while they write, almost lying on the desk, as their arms want to bend. These students also tend to swing on chairs in class, physically changing their bodily position as the position of their head moves past the midplane (the point halfway between the top of one's head and the tip of one's toes).

Miriam L. Bender (1976) finds the STNR present in 75 percent of learning-disabled students, but not present in a control group of students without learning disabilities.

The Tonic Labyrinthine Reflex (TLR)

The TLR is usually inhibited by about four to six months of age. This reflex is discernible when babies are held on their backs, as they curl up if their heads move toward their chests or extend their limbs if their heads are lowered backward (Blythe, 2017).

In students with retained TLR, we usually see poor muscle tone and development, poor posture, and poor balance, as well as spatial-reasoning problems, such as poor body awareness. The control of eye movements required for sustained and accurate visual perception and copying off the board, as well as depth perception, may also be impaired. Poor sequencing skills, such as in spelling, show up in reading difficulties and in keeping ideas in order in mathematics. These students may also squash their writing to keep their words on one line and display poor time sense and management. Some of the signs that primitive reflexes may be present in students (Blythe, 2014) are listed here.

Signs That Indicate the Presence of Primitive Reflexes

Following are signs that indicate the presence of primitive reflexes.

The Student Can't Sit Straight

Some students sit asymmetrically in chairs and appear inattentive, disrespectful, or disruptive. For some, this can indicate the presence of a retained ATNR, as when one side of the body stretches out, the other side contracts.

The Student Slumps Over While Writing

The continued presence of a retained ATNR can also affect writing posture. Typically, students slump over their writing because one arm's extension causes the other to flex. Stabilization of the paper, and their grip on a pen or pencil, can also be affected. Another common reason students slump while writing is due to poor eyesight, so we suggest they have their vision checked.

The Student Loses Track of His or Her Place When Reading

Reading involves quick and smooth movements of the eyes. Some students are unable to dissociate eye movement from head movement to localize, scan, track, and shift their gaze. They may lose their place and have difficulty locating letters, words, or sentences on a page. This will also affect keyboard use and learning mathematics.

The Student Displays Poor Running Patterns

Often, students with a retained ATNR have odd running patterns, as they find it challenging to swing their arms reciprocally.

The Student Splays When Sitting on the Floor

Students who sit on the floor in a *W* shape (with legs bent so that knees are forward and ankles are closer to either hip) may have retained their STNR.

The Student Displays Floppy Muscle Tone

Undeveloped muscle tone and strength can also indicate that the student has a retained STNR. These students may walk on their toes rather than on the soles of their feet. Others may be more likely than their peers to fall out of their seats.

Because of low levels of strength and tone, these students often prefer to lie on the floor, have trouble learning to swim, and are uncoordinated.

The Student Has Poor Impulse Control

The presence of a retained STNR can affect concentration. Some students find the pressure of the seat on their backs to be painful and so may squirm and fidget to avoid this.

Addressing Primitive Reflexes

So what can you do to address these retained reflexes and thereby improve learning? Lay down new connections that help to inhibit these primitive reflexes.

This is a fairly straightforward process of asking students to complete movements that do not include the reflexive part of the movement that was previously present. With daily exercises, for a few minutes each day over the course of thirty days, these primitive reflexes are inhibited and replaced by more usual actions (Blythe, 2014).

While referral to a physical specialist may be advisable, teachers can use these indicators to assess whether a referral is warranted (see figure 2.3). Teachers can also help develop physical skills that promote learning by implementing a program available at Integrating Thinking (www.integratingthinking.com.au).

For a comprehensive description of primitive reflexes, see *Neuromotor Immaturity in Children and Adults: The INPP Screening Test for Clinicians and Health Practitioners* (Blythe, 2014) and Tools to Grow (www.toolstogrowot.com).

Discuss your concerns and compare these results with other teachers who are familiar with this student to confirm your observations.

Please note that this list (see figure 2.3) does not contain all the main indicators of primitive reflexes. But if some of the preceding issues are present in students, you may wish to consider conducting a full assessment. If so, we recommend contacting training help, like that available at Integrated Thinking (www.integratingthinking.com.au).

Evidence That Perceptual and Motor Skills Can Be Improved

One of the rules of neuroscience is that as we, as humans, become more proficient at something, we use less of the brain's processing power to achieve the same task (Sapolsky, 2017b). As we become more proficient, we become more efficient.

The way we shift our brains toward being skilled is by integrating the parts of the brain into a neural loop, which enables us to process information more fluently and efficiently. Initially, our movements are a product of conscious thinking, as we use our frontal lobes to direct our attention. We then use mainly our parietal lobes to execute the correct movements before storing the sequence of steps in

Use this list to rate the student's primitive reflexes. Assign a score out of ten (with one being "can't do this" and ten being "great at this") for each of the statements that follow. (A student at the average level of his or her class would score a five.)

Issue	Rating
The student:	
• Has the ability to balance	
• Displays coordination skills	
• Has muscle tone and strength	
• Is able to use scissors to cut things	
• Has good posture while sitting in a desk	
• Sits on the floor with legs crossed (rather than straight out)	
• Walks on his or her heels (rather than toes)	
• Has good posture when writing	
• Can alter the direction of his or her eyes or turn his or her head without rotating his or her body	
• Can catch a ball	
• Can throw a ball	
• Can stand up from squatting	
• Can crawl on his or her hands and knees	
• Swings his or her arms normally when running	
• Demonstrates reading ability	
• Can focus	
• Is able to stop fidgeting when asked to do so	
• Generally maintains good posture or muscle control but loses that ability when tired or very stressed	

Figure 2.3: List of issues with primitive reflexes.

the cerebellum, where they become automatic. Once we have developed automaticity, we can move on to thinking about other things (Doya, 2000; Sterling & Laughlin, 2015).

How to Enhance Perceptual and Motor Skills

This is a learning strength influenced by practice, coaching, and refinement. We have done this as we've learned to crawl, then balance, and then walk. This is an area where we learn by doing. For this reason, sharing kind, supportive feedback designed to help students improve also gives them the courage to have a go and repeat their performances until they succeed.

Improving Perceptual and Motor Skills Inputs

Our mirror neurons are situated in the rear part of the prefrontal cortex. These activate when we watch other people doing intentional activities and help us learn through imitation and role modeling. Some of our most important learning happens through imitation after we watch successful people in action.

How to Improve Perceptual and Motor Skills Inputs

Some methods of improving inputs in this learning area include:

- Balance and movement practice
- Yoga
- Dance
- Aerobics
- Listening-skills training
- Origami
- Paper-plane construction
- Table tennis
- Clapping and rhythm games
- Rock climbing

Improving Perceptual and Motor Skills Processing

Some adults need to draw, knit, fiddle, or doodle in order to concentrate, and students are just the same. Students tapping, fidgeting, fiddling, rocking, or making unusual faces or gestures can upset teachers—unless they understand this can be a part of a student's process. Of course, the art is finding a way for these students to focus physically without distracting the rest of the class. Teachers should provide sufficient privacy for students with gross motor dysfunctions during their practice sessions.

Participating in hands-on experiences in small groups, manipulating materials in a science experiment, or engaging in sports can improve various neurodevelopmental functions, such as active working memory and problem solving (Johnson, Maruyama, Johnson, Nelson, & Skon, 1981; Kagan, 2013).

How to Improve Muscle Memory

Another way to facilitate the processing of perceptual and motor skills is to shift some of it to automaticity. Most adults have done this, even if they are unaware of it. After getting into a car, you don't have to think, "What do I do first?" If you pick up a pen, you don't have to ask, "Now, how do I write again?" These processes have been built through repetition over time, shifting from conscious thought to muscle memory (Colvin, 2018). When an action or a movement is so well rehearsed or practiced, like riding a bicycle or tying shoelaces, the memory of that movement is retained in the motor cortex, the basal ganglia, and the cerebellum (Clark & Mayer, 2016). It becomes an acquired skill that seems innate.

Improving Perceptual and Motor Skills Outputs

Motor output helps accomplish some important academic skills. For instance, some of the most complex muscular manipulations are needed for writing. Most fine motor activities are not accomplished at the same speed as many gross motor actions, as they require more time for planning, monitoring, and pacing.

Students with output blockages in writing may benefit from using dictation apps and a computer as soon as it is practical, but they also need consistent practice forming letters and handwriting.

How to Improve Gross Motor Functioning

Gross motor functions, such as in bending, balancing, crawling, walking, and jumping, use large muscles. Regular practice with completing obstacle courses, climbing walls, dancing, and using exercise equipment can assist development in this area (Diamond & Lee, 2011; Blythe, 2017).

How to Improve Fine Motor Functioning

Fine motor functions, which are required for squeezing, pincer grasping, and drawing, use the smaller muscles of the hand. Other fine motor activities include knitting, sewing, and stitching; picking up small objects; using scissors; drawing;

writing; and cooking. Computer games often demand speed combined with fine motor hand-eye coordination.

How to Improve the Graphomotor Skills Used in Writing

Writing efficiently involves the intricate coordination of muscles, some being used to shift the pen or pencil up and down while others move it sideways.

Students who struggle with their graphomotor skills may grip the pen or pencil with a fist or write only in block writing, often pressing too hard on the page. Placing a rubberized mouse pad beneath their paper can help these students learn how much pressure to exert when writing. Assist students who display poor pen or pencil grip by marking the positions on their fingers where the pen or pencil should touch as they hold it.

Some students lose track of where they are as they write because they look at their writing hand instead of the page. Helping them learn to write while looking away can remedy this (see table 2.2).

Table 2.2: Common Causes of Writing Blockages

Inputs	Processing	Outputs
The student:	The student:	The student:
• Focuses on too many things at once • Has restricted vocabulary • Lacks guided practice • Doesn't see patterns for spelling and punctuation	• Can't utilize feedback • Is unable to order his or her thoughts • Doesn't track his or her own progress • Can't link letters	• Lacks the confidence to write • Is avoidant and fears making mistakes • Often feels overwhelmed and gives up • Lacks a good pen grip

How to Improve Eye Tracking

The following activities will help build eye-tracking skills.

- Completing picture puzzles
- Finding many objects of the same shape around the room
- Imitating a series of motor movements made by someone else
- Playing "Simon says"
- Completing dot-to-dot pictures
- Finding the mistakes in "What's wrong with this picture?" images
- Sorting playing cards in different ways or using playing cards to find two with matching numbers

- Solving mazes
- Playing "I spy"
- Using tracing paper to trace and color simple pictures

How to Improve Auditory Processing

According to author Lesley E. Tan (1999), auditory processing disorder is a problem that affects about 5 to 10 percent of students. Because their ears and brains are not fully coordinated, students with this condition can't process what they hear in the same way as other students. A further 16 percent have hearing issues due to ear infections, colds, and flus (Treasure, 2011).

Signs of auditory-processing blockages include poor concentration, the inability to follow instructions, poor organization, daydreaming, difficulty with phonics, and a tendency to distract others. The student may also display intelligence but can't learn to read.

When attempting to improve students' auditory processing, the first question to ask is, "Can they hear properly?" If students are suspected of having hearing difficulties, two types of issues should be considered.

1. **The student can't detect softer sounds because of problems in his or her ears.** As this is usually a sensory problem, consider an audiological assessment such as the Speech Perception in Noise (SPIN) test and the Short-Term Auditory Memory (STAM) test.

2. **The student can hear instructions but does not understand what is being said.** This issue usually results from poor processing of speech and sound—the student finds it hard to derive meaning. The causes of this include background-noise levels, language overload, and listening fatigue. Strategies to address this include:
    - Stating directions simply
    - Using words like *first*, *next*, and *then* to create a sense of sequence
    - Rephrasing misunderstood directions rather than repeating them
    - Creating a ritual for when the activity changes (for example, "So now we are going to change to . . . .")
    - Using visuals, gestures, and signals, where possible
    - Asking the student to repeat your instructions in his or her own words
    - Avoiding open learning areas
    - Reducing the length of sentences and instructions (As a general guide, the number of words in any instruction should vary according to the age of the student: grades K–1, six to ten words; grades 2–3, ten to twelve words;

and grades 4–6, twelve to fifteen words. Teenagers will vary in this, as some days they can process more than fifteen words and other days much fewer.)

– Alerting the class when listening is particularly important

Difficulty in auditory processing affects students' ability to read. When digit span (the ability to recall and repeat back a series of numbers) is fewer than four, students can't hold phonemes in short-term memory. Competent readers usually have a digit span of five or more (Sapolsky, 2017b).

Some first- and second-grade students have low digit spans and therefore have problems in reading comprehension due to blockages in auditory recall (Tan, 1999). Their auditory processing needs to mature. Some helpful strategies are:

- Chunking and fragmenting materials
- Providing additional prereading activities
- Allowing for variations in readiness
- Allowing time to think and reply
- Teaching to think as they read

How to Improve Oromotor Functioning

Some students may stutter or endure other speech-articulation difficulties. It can be frustrating for these students when their mouths can't keep pace with their flow of ideas, so they often write better than they talk. These students benefit from speech pathology and therapy, while singing and music training can also be incredibly beneficial.

Perceptual and Motor Skills Cross-Fertilization Strategies

If a student has a learning strength in perceptual and motor skills, table 2.3 suggests some strategies that could be used to help extend learning in other areas. These are some key suggestions to stimulate your thinking and can be adapted to your classroom or time frame as you see fit.

Table 2.3: Extending Learning From Perceptual and Motor Skills

Learning-Strength Area	Sample Strategy
Spatial Reasoning	**Students can:** • Make learning physical and visual • Learn dance, theater, drama, and sports • Mirror other peoples' movements **Teachers can:** • Ask students to draw in response to instructions (for example, "Draw a circle; draw two triangles on top of the circle; and draw a long circle—or oval—coming from the bottom of the first circle. You have drawn a cat! Add a tail, some eyes, whiskers, a mouth, and so on.") • Ask students to practice orthogonal-views drawing—from the front, top, and side • Interpret evidence—different perspectives of visual evidence • Describe a picture or situation to someone who is not looking at it • Build structures and give instructions to others to do the same without them seeing the structures • Organize pair activities—one student describes, the other draws **At home, families can:** • Set up an art gallery • Practice photography, pottery, and model making • Play with picture dominoes
Concentration and Memory	**Students can:** • Practice when something is important to remember—point at it to link it to a movement **Teachers can:** • Copy and remember patterns • Use brain-gym activities • Use clapping and rhythm activities to increase focus • Practice balancing **At home, families can:** • Create shopping lists and checklists • Memorize a sequence of ideas • Increase the use of body memory—counting on fingers and using physical cues such as tapping to recall something • Use journey methods for memory (see page 79) • Practice origami

continued →

Learning-Strength Area	Sample Strategy
Planning and Sequencing	**Students can:** • Learn to play a musical instrument • Play a sport like soccer, softball, baseball, or hockey • Develop projects • Build things—models, playhouses, skate ramps, and so on **Teachers can:** • Map out stories • Teach students how to make notes • Teach students to identify the main idea • Use 3-D printing and 3-D pens • Use STEM or STEAM activities • Practice clay modeling **At home, families can:** • Learn dance or movement sequences • Practice building and construction projects • Rock climb • Practice gymnastics • Practice navigation and orienteering • Have a project space at home
Thinking and Logic	**Students can:** • See logical problem solving as figuring things out so that they act in useful ways • Consider what actions need to be taken, then consider what decisions need to be made before those actions • Weigh issues **Teachers can:** • Pace out problems—walk through a problem physically • Collect objects and group them by genre or category **At home, families can:** • Play matching and sorting activities—collecting toys and grouping them into categories • Use and read maps • Play with blocks

Learning-Strength Area	Sample Strategy
People Smarts	**Students can:** • Study human movement; develop expertise in how bodies move and flex • Learn body language and cold reading **Teachers can:** • Have students work in pairs or small groups to solve problems • Practice mindful walking and movements • Discuss facial expressions and appropriate touch • Promote body language and personal space • Use activities in which one student describes something while the other draws it from his or her description • Watch how people move and see what that can reveal about their feelings • Draw a portrait by looking at another person but not at the paper • Build a structure and give instructions to others to do the same without them seeing the structure **At home, families can:** • Practice art and drawing activities
Language and Word Smarts	**Students can:** • Read or write action and adventure stories • Perform improvised sketches • Read Choose Your Own Adventure stories **Teachers can:** • Act out texts • Create short films and advertisements • Have students act out parts of a story • Practice writing based on the senses • Write poetry based on art pieces • Create how-to videos for students in science and mathematics **At home, families can:** • Ask children to act out texts and create interviews with characters • Ask children with strong perceptual skills to consider stories from the perspectives of minor characters or ask them to relate stories to their own lives

continued →

Learning-Strength Area	Sample Strategy
Number Smarts	**Students can:** • Become knowledgeable about practical mathematics (for example, How tall is the average person? What is the usual span of a bridge between support structures? Is there an upper limit to how high we can build office towers? If the human race continues to get taller, what will need to change?) **Teachers can:** • Use human-sized number lines • Practice music, movement, sports statistics, blocks, dice, dominoes, and card games • Use concrete materials available in every lesson • Walk through a problem's solution • Create scale models • Watch for students who use their fingers as a concrete counting mechanism, and offer the touch mathematics technique as an alternative, in which students touch points on each number with their pencils while counting (this technique provides a concrete reinforcement for the student, while also helping to preserve the fluency of the problem) **At home, families can:** • Encourage interest in sports and activities such as skateboarding and surfing, as all these areas have numbers related to them (for example, the arc of a skate park ramp may be important to calculate before its construction)

In Summary

Learning strengths in perceptual and motor skills allow the most graceful and intricate movements to be transformed into an expressive dance or the most daring acts on a sporting field. These strengths enable chefs to taste subtle flavors and sculptors to realize images. A world deficient in perceptual and motor skills would be a world lacking in dance, mime, athletics, juggling, and touch.

Once developed, learning strengths in perceptual and motor skills can be applied to enhance success in other areas. They can be used to:

- Touch and then shape objects, such as furniture or buildings (spatial reasoning)
- Store experiences and develop skills through muscle memory (concentration and memory)
- Step through a sequence to achieve an outcome (planning and sequencing)

- Follow a flowchart in solving a problem (thinking and logic)
- Mirror facial expressions, emotions, gestures, and postures (people smarts)
- Act out a scene with dialogue (language and word smarts)
- Physically experience quantities and size of area (number smarts)

Along with spatial reasoning, perceptual and motor skills serve as another foundational building block for success in life. This positive effect on success is especially enhanced when it is linked to concentration and memory.

Reflection Questions

- What strategies will be most valuable in strengthening the perceptual and motor skills of your students?
- Which other members of staff need to be involved in this discussion?
- Should any student's parents or guardians be involved in this discussion?
- What does the information regarding perceptual and motor skills reveal?
- How can we give these insights further consideration and accommodation?
- Which classroom activities pose an advantage or disadvantage to students with perceptual and motor skills challenges?
- How can you arrange your classroom spaces to maximize learning for students with auditory-processing issues?
- How many learning activities in your classroom this week have incorporated perceptual and motor skills development?

Chapter 3
CONCENTRATION AND MEMORY

The highest correlate (0.81) of academic results is intelligence (Dreary, Strand, Smith, & Fernandes, 2007), and there is a powerful positive relationship between intelligence and memory (Ackerman, Beier, & Boyle, 2005). While correlation is not causation, it is plausible that increasing students' ability to concentrate and therefore remember is likely to increase academic results.

Careers Areas That Utilize Learning Strengths in Concentration and Memory

Aviation, train driving, air traffic control, professional chess, medicine, law, teaching, dentistry, policing, radiography, radio announcing, computer programming, postal work, data analysis, surgery, engineering, sports broadcasting, comedy, and acting are some of the career areas that utilize learning strengths in concentration and memory. Helping students consider career paths that call on their learning strengths may ease their way into a successful professional life.

Our most sophisticated concentration and memory skills involve noticing and focusing on fine or small distinctions, perceiving differences, pattern detection, mental information processing, creativity, and recall (Claxton, 1999; Popova, 2012). How we build skills in this area is an interesting journey of brain development.

Brain Systems Involved in Concentration and Memory

Different tasks require different learning skills and use distinct parts of the brain. In addition to the aims of the lesson, let all your students know what brain systems they'll be using in each lesson or activity to familiarize them with their brains. The main parts of the brain involved in concentration and memory are shown in figure 3.1.

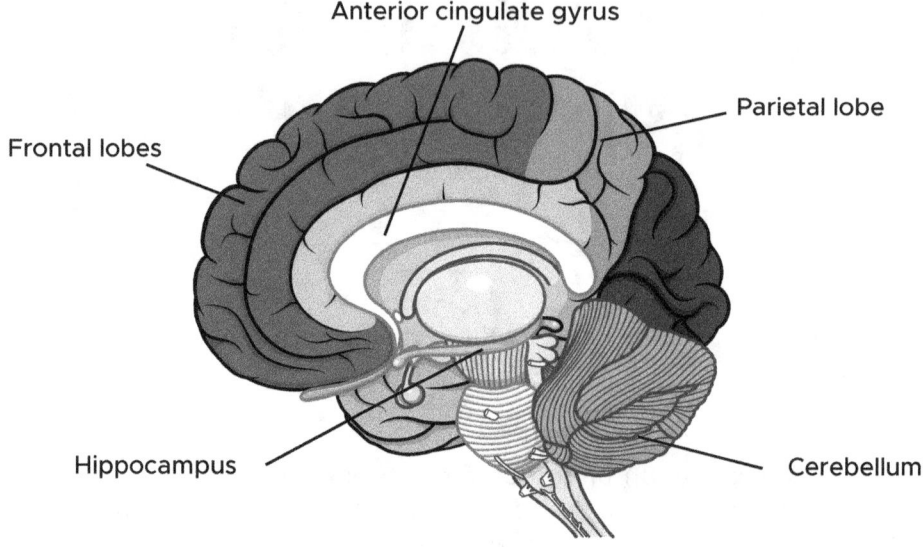

Figure 3.1: Parts of the brain involved in concentration and memory.

The anterior cingulate gyrus focuses one's concentration, the hippocampus integrates conscious memories, and the cerebellum stores habitual and unconscious memories. All these parts have to link to the frontal lobes to enable effective action.

Concentration and memory require alertness, orientation to perceptual inputs, processing of information, and the regulation of output and behavior. When our concentration and memory systems work well, we can be productive and learn to behave appropriately.

Blockages in this area tend to negatively affect reading, mathematics, reasoning, creativity, and the ability to pass tests or exams, and they can cause mayhem in life generally.

Links Between Concentration and Memory and Other Brain Systems

When concentration is unfocused, almost no other learning can occur effectively, so blockages in concentration and memory have far-reaching implications. They limit the ability to focus on and reason about spatial images, dull the awareness of motor movements and perception, make sequenced thinking and logic almost impossible, and interfere with development of language and number sense.

What Blockages in Memory and Concentration Look Like in Adulthood

When we don't develop our concentration and memory learning strengths, there are long-term consequences. Adults with blockages in concentration and memory often find it hard to focus on complex stories; find it difficult to focus on complex issues; overlook small details; forget where their cars are parked or where their keys were left; walk from one room to another and think, "Why did I come in here?"; forget birthdays and anniversaries; and will start five projects in a day and finish none of them.

Concentration and Memory Inputs

There are great benefits in concentration training. It improves memory, focus, the functioning of frontal lobes, IQ, sequencing, context, drive, and executive control (Diamond, 2013). But the most powerful way to improve your memory is focusing your attention on what you're trying to learn.

To focus your concentration like a laser, three brain and neurochemical systems are required.

1. An input system, which relies on dopamine in the frontal and parietal regions
2. An orienting system, located in the frontal temporal and anterior cingulate gyrus, which relies on the neurotransmitter acetylcholine
3. The executive frontal cortex and levels of dopamine

Concentration is like the gearshift of the human brain. While we most often think of concentration as a sharpening of focus, it is also the ability to broaden and shift our focus and actions from one activity or context to another according to different demands and contexts (Amen, 2015). This also relates to our people smarts, as it allows us to modify our behavior according to circumstances and who we are with.

Concentration requires flexible focus. At times, we need to narrow our concentration and filter out distractions and the impulse to multitask. At other times, we need to be able to broaden our concentration to increase our awareness of other possibilities. The flexibility of our filters is particularly susceptible to stress, sleep deprivation, and disturbances. Even people with very good concentration may have difficulty processing auditory sounds in a noisy environment with lots of interruptions and distractions.

Being distracted often means being otherwise attracted. Most children focus on the things that intrigue and interest them (which are not usually the things you hope they would concentrate on). For parents of children with these challenges, the typology of students with concentration issues in *Unlocking Your Child's Genius* (Fuller, 2015) may be helpful.

Concentration and Memory Processing

Some people go to a cupboard and see ingredients. Others see recipes. Patterning of thinking plays a powerful role in what we attend to and how well we recall it. Developing patterns, or schema, improves memory and is predictive of academic success (Marzano, 2007).

When we process and organize the information we are using, we strengthen our memories. If we are passive recipients of information, less is retained. Concentration and memory can best be summarized by the phrase "use it or lose it."

Encouraging students to find links between ideas, highlight information, scribble notes, or make a concept map or Venn diagram increases their ability to remember. The more actively students are involved in something, the more likely they are to remember it (see figure 3.2).

Long-Term Memory

Storing information in your long-term memory means you don't always have to learn things from scratch. It also means that eventually some processes, such as driving a car, riding a bike, and remembering your times tables, become automatic. There are three important things to know about how long-term memory works.

1. The best way to store information into long-term memory is to transform it. Putting words into pictures, or pictures into words or sounds, helps us remember information (Howard-Jones et al., 2018; Jaeggi, Buschkuehl, Jonides, & Perrig, 2008). Making flowcharts and concept maps and using graphic organizers can help with this. This is especially true when repeated over time.

    Applying knowledge to new contexts also works. For example, if you were learning about explorers in history, you might try to write a journal entry from the perspective of more modern explorers using information you have read.

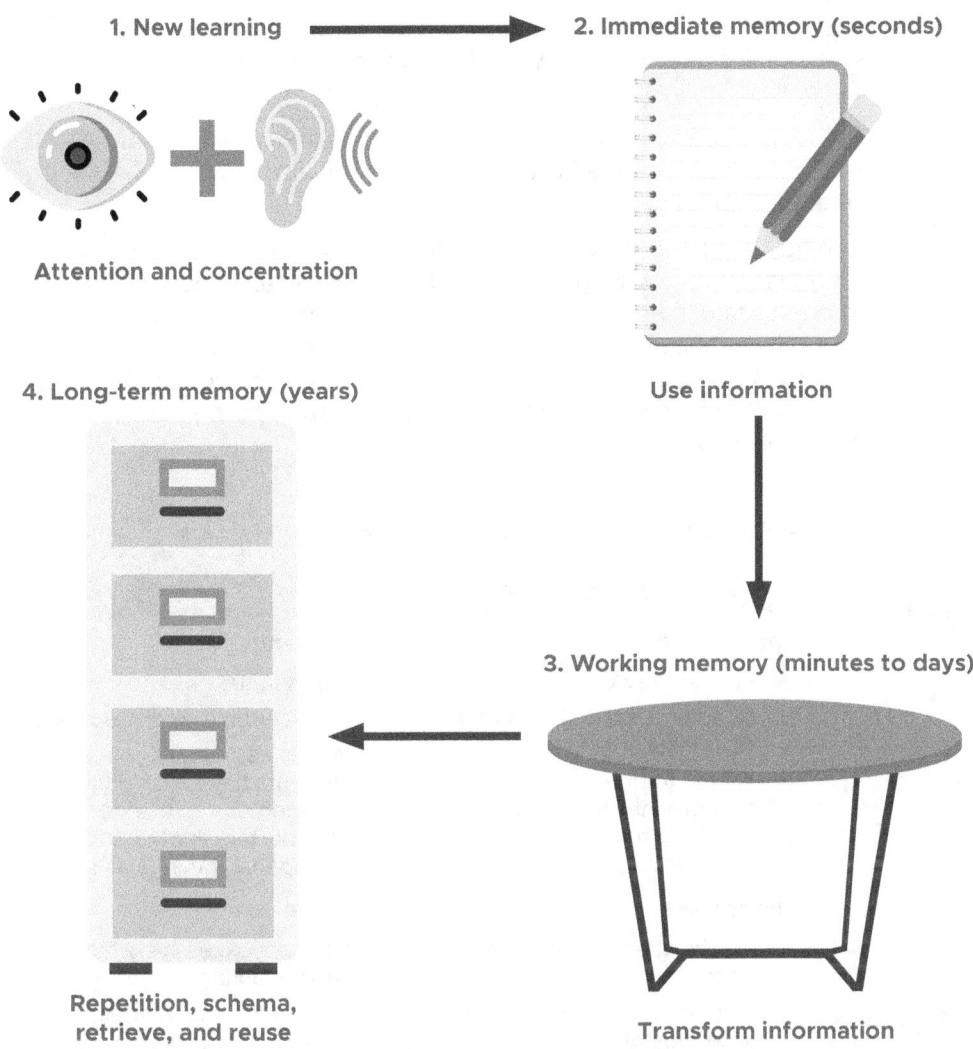

Figure 3.2: How memory works.

2. The way we store information into long-term memory (inputs) is different from the way we retrieve it (outputs; Marzano, 2007). Information gets stored in long-term memory like a filing cabinet, on the basis of its similarity to other pieces of information. The way we get information out again is based on difference.

   For example, let's say when you were a child, your family got you a pet dog. You learned and remembered the pet you had was a dog by learning about its similarities to other dogs—it has four legs, it is furry, it barks, and so on. Imagine your dog got lost and you had to go to the animal shelter to find it. You would draw on the image in your head of what your dog looks like, but using only similarities wouldn't help much. So you would use critical, distinctive aspects of your dog to find it—the spot on its left shoulder and the kink in its tail. We remember ideas in just the same way.

3. This means when we want to learn something and remember it, we need to recognize how it is similar to but also how it is different from other things.

Getting something stored into long-term memory takes time. After learning something new, the brain needs several hours to consolidate it. For students in secondary school, this is vital information, because long-term filing works best while you sleep (Walker & Stickgold, 2006). The minutes before bedtime are crucial and shouldn't be wasted flicking through social media. (See table 3.1.)

Table 3.1: Key Signs—Concentration and Memory

	Positive Signs	**Concerning Signs**
Inputs	**The student:** • Notices key details • Readily starts working and maintains effort level • Is able to demonstrate how to store information into short-term, working, and long-term memory	**The student:** • Loses focus quickly • Is susceptible to distractions • Misses key details—some students have a hard time deciding on relative degrees of importance; others focus on too many things at once
Processing	**The student:** • Works at an appropriate pace • Maintains focus for adequate stretches of time • Can abbreviate and chunk information	**The student:** • Appears excessively fatigued when working • Has trouble initiating and sticking with tasks • Experiences lapses in memory or loses his or her thread in thinking
Outputs	**The student:** • Is able to identify the most salient aspects of an issue (narrowed focus) and can consider the broader implications (open attention) • Can recall details in order	**The student:** • Is overly diverted by inconsequential factors • Has poor recall—you mention something you discussed yesterday, but the student gives you a blank look • Has recollections that are jumbled or incoherent

Ways to Assess Concentration and Memory in the Classroom

The following ideas will not replace a full psychological assessment, but they may give teachers and parents an idea if further investigations are merited.

Students' ability to complete some of the following tasks will give you an indication of their capacities or difficulties in using concentration and memory to learn well. Most of these can be used to make an assessment of specific students, but they will also benefit the entire class. Students who struggle with the following tasks over repeated trials may benefit from more specialized assessment.

General Memory Assessment

- Playing memory games (for example, asking the student to remember eight objects displayed on a tray and then recall them when the objects are concealed)
- Finding the main idea or concept after being taught how to do so
- Following a rhythm
- Playing chess, card games, or concentration games
- Completing a random letter test (for example, say each letter and ask the student to raise a finger for each of the four As: B-R-A-V-E-A-H-A-A-R-T)

Working Memory Assessment—The Digit Span Test

Ask the student to repeat a series of numbers (start with three numbers, then four, then five, then six, and so on).

Three digits: 7-8-3

Four digits: 7-9-6-2

Five digits: 6-3-8-1-7

Six digits: 4-8-3-9-7-2

Seven digits: 8-9-2-6-4-1-7

Eight digits: 7-1-9-2-8-3-5-4

- How many digits can the student recall accurately? While this is not a formal version of a memory test, as a general rule of thumb, you should see students able to correctly recall between three and seven digits.
- Ask the student to reverse the digits—for example, if you said, "Two . . . three," the student would say, "Three . . . two."
- How many digits can the student recall accurately backward?

In his foundational research on memory, cognitive psychologist George A. Miller (1956) finds the human memory storage is about seven, plus or minus two pieces of information. For young students, this might be closer to three, and for teenagers, it might be nearer to seven.

Other Memory Tests

- Recite the alphabet.
- Count by sevens; count by threes.
- Recite spelling words, such as *world*, backward from memory.
- List the names of the months, starting from the last month of the year.
- Count with interruptions. (Ask the student to count from one to one hundred, interrupting the student at thirty-two. Ask the student to wait one minute and then restart counting. Can he or she recall where to restart?)
- Count with interruptions and a separate task. (Interrupt the student at fifty-six, and then do an intervening task. Ask the student to restart counting from where he or she left off. Can the student recall where to restart?)

New Learning Assessments—Paired Associations

One way to assess memory and new learning is to present pairs of words to students that include some common pairings and some unfamiliar ones. For example, you might teach students the following pairs.

- Dog and cat
- Begonia and submarine
- Day and night
- Oxygen and brick
- Hippopotamus and roof
- Airship and carrot

After an interval of time, say the first word in the pair (for example, *dog*) and see if students can recall the matching word (*cat*). Reteach the pairs and retest after an interval. The familiar pairings should be recalled fairly easily, but the less-familiar pairings may take a few attempts before all students can recall them accurately. If you see no increase in a student's knowledge of unfamiliar pairings after several repeated exposures, you may consider if the student has blockages in his or her concentration and memory inputs.

If a student shows no memory increase in the unfamiliar pairings, you can also test to see if the information has been encoded. For example, if you said to a student, "oxygen," and his or her only response was to stare blankly, you might then say, "Do you think the word is *house* or *brick*?" If cueing the word stimulates the correct answer, this may indicate an output problem rather than an input problem.

Whether a student successfully completes or struggles to finish a series of the preceding activities will not indicate much, but these tasks will serve as a guide to his or her current level of learning strengths in concentration and memory (see table 3.2).

Table 3.2: Common Concentration Blockages

Inputs	Processing	Outputs
The student:	**The student:**	**The student:**
• Does not know what to focus on	• Can't sustain concentration	• Can't monitor and self-correct if he or she goes off on a tangent
• Goes off task if the task changes	• Has poor endurance	
• Can't link new ideas to what he or she already knows	• Can't break down tasks into smaller parts	• Lacks goals and priorities
• Can't inhibit distractors	• Can't vary the way he or she approaches a task	• Can't use self-talk to remind him- or herself
• Experiences undue stress	• Displays disjointed thinking	• Can't adapt to changing circumstances or rules
• Experiences sleep deprivation	• Is evasive and slow to explain his or her thinking	• Is forgetful
		• Is unable to elaborate on his or her thinking

Some students with memory blockages feel ashamed of their forgetfulness and make up fanciful stories or lies to cover it up. With students who habitually tell silly lies, consider if they could be experiencing memory deficits (see table 3.3, page 72, and figure 3.3, page 72). Students with traumatic histories may also often experience memory issues and reduced hippocampal functioning (Mason, Murphy, & Jackson, 2019; Sapolsky, 2004).

NEURODEVELOPMENTAL DIFFERENTIATION

Table 3.3: Common Memory Blockages

Inputs	Processing	Outputs
The student: • Is unable to determine the most important piece of information to remember • Zones in and out—can't keep up with the flow of new information • Misses details and sequences • Can't break down tasks into smaller parts • Gets distracted by irrelevant information or details • Can't switch from one task to another efficiently	**The student:** • Can't retain information long enough to work on it • Loses track of the steps involved in a task • Is unable to see patterns and relationships • Can't hold information in his or her mind long enough to copy it • Can't match language with concepts and symbols • Fails to self-correct because of losing focus and purpose	**The student:** • Recalls incorrect or irrelevant information • Can't link ideas (similarities and differences) • Does not see how information can be applied • Needs multiple prompts for retrieval • Experiences test anxiety—freezes and won't ask for help • Is slow to recall information

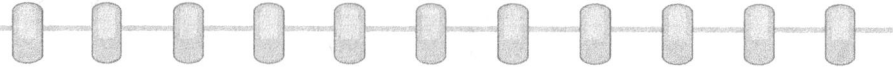

Use this list to rate the concentration and memory strengths of the student. Assign a score out of ten (with one being "can't do this" and ten being "great at this") for each of the statements that follow. (A student at the average level of his or her class would score a five.)

Issue	Rating
Inputs	
The student:	
• Can focus on the main idea	
• Can maintain attention	
• Can resist distractions	
• Can absorb new ideas and information	
• Can notice patterns and relationships	

Processing	
The student:	
• Can link new learning with prior knowledge	
• Can identify similarities and differences	
• Can break new information down into steps or manageable chunks	
• Can switch tasks and then return to the first task to complete it	
• Can sustain endurance and interest	
Outputs	
The student:	
• Has a good memory	
• Can recall links between ideas	
• Displays comprehension and understanding	
• Can summarize the most important aspects of concepts	
• Can communicate what he or she knows and what he or she is unsure of	

Figure 3.3: List of issues with concentration and memory.

Discuss your concerns and compare these results with other teachers who are familiar with this student to confirm your observations.

Evidence That Concentration and Memory Can Be Improved

If you have ever learned to play a musical instrument or had driving lessons in a manual car, you already know that concentration can be improved—but this is best done in the classroom or in real-life situations. While some great claims have been made about the power of computerized brain-training programs, it seems most of the gains usually don't transfer from the computer tasks (Restak, 2001; Restak & Kim, 2010).

How to Enhance Concentration and Memory

As stated at the beginning of this chapter, academic results are directly linked to intelligence, and the relationship between memory and intelligence is strongly positive. Memory is improved when you do something with the information you concentrate on—if you organize it or apply it, you are more likely to retain it. What follows are two methods to help achieve this.

Prioritizing

We like it when people can prioritize—if you are in a plane that is landing, you would hope the pilot is focusing on landing the plane safely rather than considering what to have for dinner. When prioritizing, the first issue is to work out what to attend to first. The art of paying attention to the most salient points is a learnable skill (Sapolsky, 2017b; Sternberg, 1996).

Provide students with artworks, historical photographs, or common problems (for example, exiting a busy shopping center or evaluating a persuasive essay), and then ask them the following.

- "What is the most important bit of information?"
- "What do we most need to know?"
- "What do we need to know or do next?"

Activities where you ask your students to select the main ideas of a concept are invaluable.

Break It Down So It Can Be Remembered

Breaking information down helps us to remember it better. It shifts us from thinking about single ideas to thinking about patterns of ideas or, as we put it earlier, from ingredients to recipes.

For example, if we asked you to remember the following series of letters, you would likely have some difficulty.

F D R B B C C I A E U F B I U K J F K N Y C U S A

But if we break it down in some way that is even slightly meaningful, it becomes easier to remember.

F D R

B B C

C I A

E U

F B I

U K

J F K

N Y C

U S A

There are a couple of ways we can help students extend their immediate memory. Have them mutter something under their breath to improve recall, or teach them to organize information by chunking it, which moves it into their working memory. Requiring students to articulate their thinking and explain their reasoning also helps. Most students, especially those around the ages of eight to eleven, love memory challenges.

Improving Concentration and Memory Inputs

Most of us can't remember much of our lives from before we could talk. This is because when we begin to put experiences into words, we put ideas into our minds. Being able to verbalize and explain the world builds our understanding of it. This is why teaching or explaining a concept to someone else strengthens our own memory of it. Memory is also particularly important for learning to read (Gopnik et al., 1999; Mason et al., 2019). These are just some of the reasons why the development of memory is so important to student success.

Most people can remember between three and seven items at any one time (Miller, 1956; Sapolsky, 2017b), which is important to have in mind when developing learning intentions. The core messages of a lesson should be composed of no more than three items.

We Remember Beginnings and Endings Better Than the Middles

We all seem to have the most difficulty remembering the middle of things (see figure 3.4, page 76). Psychology calls this *the primacy and the recency effect*. Generally, if we are trying to remember a list of things, we will recall the first and last few items but are most likely to forget the middle (Castel, 2008). The same rule applies to learning periods, class time, and homework time. Consider what this information might mean for constructing effective lesson plans and school timetables to optimize learning (Fuller, 2015; Sousa, 2009).

As we can see in figure 3.4 (page 76), twenty-minute bursts of memory time work best. Assigning homework that will drag on for endless hours is not as effective as assigning tasks that can be done in a short burst. In schools, this means teachers should divide longer lessons into twenty-minute blocks to maximize their effectiveness.

Additional Glucose

Ingesting glucose just before a test or assessment task increases concentration and memory (Mohanty & Flint, 2001; Riby, Law, Mclaughlin, & Murray, 2011). As long as it is medically safe to do so, students could eat some fruit or glucose tablets before tests.

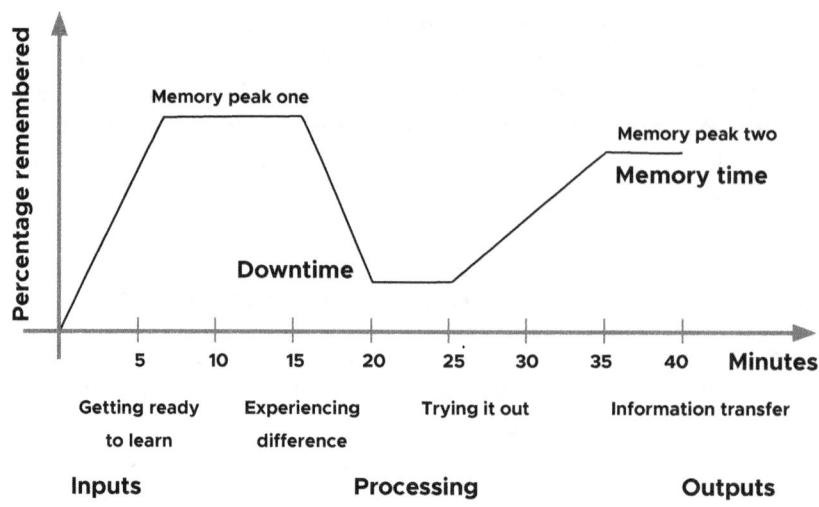

Figure 3.4: Mapping the memory across time.

Stimulation of the Vagus Nerve

Have you ever asked people for directions and seen them rub the back of their necks before answering? Colleagues who specialize in Chinese medicine have informed us that the acupressure point for the vagus nerve—a cranial nerve that links the brain stem with the abdomen and many organs in between (Porges, 2017)—is in the small hollow at the back of the neck. Stimulating the vagus nerve improves consolidation and retention of memory (Clark, Naritoku, Smith, Browning, & Jensen, 1999; Hansen, 2019).

Make It Visual

With the exception of students with serious visual impairments, students remember visuals better than words or sounds (Clark & Mayer, 2016; Marzano, 2007). In helping them learn or understand something new, include a picture, flowchart, map, drawing, or outline whenever possible.

Simplify

The way we all remember key bits of information is to break them down into simpler messages. Developing the skills of paraphrasing involves identifying the key ideas in any message. Ask students to give you summaries of their favorite stories, television shows, and films to practice this skill and keep them interested.

Challenge your students by asking them to summarize an article in one hundred words and then create a summary of the article in fifty words, twenty-five words, and so on. You can also play games like practicing elevator pitches. Ask students, "If you only had the time it takes an elevator to go from the ground floor to the tenth floor to explain a concept to someone, what would you say?" The student then has thirty seconds to explain his or her thinking to a partner.

Rest Is Best

The most powerful way to increase concentration and memory is simple—get enough sleep! Sleep resets and reboots our brains. Drowsy, tired, sleep-deprived brains can't focus, can't prioritize well, and do not consolidate memories (Walker, 2017; Walker & Stickgold, 2006).

What you do just before you go to sleep is processed in your dreams, and dreams are when your memories consolidate (Buzsáki, 2019). The initial consolidation of something new takes about six hours, so you can improve your learning by scheduling sleep (Walker & Stickgold, 2006).

When we work with students who want to achieve high levels at school, we encourage them to listen to a podcast or audio recording of the main ideas of what they have been studying before going to sleep. Enhancement, the process of improving on what you have learned, occurs during sleep. So by sleeping on what you've just learned, your brain circuits will be refreshed and your retention will increase.

A short nap is nearly as powerful a skill and memory enhancer as a full night's sleep. Encourage students to experiment with naps, as some will function best after a twenty-minute nap, while others will see better outcomes after ninety minutes (Walker & Stickgold, 2006).

Highlighting

Help students to bolster their memory by underlining or highlighting words and by going back over learned information and summarizing it. Then, encourage students to create flash cards with questions on one side and answers on the other to test themselves (Fuller, 2015; Marzano, 2007).

Improving Concentration and Memory Processing

There are two golden rules for enhancing long-term memory.

1. Make it meaningful—the more meaning you can attach to a memory, the more likely it is to be recalled.
2. Organize it—the more actively you organize information, the more likely you are to recall it.

Consider the following.

Use Aroma

Use as many senses as you can to stimulate memory. There is a link between the hippocampus, where memories are integrated, and the olfactory nerve. This is why certain aromas can elicit powerful memories (Moss, Hewitt, Moss, & Wesnes, 2008; Walsh, 2020). Lemon, basil, and rosemary are often associated with improvements in concentration and memory.

Consider Music and Language Training

Music and language training are wonderful for memory and concentration. Research shows after fifteen months, structural changes occur in brain circuits used for music processing (Griffiin, 2013). Enhanced musical ability is related to motor and auditory skills; in some instances, IQ increases as well (Griffin, 2013).

One example is the *Accelerative Integrated Methodology* Wendy Maxwell (2014) developed, which teaches language through movement and music.

Unitask

The more people multitask, the worse they perform. They become more easily distracted and have problems distinguishing relevant from irrelevant information. Multitasking is a myth: we're actually doing things sequentially, not concurrently (May & Elder, 2018). Require your students to *unitask*.

Chunk Information

For children under five years of age, the amount that can be held in immediate memory is between one and three pieces of information (Marzano, 2007; Sapolsky, 2017b). A good rule of thumb in talking to students is the *age plus one* rule—the number of words in a sentence or instruction should not exceed their age plus one.

We can increase our memory by learning to break information down into smaller bits, or *chunk it*. So rather than remembering a phone number as 0491372816, we learn to break it down to 049-137-2816. Aim to deliver important instructions in bite-size chunks.

Also remember it is the unusual things that become memorable. We know one teacher who, whenever he wanted his students to really remember what he was saying, would sing it as a Gregorian chant.

Practice

The more ways you have to access a piece of information, the easier it is to retrieve it. Schedule practice that involves recall or application. Frequently, we think we know something when we recognize it, rather than really knowing it. Recognition knowledge won't help you answer questions that ask you to integrate. If you want to retrieve information, you need to practice retrieving it using the strategies that follow.

The BASE Method

The BASE (big, active, substitute, exaggerate) method is especially useful for students with learning strengths in language and words (Lorayne, 1963). The BASE method suggests that if we want to remember something, we should imagine it as big and active, substitute it, and exaggerate it. For example, say you wanted to remember to take some fish home with you from work. You might picture yourself driving home with a gigantic fish sitting beside you and thousands of little fish flapping around in the back seat. Or if you wanted to remember to take an umbrella with you when you go out, you could imagine yourself opening the door while holding a gigantic umbrella.

The Journey Method

Leonardo da Vinci used a memory enhancement strategy known as the journey method (as cited in Konnikova, 2013).

Imagine you need to remember ten pieces of information. To recall them, think of a journey that you know so well you could almost do it with your eyes closed. Then, select ten landmarks along that journey and pair one thing you need to remember with one of those landmarks. This enables recall through thinking of that journey as a prompt to remembering the ten pieces of information.

For example, if I wanted to remember seven important art movements, I might link each to the journey I take from my home to school.

Part of Journey	>	**Art Movement**
• Turn left at the gate.	>	Realism
• Pass the neighbor's flower bed.	>	Impressionism
• Turn right at the corner.	>	Postimpressionism
• Go past the shop.	>	Cubism
• Turn left at the corner.	>	Surrealism
• Go over the crossing.	>	Abstract expressionism
• Arrive at the school gate.	>	Postmodernism

A variant of the journey method, time-traveling pairs ages and events with information to be recalled rather than landmarks.

The Peg Method

The peg method teaches people to recall anything by pairing a piece of information with each peg. These pegs need to be taught to students so well they know them thoroughly.

The problem with many pegs taught to students is that they are a bit too polite to remember. So, depending on your preference (and the age of your students), please find two sets of pegs in table 3.4—one polite and one not so polite.

Table 3.4: Types of Pegs

	Polite Pegs	Some Impolite Pegs
One	Sun	Bum
Two	Shoe	Poo
Three	Glee	Plea
Four	Ore	Gore
Five	Jive	
Six	Sticks	Sick
Seven	Heaven	
Eight	Ate	Hate
Nine	Shine	Whine
Ten	Hen	

Another way of developing pegs is to find ten memorable moments in your life and pair them—for example, from when you were one year old to when you were ten years old.

Mnemonics

Mnemonics are words, patterns, or sentences designed to aid retention. For example, each letter in the sentence "My very educated mother just served us nibbles" signifies a different piece of information to help people remember the order of the planets in relation to the Sun: Mercury, Venus, Earth, Mars, Jupiter, Saturn, Uranus, and Neptune. Another example is "Every good boy deserves fruit," which helps people remember the notes on the lines of a treble clef.

Mnemonics can be based on anything your students are interested in to aid retention, such as motorbikes, musicians, dinosaurs, or film stars' names.

Short-Term Memory Exercises

Look rapidly at a series of pictures, and then close your eyes and try to describe them. This measures both your attention and your memory.

Games are good exercise for short-term memory. Card games that require you to remember and manipulate cards exercise your general memory.

Try a game called clap your name. For example, if your name is Sarah, spell it out (S-A-R-A-H) by slapping your thigh for each of the consonants and clapping your hands for each of the vowels. This develops concentration. For an added challenge, you can do this simultaneously with someone else.

Sustained and Selective Attention Exercise

Quickly dictate a long string of randomly selected letters and numbers into an audio recorder. Later on, listen and tally only the numbers or only the letters to assess your concentration inputs. This works even better if you get someone else to read them for you, signaling only when you've heard either a letter or a number.

Exercise Your Brain With Television

Some exercises involving visual sequences that you can practice at home include the following.

- Watch a television drama while recording it, and then replay it in your mind scene by scene. Make notes about your recollection. Watch the recording again to check for accuracy against your notes (Restak & Kim, 2010).
- Do the preceding exercise with a documentary. Mentally replay the program with its interviews and commentary. Make notes. Then watch it again and check how well you recalled it.
- Watch a sports game while recording it. After a score occurs, review in your mind what you think you observed, and then play the program back and see how clearly you remembered the scoring situation.
- Exercise paying attention to small details, like the number of magazines on a table. During the day, carry a camera with you and take pictures of various scenes. You can check later what you can remember and the accuracy of your recall.
- Pattern exercises that enhance spatial reasoning include drawing free-form designs, memorizing them, and reproducing them—this is a test not only of memory but also of hand-eye coordination and motor memory.

How to Help Students Perform Better on Tests and Exams

Concentration and memory processing is improved when you practice remembering under many conditions. If your students stress out during exams, give them practice at remembering under similar conditions.

Most people experience some anxiety before a test or exam. This is partly a result of increased levels of cortisol, a chemical than can block memory in the bloodstream, and it is the reason why many people have experienced sitting in an exam and feeling like they have forgotten everything they ever learned. To reduce cortisol, we need to learn, study, and revise in repetitive, routine ways. Following a system reduces anxiety.

A few days before a test, if students are worrying, ask them to write their fears on a piece of paper. Help them learn that slowly breathing out will calm them down.

If it is possible to find out a few days before the test where students will be sitting, encourage them to go in and sit in those exact positions. Just doing this can calm fearful students.

Throughout the year (and especially for those in high school), ensure your students know how to take good notes. Help them learn how to pick out the main idea.

Each week, make a flash card (or a summary hand; see Give Your Memory a Hand, page 85) using different-colored cardboard corresponding to different learning areas. Tell students to use the cards to test themselves on a weekly basis, sorting those they get correct into one pile and those they get wrong into another. Students should then focus their studies on the ones they answered incorrectly until they get 100 percent on a retest. Then recombine the two piles, shuffle them, and retest. This means revision doesn't occur just a few weeks before a test or exam—it occurs throughout the year.

What really embeds knowledge into memory is transforming the information—in this case, from notes, to flash cards, to self-testing. Just reading over notes doesn't work. It is boring and can deceive you into believing you know or understand something when you do not.

Power Studying

From our experience, the most powerful study routine for students is as follows.

1. Study the entire subject or learning area.
2. Devise a test to assess whether you understand it.
3. Look at the areas you need to do further work on.
4. Specifically study those areas.

5. Retest.
6. Study the entire subject or learning area again.
7. Devise another test to assess whether you understand it.
8. Work specifically on the areas you don't understand. (Fuller, 2015)

Improving Concentration and Memory Outputs

In an overloaded, distracted world, a person who knows how to focus on the most important piece of information—who can pick out the idea and identify the crux of something—has a major advantage.

Note Taking

You can give each of your students this same advantage by teaching effective note taking—moving from providing full notes as models to work from, to outlines with spaces to fill in, and finally to structured sheets.

Academic achievement is linked to good note taking, but most students miss between 60 and 70 percent of the key points when taking notes from lectures or text (O'Donnell & Dansereau, 1993). Naturally, anything missed or omitted has less chance of being recalled.

Many students reread or recopy their notes in an effort to recall them, but these methods are ineffective. Two-thirds of secondary students have been found to study for tests purely by rereading their notes, with over half of them rereading them the day before the test or examination. Half of students use passive repetition of key concepts as their sole method of study (Jairam & Kiewra, 2009).

But by using a note-taking system, students increase their retention by transforming the same piece of knowledge into three different formats: (1) main notes, (2) the main idea, and (3) a visual representation.

How to Make Notes That Are Useful

Successful students have intricate systems of filing, storing, and organizing information. They methodically and systematically capture good ideas related to their interests and organize them in ways that are useful to them. One of the best ways to organize information is to create notes.

From 2001 onward, we conducted *practical intelligence projects* with teachers from around the world, looking for some of the more powerful ways to help students learn (Fuller, 2015). The note-taking system that follows evolved from those discussions (see figure 3.5, page 84). Essentially, it is an adaptation of the Cornell method of note taking and involves students dividing a page into three main sections (as cited in Fuller, 2015).

1. In the left section, students try to identify the most important piece of information or the main idea.
2. In the right section, the largest section, students write their main notes.
3. At the bottom, students convert the same knowledge into a visual representation. A Venn diagram is ideal, but a bubble or concept map can also work.

Heading or Learning Objective _____

Write the main idea here.	**Write the main notes here.**
Create a visual representation, such as a Venn diagram.	

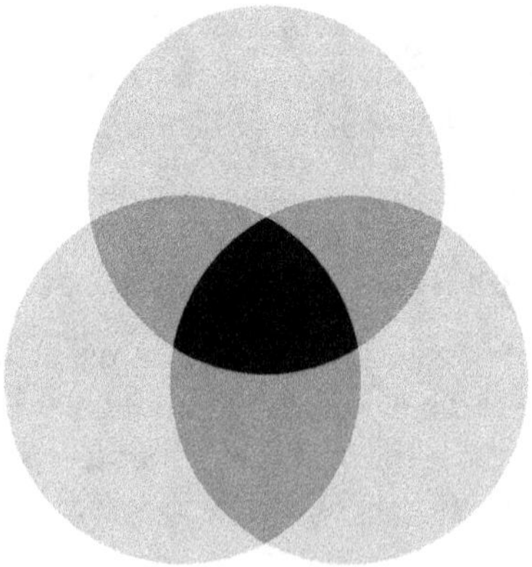

Figure 3.5: How to make effective notes.

With younger students, it can be useful for parents to take them through developing a set of notes on a book they have read. Playing games, such as identifying the main point of a film, story, or TV show, helps students learn to pick out the main ideas.

While this is the most powerful method of note taking we have observed, it still takes humans twenty-four repetitions of anything to get to 80 percent of competence (Marzano, 2007; Pitler, Hubbell, & Kuhn, 2012). But how do you get students to repeat anything twenty-four times?

Give Your Memory a Hand—One Method for Increasing Repetition

Once students have learned something, ask them to summarize it by *giving their memory a hand*.

Each student cuts out a cardboard shape of his or her hand and then writes the five most important pieces of knowledge on one side of the cardboard hand (one piece of information on each finger). In the palm area, students can either draw a Venn diagram or write a more detailed summary of the topic. They then turn the hand over and write:

- Their name
- Two questions they can use to test their memory of the area
- One question that is really tricky (assign a point value to the tricky question)

Remember to be patient. It will take students time to develop the skill of developing a good summary hand, but ideally, you will help them learn this skill over several years.

This method has been used successfully with students of all ages. It helps high school students organize and revise main ideas and prepare for exams, and it helps younger students organize their thoughts.

Every so often, have students test their memory and knowledge by trying to answer the two test questions before turning over the hand to check the answer. You can also use these in *Jeopardy!*-style games.

Using memory hands substantially increases the number of repetitions students get of key concepts.

Concentration and Memory Cross-Fertilization Strategies

If a student has a learning strength in concentration and memory, table 3.5 (page 86) suggests some strategies that could be used to help act as a lever to extend learning in other areas. These are some key suggestions to stimulate your thinking and can be adapted to your classroom or time frame as you see fit.

Table 3.5: Extending Learning From Concentration and Memory

Learning-Strength Area	Sample Strategy
Spatial Reasoning	**Students can:** • Use their minds to take pictures • Make a drawing of the facade of an intricate building **Teachers can:** • Demonstrate concept mapping • Underline key ideas in textbooks and texts • Develop graphs and maps of ideas **At home, families can:** • Play memory games • Play memory, or matching, card games • Create collages • Complete jigsaw puzzles
Perceptual and Motor Skills	**Students can:** • Increase the use of body memory—count on fingers or use physical cues, such as tapping on the sides of their foreheads, to recall something • Use their fingers to count off the five most important ideas **Teachers can:** • Use positioning in classrooms to assist students in linking their memory with location • Teach students the journey method • Demonstrate ideas through movement, song and dance, drama, and reenactments **At home, families can:** • Memorize a sequence of movements • Learn to dance • Play handball • Complete mazes • Knit • Sew • Roller-skate • Undertake construction projects • Complete jigsaw puzzles • Play board games

Learning-Strength Area	Sample Strategy
Planning and Sequencing	**Students can:** • Use their skills in planning to create a system to study and increase memory • Use computer-based reminders for recurring tasks • Create to-do lists and checklists • Develop systems to enhance memory **Teachers can:** • Guide students through topics covered at school by showing explicitly how ideas link and build on one another • Help students develop checklists and to-do lists and prioritize **At home, families can:** • Make a vacation journal with photographs and souvenirs • Use the peg and journey methods as planning tools • Create calendars of key events in their family histories • Develop world-history timelines • Plan a weekly calendar • Use diaries to write down activities
Thinking and Logic	**Students can:** • Focus on main points and debating • Learn to use prior knowledge to solve problems—always asking, "What else do I know that relates to this?" **Teachers can:** • Demonstrate mind mapping and concept mapping • Identify main ideas and linkages • Repeat key ideas to build memory • Organize information so it becomes knowledge by taking notes, creating podcasts, and mapping ideas **At home, families can:** • Remember sequences of arguments and logical structures • Practice magic tricks • Play badminton • Play table tennis • Play lacrosse • Play chess

continued →

NEURODEVELOPMENTAL DIFFERENTIATION

Learning-Strength Area	Sample Strategy
People Smarts	**Students can:** • Focus on learning about someone else—noticing eye color, using the person's name when speaking to him or her, remembering what the person says, and so on • Find out about someone else's personal timeline and refer to aspects of it in conversation **Teachers can:** • Relate ideas to key people in history • Tell students the sort of person and the types of careers that might use this knowledge • Practice "Repeat after me" • Meet new people • Have conversations with family members and friends **At home, families can:** • Help children learn the skills of reading people • Focus on detective-type skills (for example, "What clues do they give us that tell us what sort of people they are?") • Play "Simon says" • Play charades • Practice acting and improvisation
Language and Word Smarts	**Students can:** • Create cheat sheets (for example, "What are the key ideas I need to know for my test?") **Teachers can:** • Use nonfiction texts as a way to engage students in reading and ask them to write explanatory and persuasive texts using factual information • Engage in creative writing—these students could base their writing on the real world, factual experiences, and so on • Name objects in alphabetical order, by categories (for example, animals, objects, mechanical devices), and so on • Develop word meanings and technical vocabulary • Use clues to have students infer and predict about texts • Have students apply prior knowledge to suggest solutions to real-world issues **At home, families can:** • Play memory games to learn the alphabet, read words, figure out how to get ready on time, and so on • Learn poems or songs from memory • Develop stories that include a list of things they want to remember (see the BASE method, page 79)

Learning-Strength Area	Sample Strategy
Number Smarts	**Students can:** • Develop peg methods to enhance memory • Create timelines and number lines of key ideas • Use rhymes and stories to help remember key numerical information **Teachers can:** • Model key strategies and skills with examples • Use mnemonics to help recall the stages of solving common problems—some of these students will become reasonably adept not because they love numbers but because they remember how to go about solving a problem • Teach students how to focus on each step of a mathematical problem • Talk about learning to decipher mathematics **At home, families can:** • Play memory games involving numbers

In Summary

Learning strengths in concentration and memory allow us to focus on tasks and improve based on past performance. Most great gains by humanity have been a consequence of concentration and memory.

The development of learning strengths in concentration and memory plays a powerful role for all of us in our learning. Without it, we would be continually distracted and unable to sustain our attention long enough to acquire, retain, and recall new information.

Once developed, learning strengths in concentration and memory can be applied to enhance success in other areas. They can be used to:

- Recall the sequence of a series of images in a diagram, flowchart, or cartoon (spatial reasoning)
- Develop and refine motor skills (perceptual and motor skills)
- Recall and then follow a series of steps to achieve an outcome (planning and sequencing)
- Focus on a series of cause-and-effect statements (thinking and logic)
- Attend to the details of people's lives and remember their names (people smarts)

- Tell or write stories, jokes, and poems (language and word smarts)
- Recall how to calculate and solve a numerical problem (number smarts)

This positive effect on success is especially enhanced when it is linked to planning and sequencing.

Reflection Questions

- What strategies will be most valuable in strengthening the concentration and memory skills of your students?
- Which other members of staff need to be involved in this discussion?
- Should any student's parents or guardians be involved in this discussion?
- What do you already do on a regular basis that supports students strengthening their concentration and memory development?
- What else could you do?
- How do you support students in transferring new learning into long-term memory?
- Is the development of memory strategies an implicit or explicit expectation that is regularly clarified and practiced in your classroom?
- How often are concentration and memory problems misdiagnosed as low interest?
- How early should schools embed and explicitly teach memory and concentration methods in classrooms?
- What would be the benefits of helping students develop and regularly practice these skills?
- How could we help students use this knowledge in their day-to-day lives?
- How many learning activities in your classroom this week have incorporated concentration and memory development?

Chapter 4
PLANNING AND SEQUENCING

Developing ways to plan, weigh alternative ways of achieving an outcome, and consider the consequences of various actions is a remarkable skill. But many people do not do this. Instead, they act on the first thing that pops into their heads, and if that does not work, they then act on the next thing that pops into their heads. Those who do not plan can waste a lot of energy doing things that do not need to be done.

Planning relates to concentration, focus, and presence, and it develops logic and intentionality. Intentionality leads to clarity of action. Successful students and people are able to set goals and develop and follow plans to achieve them. In a world of people who seek instant gratification, it is the person who plans who stands out. The future belongs to those who plan for it and create it.

Career Areas That Utilize Learning Strengths in Planning and Sequencing

Taxi driving, choreography, project management, cooking, construction, electrical fitting, farming, forecasting, financial planning, event planning, teaching, postal work, radiography, wedding photography, delivery, forklift driving, civil engineering, surveying, and road construction are some of the career areas that utilize learning strengths in planning and sequencing skills. Helping students consider career paths that call on their learning strengths may ease their way into a successful professional life.

Our most sophisticated planning and sequencing skills involve project management, time-tabling, risk-assessment modeling, mapping, critical thinking, creative problem solving, and team coordination skills. How we build skills in this area is an interesting journey of brain development.

Planning and Sequencing Require Different Types of Thinking

Daniel Kahneman (2013) distinguishes between our need for two types of thinking: (1) fast and (2) slow. Planning often requires us to think slowly and methodically rather than quickly and reactively. To make these concepts more accessible to most students, we often talk about two brains—Rex and Albert. This is how Andrew explains it to students: "Welcome to your brain! To simplify things a bit, you have two parts of your brains. The first is the brilliant, insightful, creative, and compassionate brain that evolved most recently in humans."

Meet Albert

Now, we could call the clever, creative, brilliant, wonderful, imaginative, fantastic, and genius part of your brain the prefrontal cortex, but it's fun to call it Albert (or Alberta) in honor of Albert Einstein! (See figure 4.1.)

Figure 4.1: Albert Einstein.

Meet Rex

The second part of your brain evolved a long time ago and forms the lower part of your brain. This part keeps you alive—it keeps your heart beating while you sleep, and it keeps you at the right temperature. It does a lot of really important things. In fact, this lower part of your brain contains 80 percent of your brain cells. It knows what frightens and threatens you, and it is pretty much the same brain that dinosaurs had.

We could talk about the reticular activating system and the basal ganglia, but it's fun to call this part of the brain Rex, in honor of *Tyrannosaurus rex*! (See figure 4.2.)

Figure 4.2: Tyrannosaurus rex.

Rex is very old, can get quite grumpy, and isn't very bright. Rex does not use language. Rex does not use logic much either, and he can't be reasoned with. Rex is also incredibly easy to distract.

When Albert and Rex Meet

Now, we all like to think our inner Albert runs the show. We are all reasonable, intelligent people in control of our own destinies, right? Wrong! Rex runs the show. At times, Rex will listen to Albert, but only if it is something Rex wants to hear.

For example, your inner Albert might decide to start exercising more, but if your inner Rex wants to lie in bed and sleep in, I suggest you do not approach those scales for a while yet.

If your inner Albert says, "This issue isn't worth worrying about" but Rex detects a threat, you're likely to be up pacing the floor at four in the morning.

If your inner Albert says, "I need to prepare for a test" but Rex thinks playing computer games would be far less stressful for you and that you deserve a break, your study routine will get thrown out the window.

Rex can save your life. If something were to attack you, Rex would have you running away before Albert had even thought about it. But Rex thinks the most urgent thing to do is always the most important thing to do.

Rex's reactions are not thought through. They occur quickly and are almost automatic. Albert's strategies are more thoughtful, considered, and effective.

You can get your inner Albert to take control of matters, but only if you distract Rex with something to keep him comfortable. Food, drink, sleep, and distractions all help Rex settle down for a while.

Brain Systems Involved in Planning and Sequencing

Different tasks require different learning skills and use distinct parts of the brain. In addition to the aims of the lesson, let all your students know what brain systems they'll be using in each lesson or activity to familiarize them with their brains. The main parts of the brain involved in planning and sequencing are shown in figure 4.3.

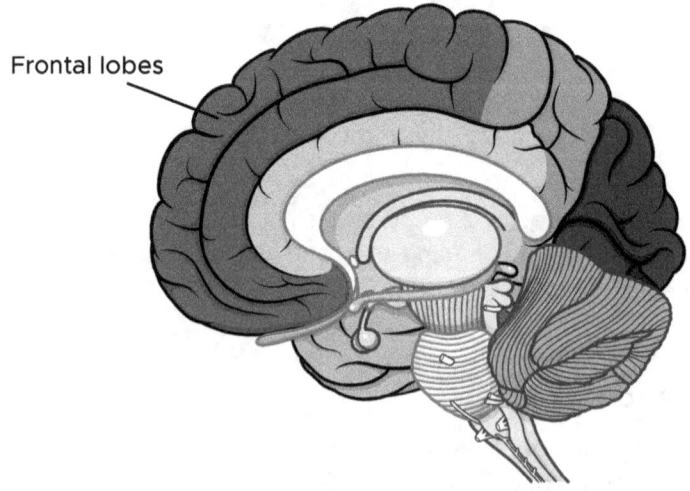

Figure 4.3: Parts of the brain involved in planning and sequencing.

The frontal lobes help us to do the hard thing first. This is the part that helps us resist that extra slice of cake or tells us to study before we watch TV. The parts of the frontal lobes especially involved in planning and decision making are the dorsolateral prefrontal cortex, which is involved in considering what needs to be done, and the ventromedial prefrontal cortex, which weighs the pros and cons of a plan or decision (Rosenbloom, Schmahmann, & Price, 2012; Sapolsky, 2017b).

Teachers often assume the connections and sequences between the steps involved in planning are being made when often they are not. So we need to ensure students are explicitly taught how to plan and sequence consciously.

How Our Frontal Lobes Determine Our Level of Success

When Walter Mischel (2014) offered young children the choice between eating one marshmallow straight away or eating two if they didn't eat the first while he was out of the room for fifteen minutes, he really started something. Only 30 percent of the children in his study were able to resist the temptation of the first marshmallow.

Resisting the temptation of the marshmallow was equated with self-control and executive functioning. The ability not to do the first thing that comes into your mind turned out to be a powerful predictor of success in life. In that famous experiment, the children who were able to resist the temptation of the first marshmallow and hold off to get the second were more likely thirty years later to be healthy, have succeeded in careers and school, have made better choices, and have kept their relationships intact.

Similarly, David M. Fergusson and John L. Horwood (2001) studied more than 1,200 children from Christchurch, New Zealand, from infancy up to their thirtieth birthdays and found that their ability to control their first impulses predicted better functioning in life and lower criminal involvement.

If we translate the marshmallow results into another context, we see that the ability to resist playing a video game before completing the study needed for a project is highly predictive of success in life. Successful people do the hard stuff first. They know that if they allow themselves to procrastinate and laze about, they'll never get to do the things that really matter.

Links Between Planning and Sequencing and Other Brain Systems

Planning and sequencing are essential in mathematics, science experiments, art projects, playing music, understanding the plot of a story, time management, and connecting new ideas to what we already know.

The frontal lobes control our executive functioning and direct our attention and efforts (Diamond, 2012, 2013). Without our frontal lobes functioning effectively, we base our actions on whatever feels good at the time, which is usually not sustained effort.

Planning and sequencing, along with chapter 5 (page 109), "Thinking and Logic," relate to frontal lobe activities called the executive functions. These are higher-order-thinking abilities that involve:

- Organizing and planning
- Shifting attention to concentrate
- Sustaining effort and persisting
- Resisting distractions and calming upsets
- Accessing memory
- Resisting impulsive acts and regulating emotions

When these areas work well, we are in good thinking shape. But when they do not work well, life can feel like a trial as we contend with one challenge after another.

What Blockages in Planning and Sequencing Look Like in Adulthood

When we don't develop our planning and sequencing learning strengths, there are long-term consequences. Adults with blockages in planning and sequencing often lose track of what to do next, can't prioritize, feel everything is equally important (which means nothing is), feel overwhelmed, find it hard to sustain the practice to improve, find it hard to save money, run late, and jump from one activity to another.

Planning and Sequencing Inputs

Planning and sequencing inputs create learning by enabling ideas to stick together. Without the ability to plan and sequence, no new information binds to anything else, so it is not retained.

One method of planning and sequencing is to *imagine forward and plan backward*. First, encourage students to decide on the outcome they are seeking and define it clearly. Then, work with them to plan backward, sequencing all the steps needed to get to their predetermined outcome. This develops a system.

While Albert is good at making plans, Rex often responds better to a system. This is why no matter how many goals we set for ourselves, we will rarely achieve them if we have no system in place to do so.

Planning and Sequencing Processing

Planning and sequencing are learnable skills. Students need to learn to ask themselves, "What is the most important thing to do right now? What do I do next? What does this change my mind about? What does this new information remind me of? What should I do next? What is the next logical step?"

All students need help as they learn to plan out what they need to do to achieve their goal in steps, rather than all at once. Well-thought-out work plans will help to facilitate this process.

Planning and Sequencing Outputs

Previewing, considering, and weighing options and adjusting the pace at which they work all help students become more considered and reflective. If students rush into doing the first thing that comes to mind, they act and answer impulsively. Students with impulsive output control problems tend to be oblivious of, or insensitive to, feedback (see table 4.1).

Table 4.1: Key Signs—Planning and Sequencing

	Positive Signs	Concerning Signs
Inputs	The student: • Plans before starting a task • Follows instructions • Links things in order	The student: • Jumps into tasks without planning • Is late for everything • Never seems to meet deadlines
Processing	The student: • Recalls the steps involved in a task • Completes tasks in logical steps • Reorders steps if they aren't making sense	The student: • Displays poor time management • Has poor rhythm • Experiences problems with everyday sequencing hurdles, such as combination locks, telephone numbers, and the interpretation of multistep instructions • Gets dressed in odd sequences
Outputs	The student: • Plans, previews, and anticipates outcomes and consequences • Self-evaluates the practice of gauging how he or she is progressing during and after an activity	The student: • Is chronically disorganized • Communicates chains of events chaotically or out of order • Doesn't anticipate future events or consequences

Ways to Assess Planning and Sequencing in the Classroom

The following ideas will not replace a full psychological assessment, but they may give teachers and parents an idea if further investigations are merited.

Students' ability to complete some of the following tasks will give you an idea of their capacities or difficulties in using planning and sequencing to learn well. Most of these can be used to make an assessment of specific students, but they will also benefit the entire class.

While ascertaining students' ability to organize and sequence tasks and ideas by considering the following issues will be helpful, their capacity for improvement after teaching assistance will be even more telling. Most students should improve their performance after instruction or coaching; if they do not demonstrate improvement after receiving assistance from their teacher, referral for specialist assessment might be warranted. Determine whether the student can:

- Be organized with his or her belongings
- Be organized with his or her time
- Complete tasks on time
- Figure out the important steps and what to do next
- Remember things or steps in order and follow a sequence of steps
- Create products in a useful or aesthetic order
- Perceive that Tuesday predictably precedes Wednesday (every week, without fail) and summer occurs before fall (year after year)
- Determine a clear sense of direction
- Learn the letters of the alphabet in the correct order
- Master problems with everyday sequencing hurdles, such as combination locks, telephone numbers, and the interpretation of multistep commands or instructions

Whether students can tackle the preceding list items will clarify your thinking about the possibility of blockages in planning and sequencing. If students display difficulties in completing the preceding activities, asking them to explain what their thinking is will often reveal whether the blockage is in their inputs (no idea where to begin), processing (rambling or wayward methods), or outputs (can't recall even when cued with leading questions).

Impulse-Control Assessments

Assessing impulse control will give you an indication of students' executive functioning, their ability to restrain themselves, and how their frontal lobes are functioning. Impulse control is such an important part of success in careers, relationships, and learning that it is best to refer students who are not developing in these areas for special assessment as early as possible. Ask questions such as the following.

- "Does the student see the task as relevant or as a priority?"
- "Is the student able to estimate the time tasks may take?"
- "Can the student delay immediate gratifications?"
- "Does the student feel overwhelmed or avoidant?"

Part of effective frontal lobe functioning is the ability to stop doing some things. You can assess this in a number of ways.

- Ask the student to place one of his or her hands on the table. Tell the student to raise a finger when you tap once and not to raise the finger when you tap twice. Using your finger, tap under the table. The student's ability to resist tapping each time is an indication of his or her impulse control.
- Play games like statues, "Simon says," and those where you stop rather than start under certain conditions; these games are good indications of the ability to control impulses.
- Ask students to complete join-the-dots and trail-making tests.
- Conduct timed tests, such as connecting numbers from one to twenty-five in order.
- Connect numbers and letters in alternating pattern (for example, 1-A-2-B-3-C . . .).

Implementation Assessments

- Can the student create a goal?
- Can the student visualize the final product?
- Does the student think the goal is important or reasonable?
- Does the student know how to set goals and subgoals?

Action Plan Assessments

- Can the student break down a big task into smaller steps?
- Can the student put steps into a logical order?
- Can the student remember the action plan steps?
- Can the student stay focused when he or she gets stuck or overcome unanticipated roadblocks?

Difficulties Following Through

- Can the student make backup plans when things get hard?
- Can the student anticipate challenges and barriers?
- Can the student identify the resources needed to achieve his or her goal?
- Does the student know when or how to ask for help?
- Does the student have or use fix-up strategies?

Sequencing Assessments

- Does the student get tasks mixed up or out of sequence?
- If the student is asked to touch his or her right thumb to the tips of his or her fingers on the right hand, can the student do it in a sequence or follow your order as you demonstrate? Repeat with the other hand (observe if the other hand moves at the same time, as mirroring could be a concerning sign of delayed motor development or a primitive reflex).

Self-Monitoring Assessments

- Can the student identify key attributes?
- Can the student use rubrics and checklists to self-assess?
- Does the student give him- or herself credit for small successes?

Whether a student successfully completes or struggles to finish a series of the preceding activities will not necessarily indicate a problem, but these tasks will serve as a guide to his or her current level of learning strengths in planning and sequencing (see figure 4.4).

Evidence That Planning and Sequencing Skills Can Be Improved

Three researchers who have focused particularly on executive functioning and planning and sequencing are Margaret Searle (2013), Adele Diamond (2013), and Robert M. Sapolsky (2017a). They show that engaging in activities, such as stop-and-start games; learning rhymes, poems, and stories; and playing physical games with rules, as well as the activities listed in the following pages, increases executive functions and specifically planning and sequencing.

Planning and Sequencing

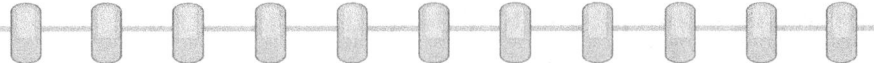

Use this list to rate the planning and sequencing strengths of the student. Assign a score out of ten (with one being "can't do this" and ten being "great at this") for each of the statements that follow. (A student at the average level of his or her class would score a five.)

Issue	Rating
Inputs	
The student:	
• Can set goals	
• Can anticipate consequences and obstacles	
• Can identity where to begin and act on that information	
• Can prioritize in terms of importance	
• Can make considered decisions	
Processing	
The student:	
• Can put steps in order	
• Can identify the next thing to do midtask	
• Can be flexible when needed	
• Can keep the desired outcome in mind	
• Can resist distractions	
Outputs	
The student:	
• Can organize his or her belongings and materials	
• Can manage his or her time	
• Can sustain effort and achieve an outcome	
• Can deliver outcomes on time	
• Can celebrate his or her successes and enjoy a sense of accomplishment	

Figure 4.4: List of issues with planning and sequencing.

Improving Planning and Sequencing Inputs

Playing rhythmic games and songs early in life can help reinforce planning and sequential ordering. Songs and rhymes about the alphabet, the months of the year, and other practical sequences are particularly effective. Music can be a powerful promoter of sequential ordering (Griffin, 2013). Go and no-go tasks, where you have to start and then stop or change direction, are good for impulse control (Diamond & Lee, 2011; Diamond, Barnett, Thomas, & Munro, 2007).

Improving Planning and Sequencing Processing

Parents of young children might watch a child getting dressed in the morning and notice there is absolutely no rationale for the order in which the child puts on his or her clothing. If the process is chaotic, teaching the sequence of activities—"We do this, and then we do this"—will help the child develop learning strengths in this area.

Remembering how to tie your shoelaces requires the ability to consolidate memories and recall motor sequences later.

Some strategies that help are the use of flowcharts, timelines, and project planners, and encouraging students to whisper a description of what they are doing under their breath.

Pose problems such as "If Tom gets home earlier than Jack, and Sue always arrives after Tom but before Jack, who gets home first, who gets home second, and who gets home last?"

Ask students to recite nursery rhymes such as "This Is the House That Jack Built" and "There Was an Old Lady Who Swallowed a Fly." These are wonderful examples of sequencing.

Playing dominoes, checkers, or chess; developing dance sequences, raps, or poetry; and constructing Rube Goldberg machines are great ways of developing this area that students will enjoy.

Improving Planning and Sequencing Outputs

Many tasks in school and in life require us to do things in a certain sequence or pattern. For example, writing an essay usually involves using a pen and placing it on some paper before beginning with a title and then an introduction, and many mathematical problems involve solving earlier calculations before coming to a main answer. For this reason, improvements in planning and sequencing outputs have major effects on performance.

Sequential Ordering

Higher sequential thinking fosters *step wisdom*. This means being able to complete the steps in a science experiment, think through the stages of a project, play scales on the piano, and track the plot of a story. These tasks require practice and repetition to get the steps in the correct order.

Sequencing

Teach rhymes for the sequences and make use of comic strip stories to combine sequencing with visual imagery. Rhythmic dance might also be helpful in reinforcing sequential ordering.

Completing actions in the correct order enables us to drive a car safely, tie our shoelaces, knit, operate machinery, and complete projects on time. This requires us to learn and recall the order of steps involved in completing recurring tasks, which is also known as motor procedural memory.

Sequential Outputs

Students with sequential output blockages are likely to tell the punch line of a joke first and may not be able to place a series of pictures into a logical sequence or to learn a dance routine. But one powerful way of helping students of all ages plan and sequence is to use ladders of understanding.

One way to help students learn sequences is to describe them like the steps we take when we go up or down a ladder. Providing this visually can be a helpful reminder for students who become confused about what needs to happen next.

If we have a five-step method of writing an essay, completing a mathematics problem, or conducting a scientific experiment, we might lay it out like a ladder and number each step, sometimes using a different color to represent each one. This method can also be used to increase students' engagement and transfer of learning.

We can then present students with a new problem in which we have worked out the first four steps of the ladder and require them to complete the last part, such as the conclusion of an essay, the last calculation in a mathematical problem, or the final step of a scientific experiment. This gives students a sense of completion and mastery, helps them see how problems are sequenced, and also enhances transfer of learning.

By laying out different tasks or problems in a ladder format, students will more easily be able to see that *this problem is almost the same as that problem* or *writing this type of essay is similar to writing that sort of essay*.

Planning and Sequencing Cross-Fertilization Strategies

If a student has a learning strength in planning and sequencing, table 4.2 suggests some strategies that could be used to help extend learning in other areas. These are some key suggestions to stimulate your thinking and can be adapted to your classroom or time frame as you see fit.

Table 4.2: Extending Learning From Planning and Sequencing

Learning-Strength Area	Sample Strategy
Spatial Reasoning	**Students can:** - Use visual planners - Have a wall calendar - Map out the key milestones in a project - Graph and chart ideas **Teachers can:** - Use de Bono's (1985) thinking hats - Have different thinking stations in a classroom and use them to solve problems - Select pictures to sequence texts **At home, families can:** - Follow stepping-stones (a marked trail) - Rearrange planning steps - Complete mazes - Invent Rube Goldberg machines - Play checkers
Perceptual and Motor Skills	**Students can:** - Learn a sequence of moves in a dance - Practice martial arts, tai chi, or yoga **Teachers can:** - Illustrate flowcharts, mind maps, mind trails, and step-by-step sequencing **At home, families can:** - Visit mazes - Practice music - Talk through sequenced actions by saying, "If we want to do this, first we'll need to . . . " - Go on a treasure hunt - Perform improvisational sketches - Build towers with cards or pipe cleaners - Practice origami - Practice skateboarding, horseback riding, and surfing

Planning and Sequencing

Learning-Strength Area	Sample Strategy
Thinking and Logic	**Students can:** • Use sticky notes, ordering them into the steps for a process • Create planning trails, such as: starting point → first thing to do → second thing to do → third thing to do → outcome or result **Teachers can:** • Brainstorm options • Weigh alternatives • Develop strategies for problem solving **At home, families can:** • Involve children in planning events, outings, vacations, and shopping trips, as well as making simple decisions
People Smarts	**Students can:** • Plan to do activities with friends • Plan ways to calm themselves down when they feel upset **Teachers can:** • Ask students to plan class events, excursions, and performances with other students • Develop experimental procedures to solve a problem • Create restorative practices for conflict resolution **At home, families can:** • Plan events the entire family will want to be involved in
Language and Word Smarts	**Students can:** • Tell a sequenced story (for example, "Once upon a time, I had to . . . and then I had to . . . ") • Write down plans and goals **Teachers can:** • Plan stories • Write and read Choose Your Own Adventure stories • Help students with comprehension, asking them to sequence jumbled-up stories or to sequence a single story before asking more complex comprehension questions **At home, families can:** • Talk through planning (for example, "Now, let's see, first we should pick up . . . ") • Write key events on a wall calendar • Write out a shopping list

continued →

Learning-Strength Area	Sample Strategy
Number Smarts	**Students can:** • Use flowcharts with numbered sequences • Develop and use checklists for frequent occurrences **Teachers can:** • Use planners to develop steps toward solutions • Deliver content in a numbered-step fashion • Ask students to predict future trends based on historical information, including numerical data **At home, families can:** • Give children a budget to manage • Provide pocket money • Encourage children to save for major purchases • Plan a weekly grocery trip • Learn to play a musical instrument

In Summary

Learning strengths in planning and sequencing enable us to embark on new ventures, systematically implement projects, and accomplish incremental progress toward a goal with an economy of effort.

The development of learning strengths in planning and sequencing plays a powerful role for all of us in our learning. Without them, we would waywardly meander toward achieving outcomes and waste inordinate amounts of time and energy on the way there.

Once developed, learning strengths in planning and sequencing can be applied to enhance success in other areas. They can be used to:

- Arrange the process of solving a problem into a visual representation, such as a ladder of understanding, or a physical representation, such as stepping-stones (spatial reasoning)
- Set and review personal skills development, such as *By the end of this year, I want to increase my long-jump distance by one foot* (perceptual and motor skills)
- Focus on possible outcomes and consequences of decisions and actions (thinking and logic)
- Think about ways to improve your own life and those of others (people smarts)

- Storyboard or graph a story, indicating the major plot points (language and word smarts)
- Appreciate that big calculations are often a series and sequence of little calculations that compound, and become aware of exponential effects in mathematics (number smarts)

This positive effect on success is especially enhanced when it is linked to thinking and logic.

Reflection Questions

- What strategies will be most valuable in strengthening the planning and sequencing skills of your students?
- Which other members of staff need to be involved in this discussion?
- Should any student's parents or guardians be involved in this discussion?
- What assumptions may be made about students who experience planning and sequencing difficulties?
- How can teachers model self-talk and demonstrate how to plan and sequence?
- How many learning activities in your classroom this week have incorporated planning and sequencing development?

Chapter 5
THINKING AND LOGIC

By the time students arrive at school every day, they have already exercised many of their thinking and logic strengths. They may well have estimated how long they can stay in bed, often to the last possible second, before having to get up to arrive at school on time. They have decided on their breakfast foods and considered the best order in which to eat them. If they have made a smoothie, they will have selected ingredients, evaluated relative amounts, and considered combinations of flavors. Decisions may also have been involved in which route to take to school or where to sit on the bus, as well as who to say "good morning" to when they reached school.

The process of thinking and logic is so inextricably intertwined with our lives it almost seems automatic and invisible. But in the preceding example, a breakdown in any of these essential thinking skills would have caused lateness and other difficulties.

Career Areas That Utilize Learning Strengths in Thinking and Logic

Law, medicine, engineering, teaching, journalism, philosophy, computer programming, city planning, mechanics, building, and nursing are some of the career areas that utilize learning strengths in thinking and logic. Helping students consider career paths that call on their learning strengths may ease their way into a successful professional life.

Our most sophisticated thinking and logic skills involve consideration, evaluation, noticing similarities and differences, reasoning, communication, creative thinking, and problem solving. How we build skills in this area is an interesting journey of brain development.

How Thinking and Logic Grow

Child psychologist Jean Piaget finds that the way we think changes as our brains mature, and he outlines the main stages of the development of thinking and logic as follows (as cited in Cherry, 2020; Inhelder & Piaget, 1999).

- **Sensorimotor stage (birth to age two):** In our earliest years, we learn rapidly by observing intently and interacting with our world. We understand actions have consequences and that people and objects are separate. Word smarts, people smarts, number smarts, and thinking and logic originate during this stage.
- **Preoperational stage (ages two to seven):** In this stage, we begin to think symbolically and start to use words and pictures to represent objects. The development of language and word smarts is a major feature of this stage of development. While we still tend to think about things in very basic terms, our vocabulary and understanding of words develop exponentially.
- **Concrete operational stage (ages seven to eleven):** In this stage, we become much more adept at using logic. Thinking becomes more logical and organized. Even so, the ability to deal with hypothetical concepts and abstract ideas, as well as the capacity to solve complex ethical situations, has yet to develop. We begin to use inductive reasoning to expand specific pieces of information into general principles.
- **Formal operational stage (ages twelve and older):** In this stage, we begin to consider multiple potential solutions to problems and think more scientifically about the world. Abstract thinking increases, as does our ability to think and reason about hypothetical problems. There is an increase in the ability to use deductive reasoning to systematically plan for the future.

Brain Systems Involved in Thinking and Logic

Different tasks require different learning skills and use distinct parts of the brain. In addition to the aims of the lesson, let all your students know what brain systems they'll be using in each lesson or activity to familiarize them with their brains. The main parts of the brain involved in thinking and logic are shown in figure 5.1.

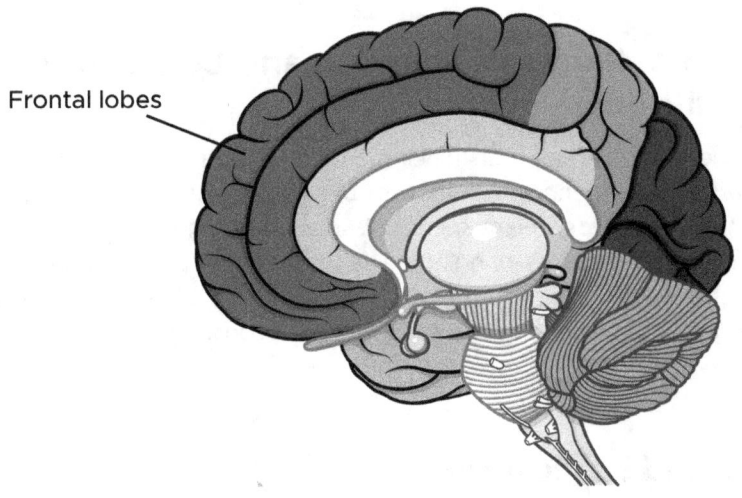

Figure 5.1: Parts of the brain involved in thinking and logic.

One of the most important aspects of thinking and logic is that this information-processing system works hard to piece together information to make accurate predictions of what might happen next. Our brains function to anticipate and predict our needs so we can survive in an unpredictable world (Buzsáki, 2019). Achieving this requires an intricate system of information pathways, of which the frontal lobes are the most adept at prediction (Sapolsky, 2017a).

The prefrontal cortex is essential for thinking about things in categories. It can not only work out that apples and oranges are both forms of a higher-order category of fruit but also help us know that apples and oranges have more in common with each other than they do with a dog.

Another feature of the prefrontal cortex is the ability to delay and persist. This restraint allows us to persevere until we solve a problem. Behaviorally, the prefrontal cortex is the area that tells us, "I wouldn't do that if I were you" (Sapolsky, 2017b).

But the intricacy of information processing in the prefrontal cortex also means it is the part of the brain most vulnerable to cognitive load. Deprive it of sleep, put it under too much stress, overload it with sugar, or numb it with boring repetitive tasks, and the quality of thinking and logic decreases dramatically (Clark, Nguyen, & Sweller, 2006).

Links Between Thinking and Logic and Other Brain Systems

Students with thinking and logic challenges often also face issues with planning, sequencing, and organizing. Concentration, memory, and impulse control can also suffer. As mentioned in chapter 4 (page 91), blockages in thinking and logic can seriously impair students' quality of life.

What Blockages in Thinking and Logic Look Like in Adulthood

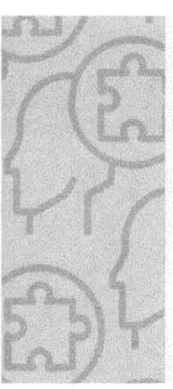

When we don't develop our thinking and logic learning strengths, there are long-term consequences. Adults with blockages in thinking and logic often find it hard to consider the nuances of issues, can be gullible, are driven by the latest ideas and impulses, bring home things that aren't needed from shopping trips, act in ways that are contrary to their interests, feel superstitious without reason, and don't see the need to review or reconsider decisions.

Thinking and Logic Inputs

Our world is shaped by the way we see it, and the way we see the world is shaped by our thoughts. So one of the fastest ways to change our world is to change our thoughts.

Many people change relationships, workplaces, or social groups and are then surprised when nothing really changes for them at all. Unless we change our thoughts, our actions remain the same, and we end up doing the same things over and over again. One of the quickest ways to improve our quality of life is to improve our thinking.

Know and Understand Simple Ideas

Most acts of great thinking and logic come from taking very simple ideas and combining them in new ways to create a whole new way of looking at things. Einstein once said imagination is more important than knowledge, and he was right, but a person needs the knowledge first (as cited in Nilsson, 2010).

Thanks to the internet and search engines, the world has become saturated with knowledge and lots of people have access to lots and lots of tiny bits of information. But being able to access information is not the same as knowing it, and knowing it is not the same as understanding how to apply it. Watching medical shows does not make a person a surgeon.

For this reason, we need to build, support, and extend the connections between pieces of information. In a complex world, it is those who can think clearly, deeply, and simply who stand out. We must develop simple ideas first. We can become intellectually paralyzed by the complexity of the world. It is helpful to realize that most great innovations had humble beginnings. Similarly, most great innovators were humble people. One way of thinking about this is that most great things had simple beginnings. We must think, "I am a simple person, so I should be able to create great things." The goal is to clear the clutter and expose what is really important, then see what's missing and identify the gaps in knowledge.

Thinking and Logic Processing

Don't believe all your thoughts. The healthy approach to the thinking and logic process is to question and evaluate your thoughts. Saying to yourself, "That's an interesting idea; I wonder if it's true" shifts you from being the victim of your thoughts to being the thinker *behind* your thoughts (Fuller, in press).

Question Yourself

Asking questions is a sign of intelligence. Socrates is reported to have said all thinking begins with wondering (as cited in Hackett, 2016). He based his entire teaching method not on providing answers but on asking questions. You can't think clearly unless you are able to ask good questions.

So learn to ask basic questions. Once you feel comfortable asking the most obvious questions, start to ask the strangest, weirdest, most out-there questions you can think of. It is by asking the questions that others think are too trivial to ask that we can come up with brilliant ideas. This enables students to then take those ideas and answers and link them in new, interesting ways.

Make Mistakes

On May 25, 1961, U.S. president John F. Kennedy challenged his nation, stating that by the end of the decade, a person would have been to the moon and safely back again. Starting work on the mission the next day, the National Aeronautics and Space Administration did not suit up an astronaut—its first goal was to hit the moon. Three years later, NASA smashed *Ranger 7* into the moon at a velocity of 5,862 miles per hour. It took fifteen more trials before the successful and gentle moon landing of *Apollo 11* in July 1969 (Adams, 2019).

The ability to make mistakes is essential. You can't get many things right until you know how to get them wrong. Learn to see mistakes as taking a step closer to getting something right, because people who don't make mistakes don't make anything. James Dyson made 5,126 prototypes of the bagless vacuum cleaner before getting it right and creating a bestseller (as cited in Brady, 2012).

In Paris, there is a festival of errors to give children experience in making mistakes and to challenge intellectual timidity. To develop the potential of all students, we need to be just as bold. Ask students to offer an answer, even if they know it is wrong, but then ask them *why* they think it is wrong. This encourages them to opt into a thinking process, rather than having them shrug and stare blankly. Learning how to move from an incorrect answer toward a solution is the way most great thinkers work.

People do not get the chance to be great before they've had the chance to be not so great. Removing the anxiety about how to be immediately successful is what allows us to play, explore, dream, and be creative.

Thinking and Logic Outputs

Thinking well is a creative undertaking, and like most creative achievements, it takes time. One of the outputs of thinking is more thoughts. Have you ever met anyone who was able to say, "Right, I'm done with this thinking business. I'm having no more thoughts"? Encouraging the flow and connectivity of someone's stream of thoughts relates to creativity and purposeful action.

Output controls sharpen throughout adolescence (Giedd, 2015). Slowing adolescent minds down so they do not have to do the first thing that comes into their heads—reflective thinking rather than impulsive action—is the basis of good outputs (see table 5.1).

Table 5.1: Key Signs—Thinking and Logic

	Positive Signs	Concerning Signs
Inputs	The student: • Solves problems in systematic ways • Notices links • Asks questions • Is more interested in curiosity than answers	The student: • Haphazardly tries to solve problems • Feels ashamed if he or she doesn't have the answer
Processing	The student: • Sees connections among and between materials from different sources and on different topics (for example, history and science) • Draws inferences from limited information • Develops an understanding of an idea by considering its components or connections to other ideas	The student: • Struggles with making connections between materials from different sources and on different topics • Struggles with inferring or reading between the lines • Has trouble understanding new things without considerable support
Outputs	The student: • Can reach logical conclusions • Can create a persuasive case for an issue or point of view • Pauses and thinks before answering • Is able to consider alternative explanations, weighing the pros and cons of those alternatives	The student: • Is overly rigid and literal—can make a decision but can't consider alternatives • Can't combine ideas to see higher-order abstractions or concepts

Ways to Assess Thinking and Logic in the Classroom

The following ideas will not replace a full psychological assessment, but they may give teachers and parents an idea if further investigations are merited.

Students' ability to complete some of the following tasks will give you an idea of their capacities or difficulties in thinking and logic. Most of these can be used to make an assessment of specific students, but they will also benefit the entire class.

- Look at students' persuasive writing; ability to follow a logical sequence; and ability to categorize, classify, sort, explain, and use and interpret flowcharts and Venn diagrams. How coherent are their contentions? Can they logically sequence assertions?

- Look over a recently covered chapter or unit in a student textbook or notebook and pick out a few key concepts. Have students tell you about these concepts, either orally or by drawing pictures or diagrams. Are they able to explain these concepts logically?

- Assess logical interpretation by asking students to interpret a proverb, such as "People in glass houses shouldn't throw stones," or by asking them to list the pros and cons of an issue. Assess their clarity of thinking and their ability to draw an abstract principle from a specific proverb (inductive reasoning).

- Conduct similarities tests, such as "What are the similarities between an apple and a banana or a table and a chair?" Move to more obscure connections, such as how a giraffe and a fly are alike. This not only helps assess thinking and logic skills but also builds capacity in higher-order thinking.

Whether a student successfully completes or struggles to finish a series of the preceding activities will not necessarily indicate a problem, but these tasks will serve as a guide to their current level of learning strengths in thinking and logic (see figure 5.2, page 116).

Use this list to rate the thinking and logic strengths of the student. Assign a score out of ten (with one being "can't do this" and ten being "great at this") for each of the statements that follow. (A student at the average level of his or her class would score a five.)

Issue	Rating
Inputs	
The student:	
• Identifies main ideas	
• Considers flaws in ideas	
• Seeks out more information when needed	
• Evaluates the validity of the sources of ideas	
• Connects ideas from different sources or schools of thought	
Processing	
The student:	
• Weighs factors in favor of and against a proposition	
• Deduces from a general idea to a specific example	
• Can methodically process an idea or issue—can classify, sort, and arrange ideas	
• Can consider different perspectives	
• Can find a general principle from some specific examples (inductive thinking)	
Outputs	
The student:	
• Reaches logical conclusions	
• Communicates the reasons for his or her conclusions	
• Communicates persuasively	
• Reviews decisions based on new information	
• Thinks and evaluates critically	

Figure 5.2: List of issues with thinking and logic.

Discuss your concerns and compare these results with other teachers who are familiar with this student to confirm your observations.

Evidence That Thinking and Logic Can Be Improved

Extensive research from Diamond (2013); Searle (2013); and Ron Ritchhart, Mark Church, and Karin Morrison (2011) demonstrates that we can all improve our levels of clear and critical thinking. The title of Richard F. Elmore's (2011) edited volume on the work of school reform, *I Used to Think—and Now I Think—*, encapsulates the shift that reflective thinking makes in our lives. Effective use of thinking and logic is about not only the ability to plan and decide well but also the ability to reflect on and reconsider the decisions and plans we have made.

By requiring students to engage in conversations and debates about ideas, create and test hypotheses, and examine and evaluate conjectures and propositions, they develop and deepen their skills in thinking and logic.

The Fine Art of Thinking Clearly

Helping your students think clearly is a long-term project. Clarity of thought not only leads to inventiveness and creativity but also helps create happy lives. Much of people's happiness will be determined by their ability to make positive plans and then make decisions and follow through on them. The process of increasing learning strengths in this area can take a lifetime, but the payoffs are enormous. Never give up on developing students' learning strengths in thinking and logic.

Improving Thinking and Logic Inputs

The following ideas are suggestions for readers to build on in helping students develop their learning strengths in thinking and logic.

Perceiving

Both considering and evaluating require people to notice or perceive distinctive elements of the area they are learning. Some activities that can improve this are playing detective games, studying spot-the-difference and find-what-is-missing drawings, playing memory games (such as remembering ten objects on a tray), interpreting photos and artworks, and solving puzzles and mysteries.

Noticing and creating links between different pieces of information is the product of thinking and logic but also promotes memory and creativity. Questions such as "How are the water supply and blood flowing through the human body similar?" and "What other time in history is most like today?" prompt students to perceive similarities they may not have considered (McDowell, 2020; Pithers & Soden, 2000; Pohl, 1997).

Evaluating

Thinking and logic require prioritization and transfer of learning. We can assist students in developing learning strengths in this area by asking questions like the following.

- "Why is this issue important?"
- "How does . . . relate to . . . ?"
- "What would be an example?"
- "What is an alternative?"
- "What do you think is true about . . . ?"
- "How do you know?"
- "Why do you think that is true?"
- "Do you have any evidence for that?"
- "What other information do you need?"
- "Could you explain your reasons to us?"
- "Are these reasons adequate?"
- "How can you find out more?"

Improving Thinking and Logic Processing

By the time students get to middle school, they have had countless experiences in empirical inductive reasoning, but they often fail to make the leap to deductive reasoning (Reif, 2008). Inductive reasoning involves using information to develop a general principle or theory, while deductive reasoning involves deriving a single solution from many pieces of information.

Tell students that a simple way to remember the difference between deductive and inductive reasoning is that *deduce* rhymes with *reduce*, so you reduce the information you have in order to come up with a single answer. *Inductive* begins with the letter *i*, as does *increase*, so you increase the pieces of information to come up with a theory or generalization.

Same, Same but Different

To us, the phrase "same, same but different" encapsulates all of human thought. The way people form concepts in their heads is through analogy and difference.

People think in patterns. George Kelly, a cognitive scientist, finds these patterns, or schema, are formed when we work out how two things are similar and then differentiate them from a third thing (as cited in Benjafield, 2008).

Just the ability to identify similarities and differences results in a 45 percent improvement in academic results (Marzano, 2007). The improvement of this skill alone can take a student from performing better than 50 percent of their class to performing better than 95 percent. Encourage students' ability to identify similarities and differences by asking questions like the following (also see table 5.2).

- "How are an apple and an orange alike?"
- "How are a dog and a giraffe alike? How are both different from a buffalo?"
- "How was the American Revolution similar to the French Revolution?"
- "How are the speed of light and the speed of sound alike? How are they different?"
- "How are subtraction and addition alike? How are they different?"
- "What is similar between these two stories? How are they different?"

Table 5.2: Thinking and Other Wild Ideas

Who . . .	does this help? does this hurt? makes decisions about this?	talks about this issue? knows about this area? is most directly affected?
What . . .	is your main point? would be an example? other information do you need? do you know for sure? are you uncertain about? evidence do you have?	are you assuming? would change your mind? do you think the main issue is here? has been done in relation to this in the past, and has that worked?
Where . . .	do we see this happen? are similar situations? is the most need for this?	are the places this doesn't happen? should we go for help with this?
When . . .	does this happen? doesn't this happen? would it cause a problem?	has this occurred in the past? did it improve? would we know if we have made a difference?
Why . . .	do you think that is true? is this relevant to me?	should people know about this? should people care? do you think this happens?
How . . .	do you know? does . . . relate to . . . ?	will we know if it improves? will we know if it gets worse? does that apply to this case?
Why not . . .	consider if you could wave a magic wand and change all of this—what would happen?	consider if you were totally wrong about this or the reverse of what you think is true—what would that mean?

Improving Thinking and Logic Outputs

The opposite of impulsivity is good problem solving. Thinking and logic require deep understanding, not just memorization and regurgitation. Using a range of thinking methods helps with this. Some, from the work of Ritchhart and colleagues (2011), are outlined in the sections that follow.

See, Think, Wonder

Teachers can use this method to develop a student's sense of curiosity. Take a picture, painting, data table, story, or graph and ask students the following questions.

- "What do you see?"
- "What do you think is going on?"
- "What does it make you wonder?"

Stop at particular points and ask, "Why did this happen? What do you think might happen next?"

Zoom In

Teachers could also show a small part of a picture and ask the following.

- "What do you see or notice?"
- "What do you think is going on?"

Keep revealing more of the image, and repeat the questions. This encourages hypothesizing and using evidence.

Think, Puzzle, Explore

Teachers can ask these questions to help students expand their thinking about an issue or a topic.

- "What do you think you know about this?"
- "What questions or puzzles do you have about this?"
- "How might we explore these questions or puzzles?"

Headlines

Ask students to write a headline that summarizes the main point of a story, report, or historical event, such as "Dinosaur Alert: Asteroid Hits Earth," "Baseball Game Goes Round and Round," or "Titanic: The Unsinkable Sinks."

Fishbowl Discussions

In these discussions, students are divided into two groups: (1) an inner group, who discusses ideas, shares opinions, and asks questions relating to a specific topic, and (2) an outer group, who listens to this discussion carefully. The two groups then swap roles. Over time, this method gives students the chance to be both active participants and observers and listeners.

Fishbowl discussions are useful for student groups who think well while moving or changing positions and as a formative assessment technique. The method also helps students consider different perspectives.

Four Corners

In this exercise, the four corners of the room represent four different responses to a contentious question or positions on an issue presented to students. Students then move to the corner that best reflects their thinking on the question or issue. You can then ask them to articulate their thinking about the choice they have made. Students can change corners if the classwide discussion convinces them of different perspectives or opinions.

Thinking and Logic Cross-Fertilization Strategies

If a student has a learning strength in thinking and logic, table 5.3 (page 122) suggests some strategies that could be used to help extend learning in other areas. These are some key suggestions to stimulate your thinking and can be adapted to your classroom or time frame as you see fit.

Table 5.3: Extending Learning From Thinking and Logic

Learning-Strength Area	Sample Strategy
Spatial Reasoning	**Students can:** • Practice drawing a sequence of pictures (or shapes) to represent the different steps involved in solving a problem • Use different colors or shapes to represent different types of issues, such as environmental, personal, financial, historical, or cultural **Teachers can:** • Map out ideas and concepts • Use graphic organizers • Take a series of photographs and create a story line • Display M. C. Escher artworks • Draw mathematics problems, including fractions, as a series of pie charts **At home, families can:** • Play chess, *Tetris*, *Monument Valley*, and *Minecraft* • Visit art galleries and museums • Display an obscure part of a picture and ask children to guess what might be going on in the whole picture • Complete puzzles • Use estimation
Perceptual and Motor Skills	**Students can:** • Walk through a problem physically, where each step taken is a different aspect of an issue they are trying to solve (at times, students can step off at different angles to represent the different possible ways of solving the problem) • Consider the thinking and logic involved in a sports game or dance sequence **Teachers can:** • Graph students—model going through a logical sequence and have students move to specific parts of the room depending on the position or option they support • Create problem-solving activities involving building (for example, create a bridge that will hold a specific object using pipe cleaners, drinking straws, and one roll of tape) **At home, families can:** • Help children realize that simple actions, such as throwing a ball, involve calculations using thinking and logic

Thinking and Logic

Learning-Strength Area	Sample Strategy
Concentration and Memory	**Students can:** • Try to identify the main idea or message of a story or a lesson • Develop chains of ideas • Notice how ideas can be similar or different (for example, find two similarities and one difference) • Consider different perspectives about a problem (for example, "Would this problem look different if I was . . . ?") **Teachers can:** • Talk about how one idea can kick-start or lead to other ideas • Map ideas • Create thinking chains • Illustrate concept maps • Ask Fermi questions • Use prior knowledge to form opinions, strategies, and solutions • Find parallel issues in history, asking, "How were they managed?" **At home, families can:** • Play chess and backgammon • Play twenty questions
Planning and Sequencing	**Students can:** • Think about logic as a series of thinking stepping-stones **Teachers can:** • Ask students, "If we were completely correct about this, what would it mean?" and "If we were completely wrong about this, what would it mean?" • Create lists of pros and cons **At home, families can:** • Work out ways to decide issues that have several options, such as where to go on vacation, where to move, and which sport to play

continued →

NEURODEVELOPMENTAL DIFFERENTIATION

Learning-Strength Area	Sample Strategy
People Smarts	**Students can:** • Try to consider the motives and reasons behind people's actions and decisions and why they might feel the way they do • Read or watch whodunits • Explore ideas, asking, "What makes you say that?" **Teachers can:** • Discuss why success is more likely if we learn to get along with others • Study people who exhibit people smarts • Try to understand the motivations and feelings of people and characters in stories • Study body language • Consider other people's perspectives on an issue or problem • Teach conflict-resolution strategies **At home, families can:** • Discuss the dilemmas faced by different people in different situations • Take a position on an issue opposite of the one they believe and argue for it
Language and Word Smarts	**Students can:** • Use facts as bridges to broaden their understanding • Link several ideas to form a theory and work out ways to test it • Read thrillers, spy stories, Choose Your Own Adventure stories, or courtroom dramas **Teachers can:** • Provide students with the opportunity to have meaningful discussions about texts and produce writing that is relevant and meaningful to the students • Teach inductive and deductive reasoning • Give students three unrelated pictures and ask them to create a story that involves them all • Teach media analysis—look at advertising and consider how images and words are used to persuade • Make persuasive arguments **At home, families can:** • Try to unpack why someone says something the student doesn't understand (for example, from a friend, teacher, or news story)

Learning-Strength Area	Sample Strategy
Number Smarts	**Students can:** • Know that mathematics is more about thinking than it is about numbers • See mathematical problems as logic challenges • Identify patterns **Teachers can:** • Use real-world problems and mathematics to think through solutions • Interpret graphs and data and use them to support a proposition • Teach the scientific method and how it can apply to thinking • Look at how mathematics contributed to major achievements, such as lunar exploration, quantum physics, and genetics **At home, families can:** • Try to develop interesting questions that have some number component—creative people ask better questions • Fix things at home

In Summary

Learning strengths in thinking and logic allow us to coherently and systematically consider and evaluate the evidence for and against specific ideas and propositions to come to a reasoned conclusion.

The development of learning strengths in thinking and logic is a hallmark of the developing maturity of students. Many of the major gains of humanity have been realized through the application of thinking and logic to solve problems and to improve the lives of people. Without these strengths, we are left with erratic and ill-considered decision making, as well as half-baked plans or efforts unlikely to be successful because they are not based on any rationale or evidence.

Once developed, learning strengths in thinking and logic can be applied to enhance success in other areas. They can be used to:

- Link the functioning of machinery, computer programs, and even human movements to the achievement of a desired result (spatial reasoning)
- Develop motor skills and movements (perceptual and motor skills)
- Consider the logical steps and sequences so we can remain focused and retain key ideas in our heads (concentration and memory)
- Implement purposeful steps to achieve an outcome (planning and sequencing)

- Take responsibility for our own actions (people smarts)
- Develop puzzles and mystery stories and decipher codes (language and word smarts)
- Think through the information needed to make a calculation (number smarts)

This positive effect on success is especially enhanced when it is linked to people smarts.

Reflection Questions

- Students with a learning strength in thinking and logic will benefit from thinking activities and routines. And even though they may find them challenging at first, students with learning strengths in other areas will also benefit from the activities in this chapter. Can you think of particular examples of thinking and problem-solving tasks or activities?
- Are there times less-developed students could benefit from those types of activities?
- What strategies will be most valuable in strengthening the thinking and logic of your students?
- Which other members of staff need to be involved in this discussion?
- Should any student's parents or guardians be involved in this discussion?
- To what extent is strengthening thinking and logic an explicit intent in every classroom?
- What benefits would come from a whole-school focus on this area?
- How many learning activities in your classroom this week have incorporated thinking and logic development?

Chapter 6
PEOPLE SMARTS

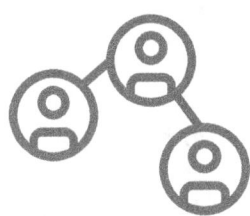

Humans are exquisitely sensitive to the presence or lack of people smarts in others, but we can be less attuned to a lack of people smarts in ourselves. People can have wonderful strengths in all other brain areas, but if they lack people smarts, it can all come to nothing. This area of learning strengths can either set us up for success or devastate even the most promising of careers and relationships.

Career Areas That Utilize Learning Strengths in People Smarts

Management, coaching, mentoring, leadership, sales, acting, social work, nursing, midwifery, teaching, hospitality, and policing are some of the career areas that utilize learning strengths in people smarts. Helping students consider career paths that call on their learning strengths may ease their way into a successful professional life.

Our most sophisticated people smarts involve emotional intelligence, people reading, emotional regulation, knowing how to calm ourselves and others, rapid de-escalation methods, stress management, constructive feedback, motivational skills, compassion, relationship building and maintenance, and clear communication. Whether students have learning strengths in people smarts, it is important to develop some skills in this area. How we acquire skills in this area is an interesting journey of brain development.

People smarts are not just for extroverts. People who are shy, reserved, or introverted can develop these skills as well. Knowing how to contribute to conversations and how to provide other people with a sense of social ease is an important aspect of leadership, collaboration, and friendship. Knowing how to deal with the times when people are upset or when frustration occurs can save everyone a lot of angst and unhappiness.

Elements of Advanced People Smarts

The strong connection between successful relationships and success in almost every aspect of life means having a high level of people smarts pays off. Three of the essential elements of strong people smarts are (1) attunement, (2) theory of mind, and (3) security.

Attunement

Inscribed in the Temple of Apollo in Delphi is the statement "Know thyself" (Best, 2018). Self-awareness is a gift that lasts a lifetime. Knowing one's learning strengths is part of this, but knowing one's own emotions and what to do with them is invaluable.

High-level people smarts enable people to align and attune themselves with others while retaining a clear sense of themselves and their values. The ability to work and live alongside others builds trust. Considerable research points to the power of attunement in successful relationships (Gottman, 2011). People able to perceive that others may have needs different from their own and tune in to those needs are more likely to have successful and enduring relationships.

Theory of Mind

Having a theory of mind allows people to realize that not everyone feels or thinks (or learns) in the same way they do (Gopnik et al., 1999; Hawkes & Hawkes, 2018). Different people need different things. A theory of mind is the difference between people being curious about and appreciative of others' differences and people insisting that everyone should be exactly like themselves.

Security

This final aspect takes the form of people using their skills of attunement and their knowledge that people learn, think, and feel differently to assist themselves and others in feeling secure. Secure people help others feel secure around them and are therefore more likely to form positive relationships.

Brain Systems Involved in People Smarts

Different tasks require different learning skills and use distinct parts of the brain. In addition to the aims of the lesson, let all your students know what brain systems they'll be using in each lesson or activity to familiarize them with their brains. The main parts of the brain involved in people smarts are shown in figure 6.1.

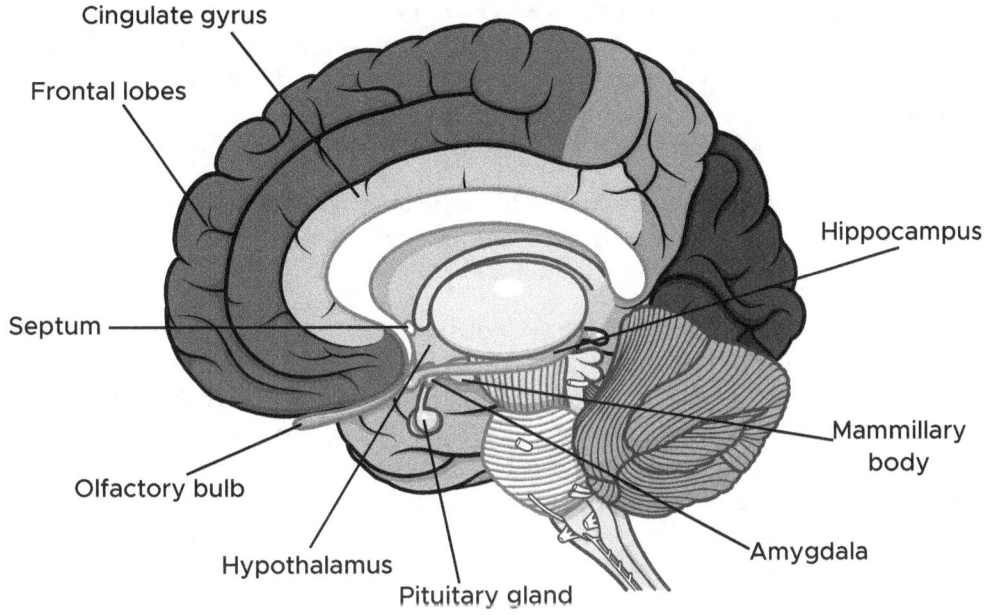

Figure 6.1: Parts of the brain involved in people smarts.

- The amygdala is the detection system that sets off the alarm bells of fear and stress.
- The limbic system (amygdala, hippocampus, and cingulate gyrus, among other structures) is where emotions are processed.
- The hypothalamus and the pituitary gland work together to release oxytocin, the hormone of trust, love, and social connectedness.
- The frontal lobes make assessments of risk versus reward, which relate to involvement with other people.
- Mirror neurons help people understand the situations and experiences of others (Sapolsky, 2017a).

As discussed, the entire human body, including the brain, is an information system. Our bodies send signals to our brains that lead to some of our feelings, and this is why many people locate some feelings in specific parts of their bodies. For example, we often feel sick in the stomach when we feel disgust, surprise is often accompanied by a sharp intake of breath, and stress is often accompanied by a feeling of butterflies in the stomach (Fuller, in press).

Links Between People Smarts and Other Brain Systems

The limbic system is the most well-known part of the brain for handling our emotions and attuning ourselves with others (Sapolsky, 2017b). Calming the agitated amygdala is essential to avoid unnecessary feelings of fear that create stress. We also use our mirror neurons to feel empathy and compassion toward others, and our frontal lobes are used to solve interpersonal problems.

The language centers are involved every time we interact with others by expressing how we feel (Broca's area) and by understanding what other people are saying to us (Wernicke's area; see figure 7.1, page 151).

People smarts can help us read other people's facial signals and postures (spatial reasoning); physically move with and around other people while maintaining a respectful personal distance (perceptual and motor skills); recall key features of other people's conversations and lives (concentration and memory); consider the needs of others when setting out to do something (planning and sequencing); communicate clearly with people (thinking and logic); enjoy conversations, debates, and stories (language and words); and think about proportions of people and their situations (number smarts).

What Blockages in People Smarts Look Like in Adulthood

When we don't develop our people-smarts learning strengths, there are long-term consequences. Adults with blockages in people smarts often are perplexed by their own feelings and mystified by the reactions of others. They may say things they later wish they could retract, find it hard to make friends and harder to keep them, don't know to settle themselves when they are upset or angry, experience upheavals in their relationships and workplaces, and may demonstrate lots of potential but find it can come to nothing.

People-Smarts Inputs

Emotional intelligence is the ability to read, interpret, and respond constructively to one's own inner world of feelings, as well as to the external world and needs of other people (Goleman, 2009).

Within Yourself

Being able to identify your own feelings accurately, and know what signals they might be giving you, is a major life advantage. Emotions are neither good nor bad—they are forms of information.

The body has six main senses: (1) touch, (2) smell, (3) taste, (4) sight, (5) hearing, and (6) haptic (the feeling of where one's body is in space, which allows a person to catch a ball, drive a car, and play tennis; Fuller, in press). These senses give us access to the external world. We also have inner senses—our emotions and feelings—that help us access our inner worlds. These are the signposts we use to learn about ourselves and, later, about others.

All human emotion stems from one of two basic states: (1) love or (2) fear and pain. The first accompanies the release of oxytocin. The latter relates to the release of corticosteroids, when the amygdala activates if we sense a threat (Sapolsky, 2017b).

Paul Ekman (2012) identifies six universal emotions: (1) anger, (2) disgust, (3) fear, (4) happiness, (5) sadness, and (6) surprise. But the range of human feelings is far greater than six, ranging from acceptance and ambition to melancholy and regret to zest.

Just as we are healthiest when our breath passes in and out of our bodies, we also function best when our feelings flow freely through us.

Toward Others

Sharpening our sensitivity to the feelings and signals exhibited by others enhances our relationships and, therefore, our quality of life.

Knowing our own emotions and being able to read the emotions of others are a major determinant of happiness and success. Humans are happiest when they do things that are meaningful to them and that also contribute to the lives of others (Hallam et al., 2013).

Social connections enrich our brains. People with larger social networks have more intricately connected brains (Sapolsky, 2017b), and their friends, siblings, parents, and peers play a dominant role in shaping them. Being curious about how other people think and see things is a powerful motivator of learning.

People-Smarts Processing

Consider the following strategies for people-smarts processing.

Within Yourself

Students can learn how to become the thinkers *behind* their own thoughts and feelings by observing, noticing, and asking questions like "That's interesting; why am I feeling like this right now?" "How long will I feel like this?" and "I must have felt like this before—what happened then?" Many people appear to believe all their thoughts and value all their feelings, but this can lead to a very cyclical existence, somewhat similar to being on an emotional roller coaster.

When people learn to evaluate their own thoughts and feelings, they possess a wonderful advantage in life. There are times when feelings influence thoughts, which then determine actions. Being someone who can say to him- or herself, "I'm feeling agitated; I wonder what has led to this feeling" is vastly more useful than being someone who says to him- or herself either "I'm feeling agitated; I wonder who is to blame" or "I am feeling agitated; I must not be coping."

Toward Others

Being able to develop kindness and see things from another person's perspective enlarges one's world. The ability to read other people's body language can give a person advance knowledge that is helpful in soothing upsets.

People-Smarts Outputs

Within Yourself

Knowing how to calm yourself and regulate your emotions, and eventually how to help other people regulate theirs, is an essential predictor of resilience, successful relationships, and life success.

Toward Others

Knowing how to express feelings and ask for help when needed is an essential part of communication and obtaining social support. Similarly, developing kindness and a willingness to help others is empowering and enabling.

Being able to verbally resolve conflicts and get along with others is essential for maintaining and repairing relationships, because collaboration is advantageous. All of us thinking together are smarter than just one of us (see table 6.1).

Table 6.1: Key Signs—People Smarts

	Positive Signs	Concerning Signs
Inputs	**The student:** • Can make friends • Can correctly identify his or her own feelings • Can calm down • Understands why others may see or feel about things differently than he or she does	**The student:** • Misreads social cues • Has poor temper or impulse control • Has little self-awareness of feelings
Processing	**The student:** • Can keep friends • Knows how to calm down • Can read and consider other people's feelings	**The student:** • Misunderstands other people's intentions • Has little concept of other people's feelings or ideas
Outputs	**The student:** • Can repair friendships • Can resolve most conflicts • Can act to help others • Is able to modify his or her behavior according to outcomes or feedback	**The student:** • Has little awareness of personal space • Has no sense that he or she has a role or responsibility in relation to others

Ways to Assess People Smarts in the Classroom

The following ideas will not replace a full psychological assessment, but they may give teachers and parents an idea if further investigations are merited.

Students' ability to complete some of the following tasks will give you an idea of their capacities or difficulties in using people smarts to learn well. Most of these can be used to make an assessment of specific students, but they will also benefit the entire class.

Essentially, people smarts rely on emotional regulation skills as well as the development of a theory of mind, which allows us to consider that other people may have thoughts, feelings, and perspectives different from our own.

Theory of Mind Assessments

In the past, *false-belief* tasks have been used to test students' theory of mind (Zeliadt, 2014). An example of a false-belief task would involve telling a student a story about two characters who put an item into a basket. When one of the characters leaves, the other hides the item in a box. If the student can reason that the first character will look for the item in the basket when he or she returns, the student passes the test. Most typically developing children pass this test by age five.

Knowledge of Self

Can the student identify how he or she is feeling and usually determine what caused that feeling to arise?

Knowledge of Others

Determine whether the student can:

- Greet people appropriately
- Ask questions to find out how other people are feeling
- Develop friendships and have the ability to resolve differences (not all students are highly sociable, so this is a matter not of popularity but of ability)
- Appreciate that others may see things, view things, or feel differently than he or she does

Ways to Deal With Issues

The student:

- Can deal with feelings of frustration constructively without lashing out, yelling, swearing, or becoming abusive
- Doesn't need to control what other people do
- Can talk through issues or find other ways to solve problems

Ways to Calm Down

The student:

- Can use physical means to calm down, such as looking away, walking away, deep breathing, or writing out problems
- Can ask for help when feeling upset
- Can discuss problems through to solutions

Whether a student successfully completes or struggles to finish a series of the preceding activities will not necessarily indicate a problem, but these tasks will serve as a guide to his or her current level of learning strengths in concentration and memory (see figure 6.2).

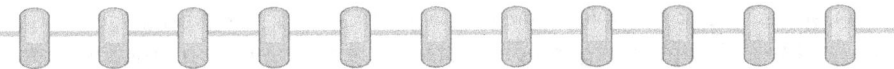

Use this list to rate the people-smarts strengths of the student. Assign a score out of ten (with one being "can't do this" and ten being "great at this") for each of the statements that follow. (A student at the average level of his or her class would score a five.)

Issue	Rating
Inputs	
The student:	
• Is aware of his or her own emotions	
• Is aware of the emotions of others	
• Considers other people's perspectives and feelings	
• Can separate his or her own feelings from other people's feelings	
• Can rely on him- or herself when appropriate	
Processing	
The student:	
• Is aware of appropriate personal space	
• Can calm him- or herself when upset	
• Can motivate him- or herself when listless or disinterested	
• Can shift to more positive feelings when needed	
• Can control his or her anger and frustration	
• Can positively support other people	
Outputs	
The student:	
• Can maintain eye contact (if appropriate)	
• Uses an appropriate voice tone and volume	
• Can alter his or her behavior when others react badly	
• Can verbally resolve conflicts	
• Demonstrates empathy for others	
• Develops and maintains friendships	
• Can seek help from others appropriately	
• Communicates clearly	

Figure 6.2: List of issues with people smarts.

When assessing people smarts in a multicultural classroom, you must be aware of the differences in perception of what is appropriate (particularly regarding personal space, communication, and eye contact). Discuss your concerns and compare these results with other teachers who are familiar with this student to confirm your observations.

Improving People-Smarts Inputs

You can improve students' learning strengths in people smarts by teaching them to understand their own and other people's feelings and to read emotions and body language.

Your Own Feelings

Our feelings are like a barometer—they can swing about depending on pressure. For younger students, fill in the barometer in figure 6.3 by writing in the feeling spectrum from *sad* to *happy*, and then ask students to mark where they on a particular day. For older students, allow them to label the barometer themselves.

You can also ask students to give you a physical signal of their feelings each day on arriving to school or to a class, such as a thumbs-up, a thumbs-down, or a thumb pointed sideways; a rating out of ten, where ten is great and one is miserable; or a point on a mood color board, where red means angry, blue means sad, yellow means happy, gray means worried, and black means rotten.

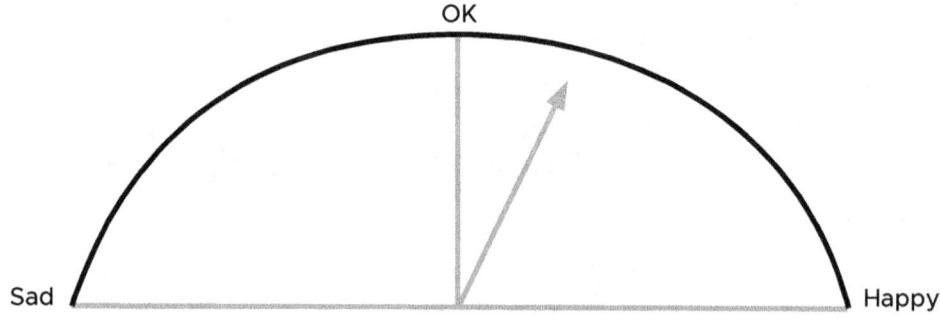

Figure 6.3: A feeling barometer template.

Other People's Feelings

Spot-the-feeling games are a powerful way of improving these skills. Show students faces displaying different emotions, and ask them to describe what people might be feeling. You can increase the challenge by masking a part of each face, such as the eyes or mouth, and asking students to determine the emotion.

Eventually, most students will become more accurate at determining emotions even when you show only the eyes of a face. Tell students this can be honed into a powerfully advanced skill, such as detecting whether people are telling the truth.

You can also have students watch short, muted video clips from films or TV shows they are not familiar with and ask them to determine what is going on between different characters. You can then replay the scene from the show with the sound on to see whether students were correct in assessing the emotions on display.

Greetings

Teach students how to greet people and talk to them while maintaining eye contact (if eye contact is appropriate). You might ask students to do an experiment of greeting someone exuberantly (you may need to demonstrate), noticing another person's eye color, and then ask the students what happened to the other person's eyes as they spoke.

Improving People-Smarts Processing

If you want to improve your people smarts, then you need to get out and meet people. Take time to meet new people and engage in conversations that will help you learn more about your newfound friends.

Reflecting on what other people like or do not like, or how their viewpoints may differ from your own, is also beneficial. *Learning* when someone else has a point of view different from your own and becoming curious rather than defensive are major life advantages.

Formulate Your Own Personal Development Plan

Consider the following to formulate your own personal development plan.

How Do You Want Your Life to Be in the Next Few Years?

As mentioned in chapter 4 (page 91), this process is one of *imagine forward and plan backward*. Imagine the type of person you wish to be, including your lifestyle, values, and priorities, and then plan backward. What are the stepping-stones to achieve that outcome?

What Are Your Plans When You Grow Older?

Write all the plans in your journal, and reflect on them whenever you can. This will keep you aware of your own emotions and desires in life.

Attuning Yourself to Other People

As in many areas of life, we form patterns of how we generally respond to hearing good news (Gable & Algoe, 2010; Gable, Reis, Impett, & Asher, 2004). Different people respond in different ways.

- **Amplifying** positive emotions. When you say something good about your life, amplifiers say things like "That's great to hear!" and will ask more about it.
- **Stalling** the conversation with little or no emotional involvement. When you say something good about your life, stallers say things like "I suppose that's good" or "That's nice for you." Typically, this shuts down the sharing of positive information, and the conversation turns to other topics.
- **Deflating** the good news by pointing out problems. When you say something good about your life, deflaters point out potential pitfalls or issues. For example, you might tell them you have a new job and will move to a great location, and they will ask, "Can you afford it?" "What about your friends?" or "Is the place as good as they make it seem, though?" This is often expressed as concern but acts like a pin of cynicism to your balloon of hopefulness and happiness.
- **Stealing** the limelight by changing the subject. Usually these people feel they have more important news, issues, and ideas than yours.

Let's use an example and refer to table 6.2: Someone comes home and says, "I've been given an award at school."

Table 6.2: Responses to Good News

	Constructive	Destructive
Active	Amplifier: "That's great! Well done—you've worked hard, and you deserve it."	Deflater: "Now you'll have to spend even more time doing work."
Passive	Staller: "That's nice."	Stealer: "Oh, is that what happened to you today? Wait until you hear what happened to me . . ."

Time to Become Your Own Language Coach

Think about your most important relationships. How much time do you spend amplifying, deflating, stalling, or stealing? How do you respond to good news from other people? How do you respond to bad news?

Take on the project of becoming someone who contributes to conversations and amplifies positive aspects. Try doing this in all the conversations you have for several weeks. Notice, but don't comment, when other people deflate, stall, or steal through their conversations.

Continue to amplify and provide contributions even in conversations in which other people are not contributing in the same way.

Improving People-Smarts Outputs

When students develop strengths in people-smarts outputs, they can match the moods and emotions of others, interpret feelings well, alter their language to fit the situation and the setting, and repair misunderstandings.

Calming Ourselves

Discuss with students how we calm ourselves down. Develop a list of the top-ten ways you do this and ask students ways they might calm themselves down (such as count back from ten, go for a walk, or play with their dog).

Calming Others

Anger is usually caused by feelings of injustice, frustration, or being controlled or thwarted, and it runs on a continuum from mild annoyance or irritation to blind rage. Stress and fear are almost always behind anger. If we can lessen these emotions and replace them with caring and positive relationships, we can avoid a lot of anger. One way to do this is by using the RESOLVE method.

The RESOLVE method can be broken down into seven steps.

1. **R**espond with respect.
2. **E**ngage.
3. **S**eek understanding.
4. **O**bserve feelings.
5. **L**ower the tone.
6. **V**alue add.
7. **E**mpower.

Respond With Respect

The aim of the RESOLVE method is to respond rather than react. If we react, we are being led by the angry person's actions. Responding involves leading and calming angry people.

The key in calming anger lies in respect. Feeling respected creates the sense of being heard and increases trust. Feelings of trust reduce anger. When we respond respectfully, we enable angry people to calm and recover. Some things you can say are as follows.

- "Wow, it looks like you've had a bad time. I'm sorry about that. Let's see if we can help."
- "I'm feeling a bit worried about you."
- "Would you like to tell me about it or just settle in first?"

Engage

If someone approaches you looking irate, be the first one to talk. Say, "Hi, you look upset about something. Can we talk about it?" Engaging with and acknowledging the person's feelings at the outset prevents the person from feeling the need to prove how he or she feels by demonstrating it.

According to the foundational research of Albert Mehrabian (1971), 93 percent of communication is nonverbal. What you do is more important than what you say. Be friendly, open, and welcoming, but also give the other person the freedom to feel what he or she is feeling. Slow your breathing (slow breaths out calm you down), and be patient.

Respect the person's territory, and, if need be, give him or her space. Maintain at least a one-and-a-half arm length's distance from an angry person. This is less likely to increase his or her anxiety, and it also reduces any danger to yourself by providing you with time to react to any sudden moves. If you can, place something—a table or a chair—between you and the upset person.

Standing right-side forward at a forty-five-degree angle, rather than directly in front of the person, can help keep a situation calm and nonadversarial. People's feet often give more information than their faces. Usually, feet point in the direction the person is most likely to move next. So a shift in a person's direction may give you an early warning that he or she is about to run away, leave, or move closer to you. If the person backs away, slowly retreat also. If he or she starts to come back, stop and wait.

Seek Understanding

Listening communicates respect. It does not necessarily mean agreeing with a person's feelings; it means acknowledging the distress or upset behind the immediate issue. If one person refuses to struggle or engage in the conflict, there can be no conflict.

Talking and calming are incompatible. It is impossible to simultaneously calm someone down, get him or her into a position of agreement, and convince him or her that the whole thing is not really your fault. If you try to verbally explain or defend yourself while trying to calm the other person, you will only send mixed messages. It is never wise to send mixed messages to an angry person.

Observe Feelings

By the time an angry person gets to you, he or she is already frustrated and may not be interested in solutions. The person may have been holding in his or her frustration all morning or throughout the school day and just wants someone to yell at to vent his or her anger.

If appropriate, allow the person to release as much energy as possible by venting verbally. Angry people are often in a rush to express their displeasure. Slow down the process. Give the person the sense that you have plenty of time to hear him or her out.

Ask the person to tell you all the things that have gone wrong (most angry people have quite a list). If you can, try to redirect his or her verbal aggression into a problem-solving approach, but this is easier said than done.

During an anger outburst, useful information can be gained. Usually, the real reason for an outburst is not what it would first appear to be. Try to listen for the feelings behind the anger. Restate the feelings and the message you inferred in order to determine whether you have understood the person correctly. One helpful strategy is to generate a list of things we often hear students say angrily and then try to imagine what it is they are fearful about, as shown in the partially filled template in figure 6.4.

What They Say	What They Fear
"You can't make me!"	"They are going to force me to do this for hours!"

Figure 6.4: Statements and the fears behind them.

Lower the Tone

In some ways, calming an angry person is similar to protecting yourself from an aggressive animal.

- Aim to give the message that you are not a threat.
- Avoid direct eye contact—glance but don't stare.
- Speak in a calm voice and breathe evenly.
- Be very still.

Try to lower the level of tension, stimulation, and adrenaline, but do not make jokes. People who are angry can't be joked out of it, and if they feel they are not being taken seriously, this may increase their anger.

People often stop yelling when you calmly and quietly ask, "Could you please speak a little slower? I'd like to understand." Repeating back to the other person what was said also does this. Listen and then paraphrase.

Value Add

Ask, "What would you like me to do?" or "How can I help you?" This unexpected question is the most useful tool for dealing with anger. Angry people either don't know or won't admit what they want you to do. To answer this question, they will have to stop and think, which is what you want them to do.

Empower

Your gut feeling of fear is something you should attend to. No animal senses fear and thinks it is nothing. If you are in a loop and getting nowhere with defusing a situation, ask someone else to help you. If you feel unsafe with an angry person, physically move away from him or her and consider removing yourself from the situation.

Finding Your Contribution

An important aspect of people smarts is learning that you have a contribution to make to others. All the research on happiness tells us the most certain way to create a happy life is through contributions to others and their well-being (Hallam et al., 2013).

Human actions occur in clusters. They are contagious, if you prefer to think of them that way. Ask students to think of a positive idea or behavior they could make contagious. Students Create the Future, a project we ran in 114 schools in Victoria, Australia, involved teams of students choosing a social improvement they could make in their school, their community, their city, or the world and then trying to influence this issue or action for one week. The results were amazingly

Learning-Strength Area	Sample Strategy

Number Smarts	**Students can:**
	- Think about how numbers relate to the people they know
	  - How many direct relatives do you have?
	  - How many close friends do you have?
	  - How many acquaintances do you have?
	  - What is the total? (That is your immediate community.)
	  - How many have blond hair?
	  - How many are left-handed?
	  - How many like dogs?
	  - How many languages are spoken by the people in your class?
	Teachers can:
	- Humanize numbers, using mathematics problems that relate to people (for example, "How does your arm span relate to your height or to the ratio between the length of your arm and your height?")
	- Instruct students to count the number of letters in their own names and compare with a friend's name to find the difference in the number of letters
	At home, families can:
	- Discuss their histories of friendship
	  - How many friends have you kept from your school days?
	  - How many friends have you made since?
	  - What is the ideal number friends?
	  - How many is too many?
	  - How many is too few?
	  - How often do you see close friends? (once a month, once a week, every two weeks, three times a year, and so on)

In Summary

Learning strengths in people smarts facilitate cooperation, teamwork, self-awareness, and the critical skill of emotional regulation, which enables us to calm ourselves when we are upset and motivate ourselves when we feel dejected or disinterested.

The development of learning strengths in people smarts is essential for knowing oneself and working well with others. Our world requires people to work and collaborate with people from many different backgrounds and cultures and who hold different beliefs. Without these strengths, we would be left with a group of self-absorbed people unable to shift their thinking or practices to accommodate people who are different from themselves. A world deficient in people smarts would be a world without kindness, compassion, consideration, and love.

Once developed, learning strengths in people smarts can be applied to enhance success in other areas. They can be used to:

- Accurately interpret the moods, facial cues, postures, and intentions of others (spatial reasoning)
- Be aware of different needs for personal space and how different actions may be viewed differently in some cultures (perceptual and motor skills)
- Focus on building and maintaining good relationships and remembering key information about people so that conversation is easier (concentration and memory)
- Consider the roles and contribution of various people as they work together to achieve an outcome (planning and sequencing)
- Consider the challenges, histories, and circumstances of other people (thinking and logic)
- Develop an understanding of how our language and words shape the way we see the world and how we talk and communicate with one another (language and word smarts)
- Apply statistical thinking to different groups of people, distribution, proportional thinking, and issues such as world poverty and epidemiology (number smarts)

People smarts is a foundation stepping-stone for building success in school and in life. This positive effect on success is especially enhanced when it is linked to language and word smarts.

Reflection Questions

- What strategies will be most valuable in strengthening the people smarts of your students?
- How do students' people smarts affect the facilitation of learning?
- How can you develop people smarts in every student?
- How can we teach students to resolve conflicts?
- Which other members of staff need to be involved in this discussion?
- Should any student's parents or guardians be involved in this discussion?
- How many learning activities in your classroom this week have incorporated people-smarts development?

Chapter 7
LANGUAGE AND WORD SMARTS

Language and words are the ways in which we connect with others, express our ideas, and understand the world around us, but the ability to read gives us access to lives and ideas beyond our own. It allows us to listen to and learn from people we've never met. If we learn to read, then we can read to learn.

In the history of humanity, we have only been writing for a relatively brief time. Writing is thought to have originated nine thousand years ago in Mesopotamia (Butterworth, 2019; Dehaene, 2009). Before then, any lessons or stories could be transmitted only by word of mouth. While knowledge could be transferred across generations, its accuracy depended on the understanding of those who it was conveyed to.

Career Areas That Utilize Learning Strengths in Language and Word Smarts

Journalism, teaching, interpreting, medicine, real estate, shopkeeping, copywriting, acting, speechwriting, slam poetry, comedy, authorship, politics, psychology, hypnotherapy, and broadcasting are some of the career areas that utilize learning strengths in language and words. Helping students consider career paths that call on their learning strengths may ease their way into a successful professional life.

Our most sophisticated language and word skills involve analysis, use of tone, rhyme, effective communication, oratory, clarity of thinking, creativity, critical thinking, and evaluation. How we acquire skills in this area is an interesting journey of brain development.

For hundreds of thousands of years, humans have possessed speaking and listening brains. These skills are vital elements in our personal and professional lives, and they allow us to develop relationships, understand others, express our opinions, consolidate our ideas, and learn. This is the basis of communication.

While our ability to speak and listen builds the foundation to develop reading and writing skills, learning to speak and learning to read are not the same thing. We learn to speak and listen through exposure to oral language. Our parents model how to speak and listen from birth, but we often do not think of this process as learning to speak.

Writing, like speaking, allows us to convince, explain, express, communicate, console, elaborate, articulate, and consolidate our ideas. Reading, like listening, allows us to learn new information and understand experiences beyond our own.

Students learn to write through the modeling of writing skills and applications. Generally, students learn to read through the explicit modeling of decoding and comprehension strategies, because reading is about understanding. It involves not only learning the code that translates speech into visual symbols—for instance, that /c/a/t/ says *cat*—but also forming an understanding of what the word means. Students who do not read much are at risk of delays in comprehension, which compound literacy difficulties and make reading, and ultimately learning, arduous.

You can't learn to read by watching someone else read. Unlike speaking and listening, reading, writing, and spelling have to be taught. Phonemic awareness— or, for example, knowing that the sound at the start of *sun* is in the middle of *pasta* and at the end of the word *cats*—relates directly to reading and comprehension. The explicit modeling of literary strategies allows students to identify what strategies they can use and when.

Brain Systems Involved in Language and Word Smarts

The brain is changed forever by learning to read, with even a small amount of literacy training having an effect (Dehaene, 2009; Konza, 2006).

As the brain learns to read, it goes on a real estate grab, shifting the boundaries of regions initially used for other purposes as it links and networks different areas (Dehaene, 2009).

In order to read, the brain has to adapt the forward part of the occipital region to recognize letters and words. One of these systems, the fusiform gyrus, is used to recognize faces. As facial recognition is more interested in shape and symmetry than left or right, this may partly explain why some beginning readers reverse their letters (especially *p* and *q*, and *b* and *d*).

To further complicate matters, the brain must also integrate what is seen with what is heard or said, and then eventually with what is meant. This process occurs gradually as we learn to read.

Different tasks require different learning skills and use distinct parts of the brain. In addition to the aims of the lesson, let all your students know what brain systems they'll be using in each lesson or activity to familiarize them with their brains. The main parts of the brain involved in language and word smarts are shown in figure 7.1.

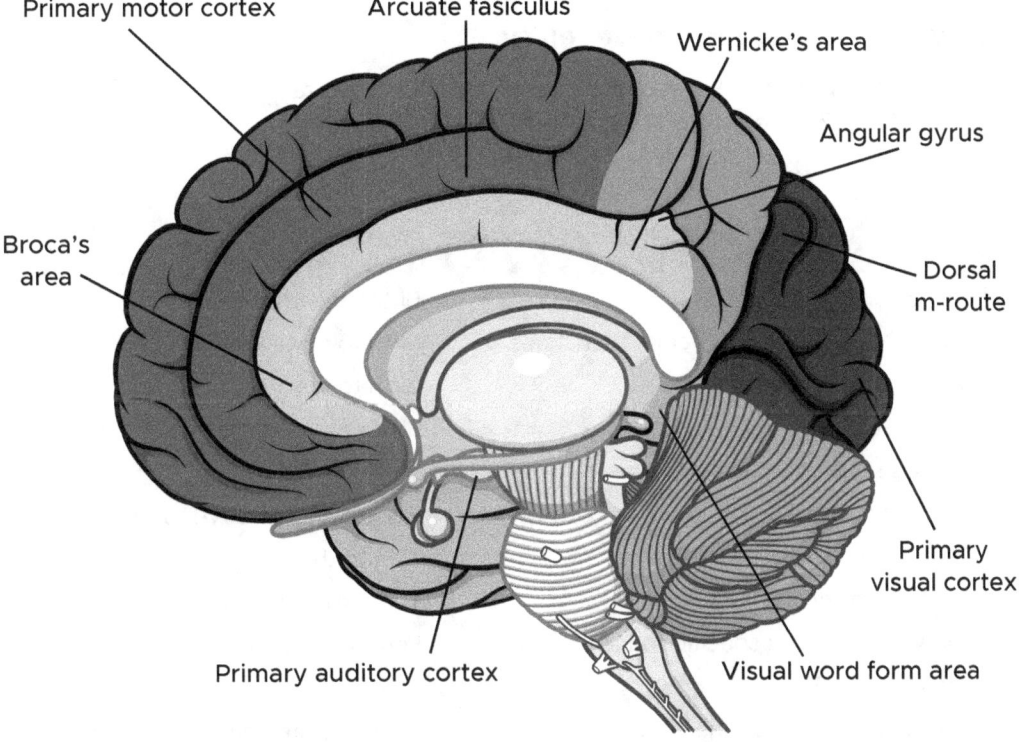

Figure 7.1: Parts of the brain involved in language and word smarts.

- The occipital lobe processes the visual information of words and letters and transmits it to different areas of the brain.
- Broca's area helps us express both verbal and written language.
- Wernicke's area helps us comprehend both written and spoken language. Broca's area and Wernicke's area are located in the left temporal lobe.

The loop between these three areas must be trained to coordinate efficiently (Frey & Fisher, 2010). This allows us to input words and language, process and comprehend them, and respond with verbal or written language.

The critical part of this loop is the ventral occipitotemporal region, located behind the left ear, which activates in response to reading written words or letters. This part of the brain processes the letters of words (Dehaene, 2009). It allows us to recognize the word *LEARN*, *Learn*, or *learn* regardless of font size or location.

This reading network involves simultaneous activation of the frontal, temporal, and parietal lobes, where information about the phonological (speech sound) and semantic (meaning) characteristics of words is processed (Dehaene, 2009).

How the Literate Brain Develops

As an approximate guide, the ages most students attain these skills are outlined in table 7.1 (Dehaene, 2009; Karten, 2017; Konza, 2006).

Table 7.1: Ages of Skill Attainment

Skill	Age
Enjoys being read to	Birth onward
Learns to recognize phoneme distinctions	Birth to eleven months
Develops oral language	Birth to two years
Says first words	Six to eleven months
Follows simple verbal directions	Twelve to seventeen months
Pronounces first vowels and most consonants	Eighteen to twenty-four months
Develops awareness of some letters	Two to three years
Can tell a story	Three to eight years
Knows letters have specific sounds	Four to seven years
Begins to read	Four to seven years
Develops complex phoneme manipulation	Four to eight years
Can gain meaning from short paragraphs	Five to nine years
Comprehends longer texts	Five to nine years

Language Telescopes

Thinking about language
Chunked language (discourse)
Sentence structure (syntax)
Word meanings (semantics)
Word bits (morphemes)
Sounds (phonemes)

Language and word smarts arise from the tiniest units, language sounds, up through fragments of words (like prefixes, roots, and plurals), entire words, whole sentences, lengthy chains of sentences, and finally to the process of not just thinking in language but also thinking *about* language.

Links Between Language and Word Smarts and Other Brain Systems

The circuitry of brain functions involved in literacy mentioned previously—Broca's area (expression of language), Wernicke's area (understanding language), and the ventral occipitotemporal region—is just the beginning. We also need to be able to see words, signs, and instructions (occipital lobes); decide what do about them (frontal lobes); and act appropriately (motor cortex and cerebellum), while resisting the urge to do something else (anterior cingulate gyrus).

Being able to extrapolate from printed words to sounds and then to create meaning helps us understand and comprehend ideas, concepts, and different perspectives. Human survival relies on collaboration, which involves communicating emotionally as well as cognitively. This means there is an overlap between the development of language and word smarts and people smarts. Language issues can also look a lot like concentration problems, as the inability to organize words impoverishes memory and attention.

What Blockages in Language and Word Smarts Look Like in Adulthood

When we don't develop our language and word smarts learning strengths, there are long-term consequences. Adults with blockages in language and word smarts often have poor social skills, feel overlooked and left out, have social anxiety, underestimate their own intelligence (usually incorrectly), feel shameful and secretive, and can't draw on the experiences of others.

Language and Word Smarts Inputs

In *Reading in the Brain*, Stanislas Dehaene (2009) identifies three stages of learning to read.

1. **Pictorial stage:** Children "photograph" a few words and treat words like pictures. Both hemispheres of the brain are involved.

    Infants extract, sort, and classify segments of speech. By two years of age, a child's vocabulary grows at a rate of twenty new words per day, which, of course, relates to how often and how much they are spoken to (Karten, 2017; Konza, 2006). The size of a child's vocabulary increases his or her speed of learning to read. The best predictor of early success in reading is letter knowledge or mastery of the alphabet.

    In order to move beyond the pictorial stage, children must learn that letters represent sounds. This allows them to decode words into component letters and link them to speech sounds (Dehaene, 2009).

2. **Phonological stage:** Children learn to decode letters or groups of letters (graphemes) into sounds (phonemes). Activation becomes more focused and slowly converges in the ventral occipitotemporal region (Dehaene, 2009).

    By five to six years of age, most children are already experts on how sounds work in language (phonology) and possess a vocabulary of several thousand words (if they have had sufficient conversations with adults).

    By age seven, the ventral occipitotemporal region begins to activate at the sight of text. Activation in this region correlates more highly with children's reading scores than their ages.

    Students who are most fluent in phonological games, such as rhyming, learn to read more quickly. Practice with speech-sound manipulations at an early age improves both phonemic awareness and reading scores.

    During the phonological stage, students become aware that speech can be segmented into sounds (Carnine, Silbert, Kame'enui, Slocum, & Travers, 2017), that *cat* rhymes with *hat*, and that the first letter of *snake* sounds like *ess*.

    Some letter-sound combinations appear to be more easily learned than others. The Carnine method (Carnine, Silbert, Kame'enui, Tarver, & Jungjohann, 2006) suggests letter sounds should be taught in a certain order to help students identify and link letters in a sequential fashion, as shown in figure 7.2.

a	m	t	s	l	f	d	r	o	g	l
h	u	c	b	n	k	v	e	w	j	p
y	T	L	M	F	D	I	N	A	R	
H	G	B	x	q	z	J	E	Q		

Source: Adapted from Carnine et al., 2006.

Figure 7.2: The Carnine method.

3. **Orthographic stage:** Word recognition becomes faster and more automatic. Several brain circuits are altered during this process, especially the left ventral occipitotemporal region.

    Vocabulary increases so that words are automatically recalled, allowing focus to shift toward decoding unfamiliar words. This enables whole-word recognition and increases fluency and comprehension. Familiar words are processed in the temporal lobe; unknown words are rehearsed mentally before having meaning attached (Dehaene, 2009).

The goal of reading instruction is to lay down an efficient neuronal hierarchy so students can recognize letters and combinations and easily turn them into speech sounds. This enables students to build on this knowledge to comprehend texts both literally and inferentially.

Whole-Word Versus Phonics Education

Welcome to the reading wars! Literacy brings out hotheaded debates, partly because people can learn in different ways and they then seem to think their way will apply to everyone.

Very few children can recognize words just by looking at them (Konza, 2011). If looking is their only strategy, learning is slower and more restricted with many failures. Trying to treat reading words like reading faces does not work.

In a review of thousands of research studies, Ken Rowe concludes that phonological skills are essential for reading (Rowe & National Inquiry Into the Teaching of Literacy, 2005).

Separate research by Dehaene (2009), Toby Karten (2017), and Deslea Konza (2006) supports this conclusion, finding that for young students to link their knowledge of speaking and writing, they must first master the alphabetic code—the system of grapheme-phoneme correspondences that link written words to how they are pronounced (Rowe & National Inquiry Into the Teaching of Literacy, 2005).

These researchers indicate that if students' reading tuition is grounded in direct, explicit, and systematic phonics instruction, followed by the practical application and practice of newly developed skills, they are greatly assisted in learning to become proficient readers (Dehaene, 2009; Karten, 2017; Konza, 2006; Rowe & National Inquiry Into the Teaching of Literacy, 2005).

Sight words are an important tool, especially for beginning readers. Visual whole-word methods are needed for about 25 percent of English words because many common words don't follow regular letter-sound rules—for example, *yacht*. But as the preceding research illustrates, a strong emphasis on phonics is far more valuable than meaning or sight-word approaches in early reading instruction.

Language and Word Smarts Processing

The goal of reading instruction is to lay down an efficient neuronal hierarchy so students can recognize letters and graphemes and easily turn them into speech sounds. All other aspects of literacy depend on this.

In order to move beyond the pictorial stage, students must learn to rapidly decode words into component letters and link them to speech sounds. This is called segmenting—that is, *cat* to /c/a/t/ or /c/at/. The reverse, blending, is required also—that is, /c/a/t/ to *cat*. Writing requires encoding.

Language and Word Smarts Outputs

Some students have difficulty writing, even though they have a lot to say. Others can be inarticulate but write fluently. Students need to be explicitly taught how to read and write, and practice should occur until these skills are automatic (see table 7.2).

Table 7.2: Key Signs—Language and Word Smarts

	Positive Signs	Concerning Signs
Inputs	The student: • Can identify sounds and code combinations of letters into words	The student: • Appears to have concentration deficits • Demonstrates insufficient matching of sounds with letters and words
Processing	The student: • Can make meaning • Can decode and encode words using knowledge of sounds and component letters and link them to speech sounds	The student: • Has difficulty with comprehension • Stumbles over words • Is unable to identify individual sounds in a word • Is unable to rhyme

	The student:	The student:
Outputs	• Can express ideas in spoken and written forms • Can think about the sequence and the selection of language to increase the impact of a message	• Has difficulty writing and forming letters • Is unable to tell a coherent story or joke • Appears to find conversations tiring • Is reluctant to read or to write

Ways to Assess Language and Word Smarts in the Classroom

The following ideas will not replace a full psychological or literacy assessment, but they may give teachers and parents an idea if further investigations are merited.

Students' ability to complete some of the following tasks will give you an idea of their capacities or difficulties in using language and word smarts to learn well. Most of these can be used to make an assessment of specific students, but they will also benefit the entire class.

By profiling each student's skill level in processing sounds, decoding words, comprehension, and analysis, as well as his or her existing vocabulary, we can focus our interventions to help the student develop learning strengths in language and word smarts.

Auditory-Processing Assessment

Provide students with a sheet of paper with different shapes on it, and ask them to color the different shapes certain colors.

Decoding Assessment

Ask students to read a passage aloud, and observe their strategies for decoding unknown words. Are they able to make logical attempts at decoding? Are they able to make logical attempts at spelling based on their understanding of letter-sound relationships?

Comprehension Assessment

Ask students to answer key questions about a text—for example, "Who was Jane's best friend?"

To test students' ability to infer from the text, ask them questions about why things happen in the story and assess their ability to use evidence from the text to make logical inferences.

To assess students' ability to summarize, synthesize, and extract information from a text, ask them to tell you what a book is about. If they provide a detailed retelling of the text, they are unable to summarize and infer. But if they tell you the text is about a specific theme, then these abilities are well developed.

Use multiple methods of assessment to provide a deeper understanding of students' comprehension. Written work does not always represent understanding for students who are more competent in expressing their understanding verbally.

Vocabulary Assessment

Ask students to brainstorm and use similes, adjectives, and verbs to create interesting writing pieces. If students are using the same words often, then perhaps their vocabulary is not as well developed as it could be.

Analysis Assessment

To assess students' ability to analyze what they are reading, use the *four-resources model* (Freebody, 1992; Freebody & Luke, 1990) as a starting point.

The four-resources model asks students to consider what the purpose of the text is; how the author has positioned the reader and what he or she has done to achieve this; what codes have been used in the text to influence the reader's opinion and to create context; and what text-to-self, text-to-text, and text-to-world connections can be made.

Whether a student successfully completes or struggles to finish a series of the preceding activities will not necessarily indicate a problem, but these tasks will serve as a guide to his or her current level of learning strengths in concentration and memory (see table 7.3).

Dyslexia

Dyslexia is a problem in connecting the sounds that make up words with the letters that represent those sounds, and it is experienced by between 6 and 17 percent of students (Butterworth, 2019). It appears to be genetic and is related to the cells that process visual and auditory inputs. While they are not identical, there are some similarities between dyslexia and dyscalculia (Butterworth, 2019). (See chapter 8, page 171, for more on dyscalculia.) Students with dyslexia have difficulty processing letter-sound relationships within the brain. This makes reading a difficult task (Stein, 2001).

Table 7.3: Common Causes of Reading Blockages

Inputs	Processing	Outputs
The student:	The student:	The student:
• Doesn't link sounds to letters • Can't break down or blend sounds • Can't break words into syllables • Can't see patterns in syllables • Is overwhelmed by paragraphs of text	• Can't infer meaning from context • Can't read in phrases • Is unable to analyze words using roots and affixes • Loses track of where he or she is on the page • Doesn't create visual images of information	• Can't recall what was read • Experiences no linkage with prior knowledge • Can't identify main messages • Demonstrates expressionless reading—no inflection or pausing when reading • Demonstrates disjointed, stumbling reading

The four main areas in the brain that relate to dyslexia are Broca's area, angular gyrus, primary auditory cortex, and Wernicke's area. People with dyslexia show disruptions in the information pathways between these areas (Stein, 2001).

It is important to note that dyslexia is not the result of bad teaching or parenting. It is also neither an indication of lower intelligence nor reversed writing. But it is just as important to note that dyslexia is also not a phase that will be outgrown.

Is It in the Eye of the Beholder?

Reading requires visual processing. When we see something, the information from our eyes splits into two main pathways (Chouake, Levy, Javitt, & Lavidor, 2012; Stein, 2001).

1. The **upper, dorsal stream** enables us to know where we are and how to move in relation to our immediate environment.

2. The **lower, ventral stream** enables us to determine, understand, and classify what we see.

Two visual pathways use different kinds of brain cells to process information.

1. **Magnocellular cells** pass information along the upper, dorsal stream of the brain. They help us understand motion. The pathway tells us all about where things are and how fast they are moving.

2. **Parvocellular cells** carry visual information along the lower, ventral stream of the brain. They help us understand the shape, size, color, clarity, contrast, and detail of things.

Magnocellular cells are important for the focusing of both visual and auditory attention. Our magnocellular circuit relates to the ability to stabilize the eyes. It locks the eyes on targets and identifies the orders of the letters. Impairment of the magnocellular system seems to delay processing of what we see and is often found in poor readers and people with dyslexia.

According to professor John Stein from Oxford University (2001), two-thirds of reading differences can be accounted for by visual sensitivity. This is why experimenting with colored screens (blue or yellow) or tinted glasses to combat dyslexia is worthwhile.

Auditory Attention

To understand someone who is speaking, you must listen to the sounds he or she is making and sequence them in your mind. This requires you to focus on each sound to understand what is being said, which is why students are at a disadvantage in noisy classrooms.

Many dyslexic and dysphasic students have a problem with their auditory magnocellular system and therefore struggle to focus their auditory attention in order to sequence sounds properly (Stein, 2001).

Essential Fatty Acids

Fatty acid deficiency is a common problem in students who can't read. These essential fatty acids are incorporated in the brain but move in and out of the membranes and into other areas. If they are not replenished, the workings of the brain can be negatively impacted. Fish oils—docosahexaenoic acid (DHA) and eicosapentaenoic acid (EPA)—chia seeds, flaxseed, and green sea algae help magnocellular cells and improve attention and reading. Inadequate nutrition can impair cognitive processing and contribute to the development of dyslexia (Bauer et al., 2011). (See figure 7.3.)

Language and Word Smarts

Use this list to rate the language and word smarts of the student. Assign a score out of ten (with one being "can't do this" and ten being "great at this") for each of the statements that follow. (A student at the average level of his or her class would score a five.)

Issue	Rating
Inputs	
The student:	
• Can comprehend written materials at an age-appropriate level	
• Can use and incorporate contextual cues to deepen understanding	
• Can evaluate ideas from texts	
• Can read with fluency and comprehension	
• Can rely on him- or herself when appropriate	
Processing	
The student:	
• Can comprehend what he or she has read	
• Can research independently	
• Can think and write creatively	
• Can interpret multiple perspectives from characters	
• Can think clearly	
• Can positively support other people	
Outputs	
The student:	
• Can write persuasively	
• Can communicate clearly	
• Can use metaphor, analogy, and similes	
• Can demonstrate a depth of understanding	
• Is expressive in communication	

Figure 7.3: List of issues with language and word smarts.

Discuss your concerns and compare these results with other teachers who are familiar with this student to confirm your observations.

Evidence That Language and Word Smarts Can Be Improved

Considerable research shows us that training in the form of conversations with parents and literacy programs in schools pay off with demonstrable increases in vocabulary, expressive language, and understanding of questions and language, and improvements in communication skills (Dehaene, 2009; Karten, 2017; Konza, 2006; Rowe & National Inquiry Into the Teaching of Literacy, 2005).

How to Enhance Language and Word Smarts

An extensive review by David Wray, Jane Medwell, Richard Fox, and Louise Poulson (2000) finds that effective teaching of literacy involves:

- Ensuring maximum student engagement in academic activities and a minimum of time spent unengaged
- A combination of whole-class, group, and individual teaching with about half of the time spent in whole-class activities
- Matching tasks to the abilities of the students
- Large amounts of revision and practice for high achievers and a high level of knowledge acquisition for low attainers
- Teaching letter sounds and names (looking at letter sounds in the context of reading)
- Including other adults in the teaching of reading
- The use of letter-string exercises, interactive writing, writing for an audience beyond the teacher, flash cards, sequencing activities, big books, reading scheme books, and phonic exercises

Improving Language and Word Smarts Inputs

From a young age, students need to develop their learning strengths in language and word smarts. They can do this by continuing to read and write; becoming familiar with words and sentences; and engaging in conversations about stories and ideas, independent reading, and free-writing sessions. Crossword puzzles and other word games can have a similar positive impact.

Spelling

Consider the following when it comes to spelling.

- Teach spelling explicitly. Teach a few words at a time, beginning with high-frequency words. Use phonics and letter-word families as a way of helping with spelling.
- Create word-family lists. Keep them on display for easy reference.

- Use games, such as word searches.
- Develop personal dictionaries.
- Conduct peer tutoring.
- Break words into syllables.
- Teach word families and "demon" words—lists of words that are hard to spell.

The following strategies are adapted from the Spelling Mastery program (McGraw-Hill, 2006), which uses a direct-instruction method.

Fold-and-Write Method

Fold a piece of paper into five columns, and write a list of words in the left-hand column. After looking at and spelling each word aloud, students fold the left-hand column under and try to write the word in the second column. Check for accuracy. Fold under and repeat for the misspelled words.

Take-a-Picture Method

Write a word on the board and have students read it aloud. Have students write the word on a piece of paper and take a picture of it in their mind. Ask students to turn their papers over and then rewrite the word. Check for accuracy.

Cloze-Spelling Method

Show students a word, and have them study the letter order. Then show them the same word without the vowels. Have your students write down the complete word, including the missing vowels. Then show them the word without consonants. Have your students write the complete word, including the missing consonants. Check for accuracy.

Comprehension

- Use context clues. Ask questions to assess the student's understanding of the context, such as "Was it night or day?" and "What was the weather like?"
- Prerecord the material and listen as well as read it. Ask the student about the content.
- Prompt the student to stop and think about the meaning after a paragraph is read.
- Ask for predictions about what might happen next.
- Ask the student to identify key words.
- Make notes.

- Play get-the-gist games.
- Use outlines, flowcharts, and concept mapping.
- Use free reading, where students summarize main ideas and circle words that are new to them.
- Use sticky notes to track ideas and thinking.

Improving Language and Word Smarts Processing

Academically successful students do not necessarily have larger vocabularies than their classmates. What really differentiates many top students is that they understand the meanings of the words they know better than those other students know, and they tend to use those words fluently, frequently, and effectively in oral and written language (Dehaene, 2009).

Language processing relates to memory and involves decoding, sequencing, comprehending, and reassembling words, ideas, and syllables. This is the "playing" with language that ultimately builds great communication and literature. The Finnish literacy game *GraphoGame* has achieved remarkable outcomes in word and language processing (Howard-Jones, 2014). Another promising approach is QuickSmart Literacy, developed by professor John Pegg and his colleagues at the University of New England (Graham, 2009; Graham & Pegg, 2011; Pegg & Graham, 2013).

Understanding the basis of stories and how to analyze them enhances students' processing of literature (Hutton, Dudley, Horowitz-Kraus, DeWitt, & Holland, 2019). Christopher Booker's (2004) remarkable analysis suggests there are only seven basic plots: (1) overcoming the monster, (2) rags to riches, (3) the quest, (4) voyage and return, (5) comedy, (6) tragedy, and (7) rebirth. Gaining an understanding of these major themes of literature assists students in identifying themes and styles of stories.

Improving Language and Word Smarts Outputs

Effective verbal expressive language correlates highly with writing skills, so our modern reliance on computers risks an accompanying decline in verbal eloquence and fluency (Greenleaf, Schoenbach, Cziko, & Mueller, 2001). Using less technology and having more thoughtful conversations could counteract this.

Modeling by teachers is essential. Read aloud to the class, and then stop and say aloud what you are thinking and anticipating. Ensure your students are constructing answers in complete sentences and not using slang or text-based abbreviations.

Note Taking

As mentioned in chapter 3 (page 63), good note taking is linked to academic achievement.

Word Finds

Word finds can be used to increase vocabulary and word knowledge. Define pronouns, nouns, verbs, adverbs, and adjectives with the class, and then ask students to identify different types of words in a piece of writing. Use a magazine or newspaper article, and have teams of students find different types of words. As a group, discuss which types of words were the most frequent.

Listening Teams

The ability to create a coherent story correlates with literacy skills (Konza, 2006). One person tells or reads aloud a story or speaks about something that happened to him or her. Two people listen intently to the person and then present the same story as accurately as they can to the group. A second version requires the pairs to present a five-word summary of the story. Ask teams to discuss how close the summaries were. This activity builds literacy, confidence, and summarizing and listening skills.

Team Poetry

In groups of five, each student writes the line of a poem (or the first thing that comes into his or her head—and if a student says, "I don't know what to write," he or she should use that as the first line). The first student writes a line and hands it to the second student. After adding a line, the second student folds the page over, leaving only his or her line showing, and passes it to the third student, who adds a line, folds the paper again, and so on. Ask the teams to read out their poems. Repeating this activity several times over a few weeks pays off!

Language and Word Smarts Cross-Fertilization Strategies

If a student has a learning strength in language and word smarts, table 7.4 (page 166) suggests some strategies that could be used to help open up and extend learning in other areas. These are some key suggestions to stimulate your thinking and can be adapted to your classroom or time frame as you see fit.

Table 7.4: Extending Learning From Language and Word Smarts

Learning-Strength Area	Sample Strategy
Spatial Reasoning	**Students can:** • Increase the amount of sensation and imagery in written stories—use descriptive language • Learn how authors use descriptive phrases and imagery to create pictures in their readers' minds • Use words to tell the stories of images and shapes (for example, "In the beginning was the circle. The circle was very useful because it was the shape of . . . . Then along came a square. There were lots of things squares could be, including . . . . Together, the circle and the square were powerful because they could make a . . . .") **Teachers can:** • Teach students to look at a word, take a picture of it with their minds, look away, and write the word from memory • Use Venn diagrams • Analyze great opening lines in books and inquire as to what images they invoke in readers • Discuss the use of sentence structure to create different effects, such as suspense, mystery, and dramatic tension **At home, families can:** • Describe the shape of objects • Develop a rich language of spatial relationships—*over*, *under*, *beside*, *near*, *adjoining*, *adjacent*, *beneath*, *at right angles*, *top left*, *bottom right*, *at a twenty-degree tilt*, and so on • Play Pictionary
Perceptual and Motor Skills	**Students can:** • Create a commentary of a sports event or a dance • Develop raps with music **Teachers can:** • Use *plus, minus, interesting* charts—list words associated with each step in resolving an issue • Study sports events and sports journalism • Integrate rhythm and clapping games with words • Introduce drama activities in which one student instructs another using action words (for example, *walk on tiptoe*, *jump over the line*, *lean left*, or *pick up a round shape*) **At home, families can:** • Teach dance steps verbally • Practice charades and improvisational sketches • Walk together and create a story about some of the people and things they see • Play "Simon says" • Add physical movements and gestures into stories

Language and Word Smarts

Learning-Strength Area	Sample Strategy
Concentration and Memory	**Students can:** • Create stories about the things they want to remember **Teachers can:** • Invent stories that contain given key concepts to develop memory • Teach students how to listen, looking at the teacher with lips together, hands and feet still, and ears open • Teach students note taking and identifying the main ideas in a lesson • Use the BASE method (see page 79) • Show students five objects and ask them to create a story about them (share the story and test their memory; increase the number of objects on subsequent trials) • Relate concepts to stories **At home, families can:** • After reading a book or watching a movie or TV show, ask each other to explain the plot, the main parts of the story, and the parts each liked the best and why
Thinking and Logic	**Students can:** • Practice debating • List the pros and cons of an issue • Watch courtroom dramas • Read detective novels **Teachers can:** • Put stories into timelines of key events • Challenge students to convince them using descriptive language • Ask students to write persuasive essays **At home, families can:** • Discuss issues that are complex with arguments for and against • Show children how to weigh and think through issues aloud • Read Choose Your Own Adventure stories
People Smarts	**Students can:** • Practice being better conversationalists—greet people in a friendly way, ask questions, be positive, and so on **Teachers can:** • Create stories, jokes, and entertaining anecdotes • Study ways to greet people • Brainstorm and practice the best thing to say to someone who has lost his or her dog, missed the train, gotten wet in a storm, won the lottery, or lost a close sports game **At home, families can:** • Interact with a range of people—the more children see their parents converse, the better they learn how to do so themselves

continued →

Learning-Strength Area	Sample Strategy
Number Smarts	**Students can:** • See whether they can find an area of life where numbers are not important (this should help students realize numbers are involved in all aspects of life) • Practice number thinking every day • Notice how numbers relate to sports, stories, biology, history, cooking, and science **Teachers can:** • Use real-world problems and apply thinking in numbers to solve those issues (sustainability is a great theme for this) • Write out mathematical problems in words • Create a story about a mathematical problem • Solve word-based mathematical problems **At home, families can:** • Speak positively about learning to use numbers in thinking (for example, go shopping and discuss quantities required and amounts of money—financial security relies on this)

In Summary

Learning strengths in language and word smarts allow us to be expressive and to communicate well with others.

The development of learning strengths in language and word smarts shapes our memories, our focus, and our perceptual awareness. It is hard to fully understand experiences we can't put into words. Without these strengths, we are inarticulate and often feel misunderstood by others because of the poor quality of our communication skills. A world deficient in language and word smarts would be an impoverished world deprived of jokes, stories, poems, and song lyrics.

Once developed, learning strengths in language and word smarts can be applied to enhance success in other areas. They can be used to:

- Create verbal monologues as we look at a series of pictures and images, thereby deepening our appreciation and understanding of them (spatial reasoning)
- Describe the sequence of movements required to accomplish a skill (perceptual and motor skills)
- Articulate when we have lost focus and also link ideas into patterns and stories to increase our recall of information (concentration and memory)
- Talk ourselves through the steps involved in reaching an outcome (planning and sequencing)

- Consider the advantages and disadvantages of an issue (thinking and logic)
- Apply mathematical problem solving to real-world issues, such as how long you will need to save up to buy something (number smarts)

While often viewed as almost diametrically opposed, the positive effect of language and word smarts on success is especially enhanced when it is linked to number smarts.

Reflection Questions

- What can be done to encourage reluctant readers?
- How can you orchestrate more reading activities?
- Which other members of staff need to be involved in this discussion?
- Should any student's parents or guardians be involved in this discussion?
- What insights does this information provide for you?
- What actions will you implement to support your students' optimal learning?
- How would you know if your students had dyslexia?
- What support would be available?
- What questions does this raise for schools' efforts to make learning accessible and optimal for all students?
- What mix of individual teacher differentiation efforts and whole-school pedagogy commitments are required?
- What strategies will be most valuable in strengthening the language and word smarts of your students?
- How many learning activities in your classroom this week have incorporated language and word smarts development?

Chapter 8
NUMBER SMARTS

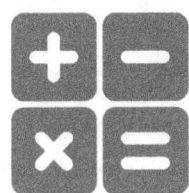

You set your alarm at 7:00 a.m. because you know it will take around ten minutes to make and eat breakfast, ten minutes to shower and get dressed, two minutes to brush your teeth, and around five minutes to get your things organized to get out the door (plus an extra ten minutes for just-in-case emergencies). You leave the house at around 7:40 a.m., knowing it will take twenty minutes to get to work, given the traffic is usually pretty bad at that time and you want to buy a coffee at the café before work.

If this is similar to your daily routine, you have already used several key numeracy skills by the time you arrive at work. You will have read the time, estimated how long it would take to get ready and get to work, calculated the amount of money needed to pay for your coffee, and checked the change you were given. Numbers are all around us. We use mathematics so often in our everyday lives as adults that we don't even realize when we are using it.

Mathematics has been the basis of great scientific discoveries, and it forms the bedrock of art and music. Once we move past the idea that mathematics is about the memorization of facts and the application and understanding of those facts, we can see it as a highly effective way of gaining a greater understanding of the world around us.

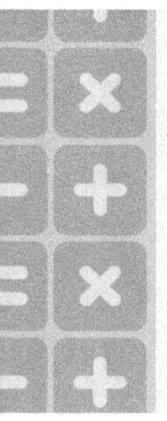

Career Areas That Utilize Learning Strengths in Number Smarts

Engineering, business management, accountancy, physics, mathematics, cooking, astronautical engineering, aviation, bookmaking, teaching, academic research, financial planning, epidemiology, actuarial science, architecture, shopkeeping, farming, and economics are some of the career areas that utilize learning strengths in number smarts. Helping students consider career paths that call on their learning strengths may ease their way into a successful professional life.

Our most sophisticated numerical skills involve problem solving, predicting, estimating, analyzing, reasoning, recognizing multiple ways of solving problems, pattern recognition, logical and lateral thinking, and algebraic skills. How we build skills in this area is an interesting journey of brain development.

Students develop a sense of numbers from a young age, but once they arrive at school, they often fail to see a connection between what they are learning in the classroom and the mathematics we use in everyday life. The problem is that we have quarantined number smarts to the mathematics classroom. As a result, some people look forward to thinking in numbers with the same relish they might look forward to having a root canal.

Number Sense

Human beings have an innate sense of numbers (Dehaene, 2011). And from birth onward, the sophistication of our number smarts increases. As students develop more intricate number skills, they are able to read a problem involving numbers, identify multiple ways of solving it, choose the most appropriate way to solve it, and then justify their answer using logical mathematical reasoning. They are also able to apply what they already know to what they do not to make logical attempts at solving a problem. Once students are at this stage, they are able to see the concepts within mathematics as interconnected (Butterworth, 2019).

In order to increase their number smarts, students need to develop an understanding of the big ideas in mathematics, such as trusting the count, place value, equivalence, proportional reasoning, and additive and multiplicative thinking.

But we often see students who just do not get it or can't remember what they learned the day before. It is therefore important to introduce concepts in a sequential and meaningful way by beginning with the use of materials and real-world learning before moving to the more abstract (Butterworth, 2019; Dehaene, 2011). If a student does not get it, go back a step, get some materials, and relate it to his or her life.

Brain Systems Involved in Number Smarts

Different tasks require different learning skills and use distinct parts of the brain. In addition to the aims of the lesson, let all your students know what brain systems they'll be using in each lesson or activity to familiarize them with their brains (see figure 8.1).

The main location of the number system in our brains is a relatively small area beneath the crown on both sides of the head called the intraparietal sulcus, which activates whenever we think of a number (Dehaene, 2011). Interestingly, this part of the brain is also involved in movement, rhythm, and music. Students with dyscalculia often have structural and functional deficits of the intraparietal sulcus (Butterworth, 2019).

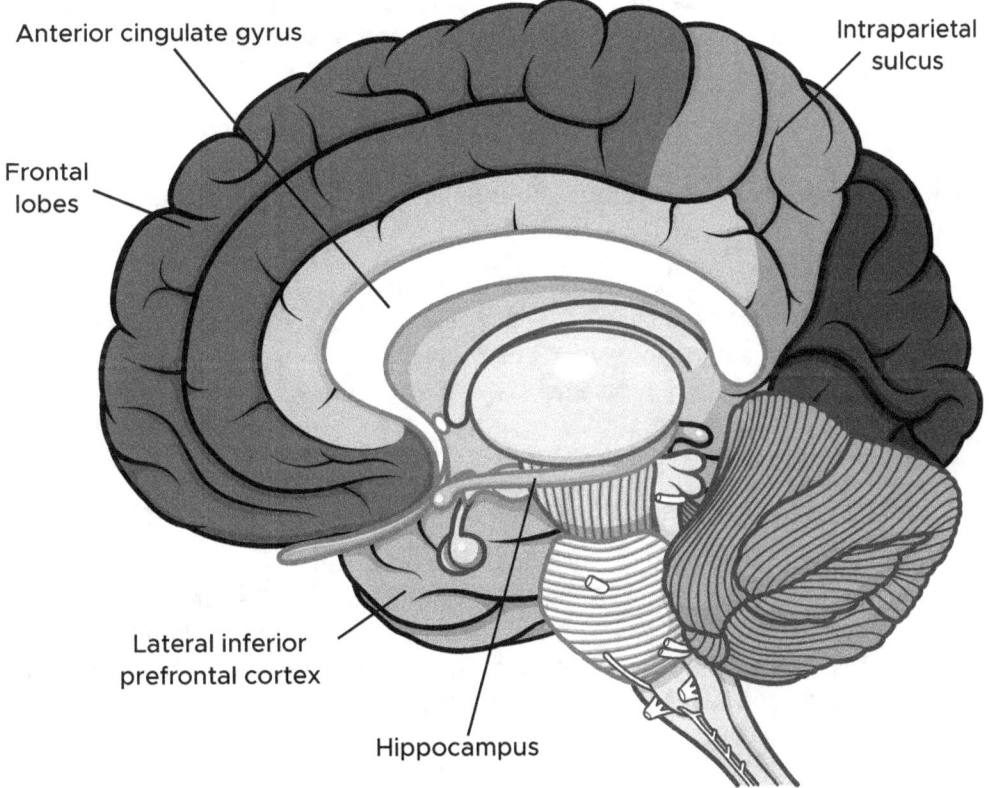

Figure 8.1: Parts of the brain involved in number smarts.

When the brain is numerate, the intraparietal sulcus recruits other parts of the brain to solve problems. Visuospatial and auditory working memory must work together for us to successfully solve problems. We also need to focus our attention (using the anterior cingulate gyrus), order tasks (using the frontal lobes), recall memories from long-term memory (using the hippocampus), inhibit distractions, and link new concepts to existing understanding or schema (Dehaene, 2011).

Being number smart involves different parts of the brain coordinating. In addition to the intraparietal sulcus, a frontal part of the brain called the lateral inferior prefrontal cortex becomes involved in solving mathematical problems. Our language areas and memory structures also provide assistance, including the hippocampus and Broca's area, as we think through problems.

When we solve complex mathematics problems, the parietal area is active. When we are proficient in mathematics, the lateral inferior prefrontal cortex is active. Thinking about numbers uses a lot of brainpower!

Links Between Number Smarts and Other Brain Systems

The way brains solve mathematical problems is very different from how our brains process language. Solving mathematical problems involves the prefrontal, parietal, and inferior temporal regions.

To confidently approach numeracy questions, students need to have several key skills that allow them to identify what the question is asking of them and what mathematics is involved in solving the problem. Because all brains are different, some students will have difficulty with this.

Some students who experience difficulties with numbers may also have challenges with memory, spatial reasoning, planning and sequencing, thinking and logic, and language and word smarts as they struggle with the input of information provided in numeracy problems.

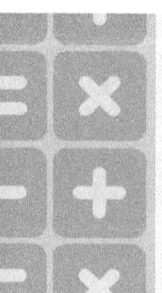

What Blockages in Number Smarts Look Like in Adulthood

When we don't develop our number-smarts learning strengths, there are long-term consequences. Adults with blockages in number smarts often find tax time a nightmare, have difficulty making a budget, find it hard to follow a recipe, have estimation problems, freeze when they have to think about numbers, and have financial-literacy problems.

Number-Smarts Inputs

Improving numeracy is a powerful way of building financial literacy and, therefore, protects people from poverty. But no other learning area seems to invoke as much trepidation and anxiety as mathematics. Therefore, we need to calm students so they can start to enjoy thinking with numbers in all areas of their learning.

Create a Risk-Taking Classroom

Focusing only on getting the correct answer actually inhibits the ability to get the answer right and causes mathematics anxiety (Butterworth, 2019). So reduce the need for speed, and instead reward considered theories, even if they are incorrect. Create a culture of learning and ideas so students shift their focus from "I'm not good at mathematics" to "I'm still working out how to do this."

The Best Doozy

One of the best ways to learn is through making mistakes. One great teacher we know introduced the idea of the *best doozy* in her classroom by bringing in a mathematics problem she had really mucked up and asking her students to figure out where she had gone wrong. She then asked them to identify what they could have done differently to solve the problem. By highlighting that even a teacher makes mistakes, her students learned it is normal to get things wrong. She then invited students to share their best doozies, and together the class worked out where each student had made the mistake and what he or she could do differently the next time.

Work Together

Modeling and creating a culture of learning, as opposed to a culture of getting it right, allow students to support one another in their learning. If the focus is placed on the process rather than the answer, then the less-competent students seek to learn and the more-competent students provide them with support. Having mixed-ability groups is an advantage to all students. Research shows streaming (or ability grouping) harms low-achieving students while not supporting high-attaining students (Linchevski & Kutscher, 1998).

There Are Many Routes to the Same Destination

There are many different strategies for solving number problems. Invite the sharing of different methods in your classroom so students can be exposed to and develop a range of different strategies.

Having a tool kit of numeracy strategies allows students to solve a problem in a range of different contexts and enables them to connect what they do know to what they do not and make logical attempts in solving a problem.

Give Students the Time to Work It Out

The Shanghai mastery method of mathematics slows down the delivery of numeracy content to allow all students the time to master key concepts before moving on. This method has been adopted widely in the United Kingdom, and there are ways to adapt this method to suit schools in other countries (National Centre for Excellence in the Teaching of Mathematics, n.d.).

Make It Spatial

There is a strong relationship between spatial reasoning and mathematics learning (Lowrie & Jorgensen, 2017). Spatial visualization is used in many areas of mathematics, including number sense, quantification, quantity comparison, and arithmetic. Highly advanced mathematicians often visualize numbers and quantities and often think about numbers in a spatial number line (Mighton, 2011; Tosto et al., 2014).

Spatial reasoning skills are predictive of later mathematics achievement and are also linked to the skills used in STEAM (science, technology, engineering, arts, and mathematics; Harris & Lowrie, 2018). Several studies show our spatial reasoning improves with training and that these gains are durable and transfer to other areas (Newcombe & Frick, 2010). Therefore, using hands-on, movement-based activities is an essential component in all successful numeracy classrooms.

The Singapore bar method is an exemplary way of integrating spatial reasoning and number smarts. It uses visual methods for demonstrating the parts of calculations (Clement, 2017).

Active Learning

When students are actively learning, they use their frontal lobes to determine what needs to happen next and to organize the information, as well as the motor regions of the brain to carry it out (Kagan, 2013).

Active learning has students, after some explicit instruction, *doing* mathematics rather than *learning* mathematics. Movement-based mathematics means using human-sized number lines to solve addition and subtraction problems; designing, measuring, and creating a new product using cardboard while creating the least amount of waste possible; measuring the length of your classroom using the students in your class; and building 3-D shapes using straws and manipulatives (Day & Lovitt, 2011).

Use Fingers

There is a relationship between the bodily awareness of our fingers (called finger gnosis) and mathematics ability (Mighton, 2011). The brain regions associated with the representation of fingers are also activated during tasks requiring the representation of numbers. Damage to or disruption of these areas affects both finger gnosis and tasks requiring the representation of numbers (Penner-Wilger & Anderson, 2013).

Allowing younger students to use their fingers as a method of counting supports the development of later mental strategies rather than hindering them. Additionally, using fingers as a unit of informal measurement is beneficial in building the foundations for learning experiences focused on formal metric measurement (Mighton, 2011).

The practical application of this is to provide students with tactile numeracy experiences that allow them to sort, classify, organize, design, create, manipulate, and construct. Drawing and manipulating objects as a method of problem solving can be beneficial in developing an understanding of complex or abstract numeracy concepts at all grade levels. This is supported by the Singapore bar method (Clement, 2017).

For older students, practical applications of this are to provide opportunities for them to write out whole questions rather than using computer-based mathematics programs and filling out work questions. Another promising approach is QuickSmart Numeracy, developed by professor John Pegg and his colleagues at the University of New England (Graham & Pegg, 2011).

Number-Smarts Processing

Consider the following strategies for number-smarts processing.

Optimize Information Processing

When we learn something new, a new information pathway is formed between neurons. With repetition and practice, this new pathway becomes more efficient in processing information, and it is more likely that the new knowledge will become stored in long-term memory.

Teachers can support this process by presenting numeracy concepts as interconnected. For example, allow students to inquire into the multiplicative nature of fractions by folding a piece of paper in half as many times as possible and describing what they observe.

Presenting concepts in a range of different ways and allowing students to tackle problems from a variety of angles strengthens conceptual understanding and helps the brain make neural connections between different mathematical concepts (Marzano, 2007).

Reps Pay Off—Big-Time!

There are learning areas you can fall behind in and still catch up, but mathematics isn't one of them. It is better to complete a few numeracy problems every day than a lot at once.

The creation and strengthening of neural pathways involve repetition. Repetition builds automaticity—when we repeat activities, we develop habits and skills that can occur automatically with minimal thinking or use of working memory (Marzano, 2007; Sapolsky, 2017b). Share this information with your students so they understand the importance of regular practice.

For example, if we give students flash cards of times tables and ask them to chant along as we recite them, they develop automaticity. If we can visually chart their progress, they can see how much faster they are getting. All of this frees working memory for higher levels of mathematics later.

Increasing Conceptual Understanding

Working memory is a big challenge for many students in mathematics. If you can't hold new information in your mind, you can't process it. And if information is not getting processed, it is not being integrated into the larger schema that builds understanding. The best way to support students struggling with working memory and mathematics is to:

- Model the key skills and strategies in the introduction, providing multiple examples
- Invite students to discuss and share their knowledge of the concept
- Use concrete materials to consolidate understanding
- Use examples to help students relate the concept to their own lives
- Provide an opportunity for students to practice the concept in multiple contexts
- Provide an opportunity for students to solve the problem without your help
- Reflect on learning by identifying the strategies used and key ideas learned either through self-assessment methods, such as KWL ("what I *know*," "what I *want to know*," "what I *learned*") charts, or through discussion
- Reflect on the previous lesson at the beginning of each lesson (Butterworth, 2019; Day & Lovitt, 2011)

Get Creative

Provide experiences for students to be creative with mathematics. Ask them to create a work of art using triangles in which the angles add up to a given amount, or to design a cardboard model of a machine, focusing on the measurement of each aspect of the machine. Charles Lovitt's wonderful Maths300 (n.d.), a collection of three hundred of the best interactive mathematics activities, provides many great examples of this.

Number-Smarts Outputs

Mathematics is about counting, classifying, patterns, and cause-and-effect chains of reasoning. Encourage students to disclose their own understanding of what they have learned and to show connections between the concepts they have learned. Include student explanations of their thinking and reasoning as a part of your lessons (see table 8.1).

Table 8.1: Key Signs—Number Smarts

	Positive Signs	Concerning Signs
Inputs	The student: • Develops number sense • Understands numbers and number values and has an awareness of the basic patterns in numbers	The student: • Demonstrates little recognition of number value or concepts • Does not have a strong number sense
Processing	The student: • Is able to explain what the problem is when asked to do so in words • Is able to reason sequentially • Uses spatial reasoning to help solve mathematical problems—with drawings, blocks, dice, and algebra blocks	The student: • Is unable to explain what the problem is when asked to do so • Becomes overwhelmed by anxiety so that memory and reasoning are impaired
Outputs	The student: • Can reason mathematically • Can think abstractly about rules and formulas and apply them correctly	The student: • Appears to expect answers will either magically pop up or forever remain a mystery

Ways to Assess Number Smarts in the Classroom

The following ideas will not replace a full psychological assessment, but they may give teachers and parents an idea if further investigations are merited.

Students' ability to complete some of the following tasks will give you an idea of their capacities or difficulties in using number smarts to learn well. Most of these can be used to make an assessment of specific students, but they will also benefit the entire class.

Building a profile of areas students understand, as well as where they have misunderstandings and anxieties, is beneficial in developing learning strengths in number smarts. The activities that follow will help you build this profile. But blockages will only become obvious when a student does not seem able to apply new understandings after helpful input (see table 8.2). In these instances, it is wise to try different approaches in helping the student to discover a way of understanding the concept before referring him or her for specialist assessment and intervention.

Table 8.2: Common Causes of Mathematics Blockages

Inputs	Processing	Outputs
The student:	**The student:**	**The student:**
• Can't break problems down into substeps	• Can't restate problems in his or her own words	• Can't estimate a reasonable answer
• Can't visualize numbers and their relationships	• Can't identify correct operations or useful data	• Rushes his or her work—thinks finishing first is important
• Does not demonstrate conjecture or justify his or her thinking	• Does not track or review progress	• Demonstrates no awareness of real-world applications
• Does not know or can't apply strategies	• Does not apply strategies correctly	• Does not check over his or her own answers
• Has an "I can't" attitude	• Displays little or no linkage of skills	• Can't explain how he or she went about solving a problem
• Demonstrates anxiety and avoidance	• Does not use concrete materials	• Considers mathematical success a matter of luck

Clock-Based Assessment

Have the student draw a clockface and write the numbers in their correct positions around it. Ask the student to draw clock hands that show a time of 11:10 and 2:50. Can the student use the numbers on the clockface to do this?

Estimation Activities

- What is the height of an average woman? What would be your high and low estimation (a range)?
- How many cars are there in the world? (This involves a series of thinking steps involving numbers, such as "How many people are there on earth?" "How many are of driving age?" "What percentage might own a car?" and "What percentage might have more than one car?")
- What is the best-paid job?
- What percentage of people have dark hair? In this class? In the school? In the world? Can the student estimate a logical answer? Is he or she able to develop an estimated range?
- Place a list of fractions in order of size.
- Pose problems such as:
    - Together Sam and Sally have twenty-five books. Sally has five more books than Sam (relation). How many books does each one have (quantity)?
    - Place a peg on a piece of string to indicate the position of a fraction on a number line.

Combine Problems

Heath has three yellow stickers and eleven purple stickers. How many stickers does Heath have all together?

Change Problems

Sarah had eight buttons, but she lost five. How many buttons does she have now?

Comparison Problems

- Without using numbers, you know you are taller than Carina because you are taller than your friend Tom, and Tom is taller than Carina. You know this, even if you have never met Carina. So we can think about relations between quantities without having a number to represent them. But when relations are represented with numbers, it is possible for us to know more: if you know Tom is one inch taller than Carina and you are four inches taller than Tom, the difference between yours and Carina's height is five inches.
- Adjit has three stamps, and Mona has seven stamps. How many fewer stamps does Adjit have than Mona?

- Charles has thirty-four pencils. How many pencils does Erin have if Charles has eighteen fewer pencils than she does?
- Jim rides his bicycle five miles from school to his home. If Jim stops for a drink of water after one mile, how can we work out how much farther he has to go?
- Timothy, Philip, and Marsha combined their sequins for a costume. Philip and Marsha together had ninety-seven more sequins than Timothy. Marsha had seventeen sequins. Timothy had twenty-five sequins. How many sequins did Philip have?

Dyscalculia

Dyscalculia involves persistent difficulty in learning number skills for at least six months, despite interventions targeting the area. Between 4 and 7 percent of students have dyscalculia, which can reduce lifetime earnings as well as academic results (Butterworth, 2019).

Students with dyscalculia have structurally different brains than numerically able students—specifically, the left intraparietal sulcus (the area involved in basic numerical processing) has lower gray-matter density. Lower activation and fewer white-matter links between the parietal lobes and the frontal areas are also present (Butterworth, 2019; Dehaene, 2011).

Three skills that predict how well students will learn mathematics, and that dyscalculic students will find difficult, are:

1. Assessing two dots arrays accurately (that is, which array has more dots; see figure 8.2)

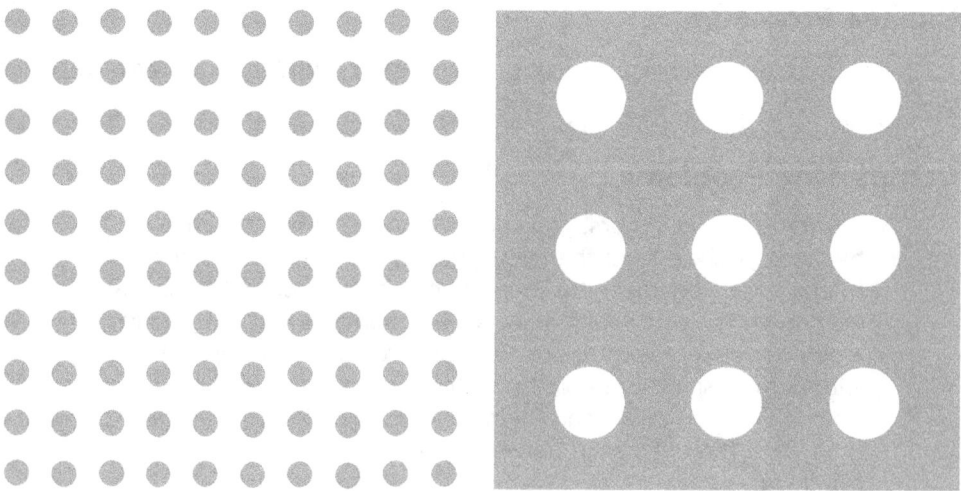

Figure 8.2: Dot arrays.

2. Saying the number of dots with speed and accuracy
3. Marking a number line accurately (see figure 8.3)

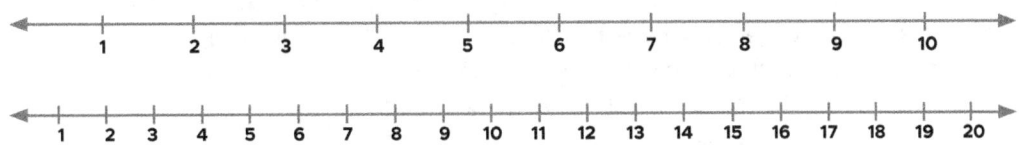

Figure 8.3: Number lines.

Some ways we can test for dyscalculia include the following.

- Panamath (https://panamath.org) has a free assessment of number sense.
- The Dyscalculia Screener (www.mathematicalbrain.com/pdf/Dyscalculia_Screener_Manual.PDF) is an online screening tool for students aged six to fourteen years.
- The Numeracy Screener (www.numeracyscreener.org) assesses if students can identify which of two numbers is larger.
- The Dyscalculia Test (www.cognifit.com/cognitive-assessment/dyscalculia-test) can help to identify the exact areas a student is struggling in.
- Brian Butterworth's (2019) book *Dyscalculia: From Science to Education* is an excellent resource.

Whether a student successfully completes or struggles to finish a series of the preceding activities will not necessarily indicate a problem, but these tasks will serve as a guide to his or her current level of learning strengths in number smarts (see figure 8.4).

NEURODEVELOPMENTAL DIFFERENTIATION

Use this list to rate the number-smarts strengths of the student. Assign a score out of ten (with one being "can't do this" and ten being "great at this") for each of the statements that follow. (A student at the average level of his or her class would score a five.)

Issue	Rating
Inputs	
The student:	
• Can identify what a mathematical problem is asking him or her to do	
• Is able to sequence the steps involved in solving a problem	
• Can predict or estimate an approximate answer	
• Can complete basic mathematical functions (addition, subtraction, division, and multiplication)	
• Can consider multiple ways of solving a problem	
Processing	
The student:	
• Can identify an appropriate strategy for solving a mathematical problem	
• Has developed automaticity with times tables	
• Has developed automaticity with addition	
• Has developed automaticity with subtraction	
• Has developed automaticity with multiplication	
• Has developed automaticity with division	
• Can think using fractions, place value, and proportions	
• Can visualize or map out a mathematical problem	
• Can draw a diagram to create a mathematical model	
• Can manipulate numbers	
Outputs	
The student:	
• Can communicate ideas	
• Can self-correct	
• Can reason mathematically	
• Can restate numerical problems in words	
• Can think algebraically	

Figure 8.4: List of issues with number smarts.

Discuss your concerns and compare these results with other teachers who are familiar with this student to confirm your observations.

Evidence That Number Smarts Can Be Improved

Comprehensive analysis of improving number smarts can be found in research from Butterworth (2019), Geoff F. Clement (2017), Stanislas Dehaene (2011), and John Mighton (2011). The process begins by assessing common areas of misconceptions and tailoring teaching interventions to a student's current level of understanding. Approaches to improving number smarts then need to minimize memorizing and guessing and encourage thinking and theorizing about numbers. Number smarts do not stand alone; the world is full of numbers. Helping students count, often using their fingers (Mighton, 2011), and helping students comprehend the nature of sets (the number of items in a group) and the relationship between sets assist in strengthening number sense. Essentially, this helps create a realization that numbers are composed of other numbers (Butterworth, 2019). There is also evidence that the use of diagrams, drawings, and concrete materials, including blocks, dice, dominoes, and algebra tiles, promotes improvement in number smarts (Day & Lovitt, 2011).

Improving Number-Smarts Inputs

Mathematics requires decoding of words, symbols, charts, and graphs. Have students preview the text and ask themselves, "What do I need to know when I solve this problem?" Have them write a declarative sentence with a blank space in it that draws attention to the answer they need to find. The following strategies can help support students in developing mathematical inputs.

- At the beginning of lessons, present students with example questions and ask, "What mathematics are we going to use to solve this problem?" Check at the end of the lesson whether other strategies were used.
- Ask students, "What do we already know about . . . ? How could we use that information to solve this problem?"
- Solve numerical word problems as a whole class, and ask students to identify the key information within a problem while you highlight their findings on the board.
- Support students by focusing more on understanding concepts and making logical attempts at solving a problem rather than on getting the correct answer.
- Help students identify the language of mathematics. Use the origin of words to help students remember the language and associate it with the concept—for example, "*Percent* means per one hundred, and *century* means one hundred years because *centi-* comes from the Latin root meaning one hundred."

- Help students understand the four operations and when to apply them.

- Promote additive and multiplicative thinking through the identification of patterns and strategies, and provide students with a wide variety of contexts in which to practice these skills.

- Help students understand symbols within numeracy. Help students by using a *make, name, and record* approach by asking students to *make* using materials, *name* using language, and *record* using symbols so students build a solid understanding of which symbols correspond with which concept.

- Help students organize and reorganize information within numeracy problems in order to identify how to solve them and make them easier to solve. This is particularly useful for numerical word problems, where the language can sometimes be difficult to decipher and there may be additional information to trick students. This is also useful in preparation for standardized exams, in which the students' regular teacher isn't writing the questions.

Encourage as many teachers as possible to write problems or issues in non-mathematics learning areas using symbols, numbers, and algorithms.

Improving Number-Smarts Processing

Teach students how to break mathematics problems down into steps to be solved by working with the entire class on sample problems. First, model a step-wise approach by verbalizing the steps you take and explaining how you think through each one. Then, have students identify what needs to be done first, what action or operation should follow next, and so on. Improving number-processing skills includes helping students develop:

- The ability to tackle challenging mathematics problems using a range of strategies (for example, "I don't know what 7×9 is, but I know $5 \times 9 = 45$ and $45 + 20 = 65 - 2$ is 63")

- The ability to make, name, and record (for example, using a place-value chart to make the number 63 by placing six bundles of ten Popsicle sticks in the tens column and three Popsicle sticks in the ones column, saying, "I have six tens and three ones," and recording "6 tens and 3 ones, or 63")

- An understanding of how to use pictures or drawings to represent numbers (for example, beginning multiplication using *groups of* drawings before moving on to *arrays* and *regions*)

- Skills in writing equations vertically from the beginning

Improving Number-Smarts Outputs

Number smarts are built on a logical structure of patterns, rules, and procedures. The use of basic rules and sequences of steps (algorithms) helps students compute mathematics more effectively.

To integrate spatial concepts, use hands-on activities and verbal explanations of mathematics concepts. For example, have students use pattern blocks or geoboards to make geometric shapes, then discuss and write down the characteristics of the shapes, such as the number of sides and types of angles.

Ask students to draw pictures that represent a numerical word problem. Students may draw actual objects (for example, three T-shirts, a twenty-by-forty-foot garden plot, and so on) or represent objects with symbols, such as ticks or dots.

Incorporate problem-solving activities using maps, diagrams, graphs, and tables to strengthen students' use of visual or spatial materials. For example, have students calculate the distances of trips taken by students in the class, and then display this information in a graph or table format.

Activities That Promote Confidence in Numeracy

Consider the following activities that promote confidence in numeracy.

Goal Setting

At the beginning of each semester, provide an opportunity for each student to set a goal in numeracy to achieve by the end of that semester. This could be completed with his or her homeroom teacher or mathematics teacher and shared with all of the student's teachers to develop an individualized learning plan to meet the goal. This can be modified to suit a range of different levels, but an example and template for this is as follows.

- My numeracy goal for this semester is . . .
- Three ways I will work to achieve my goal are . . .
- Three ways my teachers can help me achieve my goal are . . .

At the end of the semester, ask students to look at their goals and think about whether they have achieved them. If they have not, ask them to think about whether they are on their way to achieving their goals.

Reflecting on Learning at the End of the Semester

At the end of the semester, students can write down three things they have learned in mathematics they did not know at the start of the semester. It is helpful for students to reflect on the learning achieved across a whole year.

More Estimation Activities

The following activities will help familiarize students with thinking in numbers, estimating, and creating ranges.

Pack-Up Time

Ask students to estimate the time it will take them to pack up the classroom at the end of the day and write it on a sticky note. The student who estimates most accurately chooses a game to play at the end of the day just before the bell. This can also be played during setup time and can be done in table groups or teams.

Plan a Virtual Trip Around the Country

In this activity, students pretend they are going to drive a van around the country. The trip can take up to six months, but they need to decide where they are going to go, what they are going to do, and how long they are going to spend in each destination. This is a complex activity and may take several lessons, but the activity can be adapted so students only have to plan a short trip.

Action Estimation

Working as a whole class, and leaving no student behind, students need to estimate how long it will take them to walk in slow motion around a basketball court. They then estimate how long it will take them to dance around a basketball court as a class. After this, the teacher measures the amount of time it takes using a stopwatch. Remind students this isn't a race—rather, it is about accurate estimation. You can stipulate different actions, but walking in slow motion and dancing have been chosen deliberately to remove the idea of being the fastest.

Other estimation activities include estimating how many students can stand in a one-square-yard space, how many blocks would fit into a one-square-yard cube, and how big a cube would be needed to fit one thousand one-square-inch blocks.

Number-Smarts Cross-Fertilization Strategies

If a student has a learning strength in number smarts, table 8.3 suggests some strategies that could be used to help open up and extend learning in other areas. These are some key suggestions to stimulate your thinking and can be adapted to your classroom or time frame as you see fit.

Table 8.3: Extending Learning From Number Smarts

Learning-Strength Area	Sample Strategy
Spatial Reasoning	**Students can:** • Use blocks, cardboard pie segments, and dominoes to represent different numbers • Create drawings of key concepts **Teachers can:** • Categorize activities that involve numbers (for example, odds, evens, prime numbers, and numbers that are divisible by seven) • Create maps including distances and angles • Estimate measurements, volume, weight, or capacity • Practice measurement activities and jigsaws • Manipulate blocks, dice, and dominoes • Describe perspectives in art • Investigate art history timelines • Draw objects to scale • Create geometric artworks using different shapes of paper **At home, families can:** • Play card games, *Monopoly*, and backgammon to promote number awareness • Study photography—F-stops, aperture, shutter speed, and resolution • Create art projects • Create maps • Practice orienteering

continued →

NEURODEVELOPMENTAL DIFFERENTIATION

Learning-Strength Area	Sample Strategy
Perceptual and Motor Skills	**Students can:** - Learn sports league tables, scores, percentages, and averages - Step out numbers so they know roughly how long a yard or mile is **Teachers can:** - Use flash cards, rhythms, rapping, and singing - Practice finger movements and counting - Use different parts of their bodies to represent different parts of a formula (body mathematics) - Practice circuit training—number of students, time, and averages - Practice dance and gym sports related to numbers - Investigate history of sports timelines and records - Create data representations of training and weights - Practice the touch mathematics technique, where the student touches points on each number with his or her pencil while counting—this technique provides a concrete reinforcement for the student, while also helping preserve the fluency of the problem - Create human-sized number lines and graphs **At home, families can:** - Cook by following recipes - Learn to play a musical instrument - Practice orienteering and using a compass
Concentration and Memory	**Students can:** - Use the journey method, substituting numbers instead of landmarks - Create flowcharts and checklists with numbers **Teachers can:** - Tell students, "Softly repeat each fact as I give it to you before writing it down" (if the ears hear, the brain remembers) - Explain that recipes and memories are like equations—add the ingredients in the right quantities and in the right order, and you will get the desired outcome - Use Venn diagrams to highlight similarities and differences **At home, families can:** - Encourage collections and hobbies involving numbers - Play matching card games - Make a shopping list by asking, "How many apples do we need? How many oranges?"

Learning-Strength Area	Sample Strategy
Planning and Sequencing	**Students can:** • Use ladders of understanding (see Sequential Outputs, page 103) • Play solitaire • Use numbered sticky notes **Teachers can:** • Use worked examples • Provide jump starts to help students get going (for example, start one or more mathematics problems, provide the first fact in a sequence, and so on) • Look at mathematics like it is a recipe—there are ingredients, there is a process, and there is a desired outcome • Identify the steps involved in mathematical procedures **At home, families can:** • Play games like *Battleship* and other tactical games to promote numbers and planning and sequencing • Read maps and find coordinates • Let the children take charge of finding the way to places (how many streets, how many left turns, and so on)

continued →

Learning-Strength Area	Sample Strategy
Thinking and Logic	**Students can:** - Know that solving problems is like creating a number sequence of steps or a formula **Teachers can:** - Introduce Fermi questions involving numbers and estimation - Ask questions that have more than one answer - Encourage students to offer a wrong answer and then work out (with teachers) why it is wrong - Allow students to keep fact tables on hand for reference during mathematics activities (as mathematics facts are mastered, remove the supportive prompts) - Link logic with equations (for example, ask, "What is the next thing we need to work out?") - Help students deconstruct problems, teaching them how to break big problems into a series of smaller problems, not just how to solve a mathematical problem - Teach students how to start solving a problem (for example, "If we need to find out how many pieces of candy we have all together, what sort of mathematics will we be using?") - Use real-life problem solving to help students connect concepts in higher mathematics (for example, when students are exploring the question of how a spacecraft stays in orbit around the earth, they will use formulas for gravity and proportion, as well as geometric concepts) - Explain that the background for the study of algebra begins with thinking and logic (the simple equation $3 + 2 = ?$, for example, uses the algebraic concept of an unknown [?] representing a quantity [in this case 5] and is also a stepping-stone for answering $3 + ? = 5$, $? + 2 = 5$, and $5 = ? - 2$) **At home, families can:** - Ask, "How many jelly beans are in this jar?" - Ask, "How many people could fit into a small car?" - Rank their top-ten songs, movies, or types of animals - Evaluate the pros and cons of ideas and options

Number Smarts

Learning-Strength Area	Sample Strategy
People Smarts	**Students can:** • Link numbers to people they know • Consider, "What is your favorite number?" • Think about what percentages of people do different things (for example, play a sport, own a car, have pets, come from overseas, and so on) **Teachers can:** • Think about event management (for example, "What will you need? How many?") • Ask students to develop a formula for friendship and a recipe for happiness • Encourage students to say five positive things every day • Encourage students to smile at ten people a day • Practice human graphing **At home, families can:** • Highlight the association of people and numbers (for example, ask, "How many people are in this shopping center? How many have black hair? Let's categorize the next twenty people we see as having dark hair or not," and see what percentage it is) • Explain finances—calculating costs, savings, interest rates, and budgets • Read bus and tram timetables
Language and Word Smarts	**Students can:** • Write mathematics formulas as sentences • Create stories around some numbers • Learn words used frequently and infrequently **Teachers can:** • Use books about numbers to stimulate interest, such as *Counting on Frank* by Rod Clement (1991), which discusses the history of mathematical reasoning and geometry, as well as concepts like the golden ratio • Use nonfiction texts that focus on factual information and statistics • Encourage students to use statistical information when writing to persuade readers • Investigate the story of numbers and the history of Pythagoras • Use equations to represent successful essay techniques (for example, 1 + 2 + 3 + 4 + 5 + 6 = A+ essay, where 1 = catchy introduction, 2 = topic sentences, 3 = explanations and quotes, 4 = conjunctions and sequencing, 5 = climax or major event, and 6 = resolution or conclusion) **At home, families can:** • Read and tell stories, jokes, and limericks involving numbers

In Summary

Learning strengths in number smarts allow us to calculate trajectories, travel in space, navigate across distances, save money, go shopping, live within our means, and think through the probability of different outcomes.

The development of learning strengths in number smarts sharpens our knowledge of how to make things work. Whether it is air flight, the use of perspective in art, the construction of large buildings, the development of public health movements to alleviate suffering, quantum physics, or agricultural practices that feed the world, numbers form the foundation. A world deficient in number smarts would be a limited world without a research basis to develop any of the aforementioned activities.

Once developed, learning strengths in number smarts can be applied to enhance success in other areas. They can be used to:

- Describe different quantities, perspectives, and proportions visually (spatial reasoning)
- Use our bodies—arm lengths, steps to measure distances and areas, and so on (perceptual and motor skills)
- Rank ideas in terms of importance (concentration and memory)
- Prioritize and assign different values to a variety of ideas (planning and sequencing)
- Develop sequential algorithms, checklists, and decision-making trees (thinking and logic)
- Think about different types of people and their preferences, lifestyles, and attitudes, to appreciate the differences among us (people smarts)
- Think about the world in numerical terms, such as height, depth, qualities, and interrelationships, which enriches our ability to describe and communicate (language and word smarts)

Reflection Questions

- When mathematics makes sense to us and not our students, how do we bridge the gap?
- Is this the real work of teaching?
- What strategies will be most valuable in strengthening the number smarts of your students?
- Which other members of staff need to be involved in this discussion?
- Should any student's parents or guardians be involved in this discussion?

Chapter 9
IMPLEMENTING NEURODEVELOPMENTAL DIFFERENTIATION

The implementation of neurodevelopmental differentiation is always done tentatively as schools and parents work out whether it is an approach that works for them. Initially, teachers can feel like it will be more work for them. However, knowing the learning strengths of a student, a class, or a grade level offers teachers ways to engage and involve students more powerfully. Ultimately, it shifts students from engagement to empowerment.

Once they know their students' learning strengths, teachers can use neurodevelopmental differentiation as much as they feel is appropriate for their teaching and their class. Not every reader of this book will be in a position to change the way his or her school functions, so let's start with some classroom-level changes first.

Introducing Neurodevelopmental Differentiation to the Teachers at a School

Most schools begin their journey toward neurodevelopmental differentiation following these steps. Teachers complete an analysis of their own learning strengths at My Learning Strengths (www.mylearningstrengths.com) and bring their letters to a staff meeting.

1. Group teachers at a staff meeting according to the first learning strength mentioned in the letter they received. Ask them to

reflect on what this may or may not tell us about what the school may already be good at developing in students. Discuss and share thoughts.

2. Remaining in their learning-strength groups, teachers complete the "Learning or Subject-Area Profile Tool" for the subjects they teach (see figure 9.1 and also page 202 for a reproducible version of this tool). Discuss and share thoughts.

3. Then complete the "Individual Learning Strength Student Tool" (see figure 9.2 and also page 203 for a reproducible version of this tool) to consider a specific student who may currently not be achieving as well as he or she might in this subject area. Write out the student's strengths as well as his or her blockages in each of the eight areas. Discuss and share thoughts.

4. Once teachers are familiar with the concept, they can then start to directly involve students and parents.

Learning or Subject-Area Profile Tool

In the profile tool in figure 9.1, note some common tasks in your learning area or subject area that rely on a specific learning strength. See page 202 for a reproducible version of this figure.

Neurodevelopmental Profile	Spatial Reasoning	Perceptual and Motor Skills	Concentration and Memory
	Planning and Sequencing	Learning Area or Subject Names	Thinking and Logic
	People Smarts	Language and Word Smarts	Number Smarts

Figure 9.1: Learning or subject-area profile tool.

Consider the profile.

- What learning strengths would help a student succeed most effectively in this subject? (Think about the skills and knowledge of an exemplary student in this subject area.)
- What common tasks in this subject area would be most challenging for students who have blockages in some of the eight areas?

- What could teachers in your learning or subject area do to address these challenges?
- What skills or strengths from this subject area can be transported or cross-fertilized into other learning or subject areas? (You might refer teachers to the cross-fertilization tables in each chapter of this book to guide their thinking.) Discuss and share thoughts.

Individual Learning Strength Student Tool

Think of a student who is currently not achieving well in your subject area. Note down his or her strengths and blockages in each of the eight areas (see figure 9.2). See page 203 for a reproducible version of this figure.

Neurodevelopmental Profile			
	Spatial Reasoning	Perceptual and Motor Skills	Concentration and Memory
	Planning and Sequencing	Learning Area or Subject Names	Thinking and Logic
	People Smarts	Language and Word Smarts	Number Smarts

Figure 9.2: Individual learning strength student tool.

Consider the profile.

- How could you use this information to help the student understand his or her learning strengths and how to utilize them?
- How can you use this information to help the student understand the area he or she has yet to develop learning strengths in, and how to use his or her existing learning strengths to improve? (You might refer teachers to the cross-fertilization tables in each chapter of this book to guide their thinking.)
- Discuss and share thoughts.

The Neurodevelopmental Differentiation Approach

The method for implementing neurodevelopmental differentiation in schools we outline is a step-by-step process to ensure every student uses his or her specific learning strengths to support learning across all areas. By familiarizing themselves with this process, teachers can begin to implement the neurodevelopmental differentiation approach across all grade levels and learning areas as they pledge to become a school in which everyone gets smart. This neurodevelopmental differentiation approach comprises four critical elements.

1. The learning-strengths analysis
2. An individualized learning plan
3. Differentiated teaching
4. Specialized coaching

Learning-Strengths Analysis

Identifying each student's learning strengths is the first step in implementing a neurodevelopmental differentiation approach in the classroom. Teachers can either determine the student's learning strengths in their classroom by using this resource or have students and their parents visit My Learning Strengths (www.mylearningstrengths.com) to complete the online learning-strengths analysis. While the free letter is sufficient, a full report is available at a nominal fee, outlining all eight areas in order, strategies, and possible career paths.

Individualized Learning Plan

Use the next scheduled parent-teacher-student meeting to have an open discussion about the student's learning-strengths analysis and the letter he or she received from My Learning Strengths (www.mylearningstrengths.com). Use this time to collaboratively and proactively plan which of the student's learning strengths to capitalize on in his or her classes and how to use them to improve areas he or she has yet to develop.

Teachers can then refer to the cross-fertilization strategies tables in the chapters that correspond with the student's identified learning strengths to increase his or her engagement and success in an area that has yet to be developed.

Teachers should actively engage students' parents or guardians as coeducators. Ask them to discuss the activities outlined in their children's learning-strengths areas, as well as the areas that have been identified as yet to develop, and then take on and trial some of them at home.

Ultimately, the individualized learning plan should specify students' learning strengths in order of strength and develop strategies for improving each area.

We recommend the learning-strengths analysis be readministered once per semester and the full individualized learning plan be redrafted at least once per year. An example of an individualized learning plan is in figure 9.3 (and also see page 204 for a reproducible version of this plan).

Student's name: *Robin Hood*

Date: *May 14* **Grade level:** *8*

This information can be obtained from completing the learning-strengths analysis at My Learning Strengths (www.mylearningstrengths.com).

Issue	Rating
Spatial reasoning	*1*
Perceptual and motor skills	*4*
Concentration and memory	*7*
Planning and sequencing	*6*
Thinking and logic	*5*
People smarts	*2*
Language and word smarts	*3*
Number smarts	*8*

Inputs, processing, and outputs	Rating
Inputs	*52*
Processing	*38*
Outputs	*43*

Blockages we will work on in the coming semester		
Inputs	Processing	Outputs
Focusing with numbers	*Using shapes to represent numbers*	*Thinking about how numbers apply to people*

Key strategies we will use: *Encourage Robin to think about using existing learning strengths of spatial reasoning and people smarts in thinking about people by using shapes, symbols, and diagrams to represent numbers as they apply to people.*

Key people involved: *Robin, Mr. and Mrs. Hood, Ms. Rodriguez (teacher)*

Review date: *Next parent-teacher meeting*

Figure 9.3: Sample individualized learning plan.

Differentiated Teaching

Teachers can actively utilize the learning strengths of students in guiding the types of activities and groupings of students for completing tasks.

If they have not already done so, teachers should complete their own analysis at My Learning Strengths (www.mylearningstrengths.com) and consider what implicit biases they might bring to their work. Teachers who are aware of their own learning strengths are more able to call on the learning strengths of different students in the class to provide a range of approaches to a problem.

In table I.2 (page 17), we showed you an example of how a teacher collated six students' learning-strengths analyses to provide an overview of their learning strengths. The teacher can see most of these students have strengths in spatial reasoning, number smarts, and concentration and memory. The teacher now knows that presenting information about numbers pictorially and using it to generate concentration and memory challenges is likely to engage most of the class.

The teacher can also see Nitika is not yet strong in spatial reasoning but has learning strengths in planning and sequencing and word smarts. The teacher can use the cross-fertilization activities tables in this book to help Nitika and her parents develop strategies that use her current learning strengths to build her nascent learning strength in spatial reasoning. The teacher may also choose to pair Nitika with a student who is strong in spatial reasoning or may call on her to plan sequences and stories that will help the rest of the class understand concepts.

Overall, the class is relatively low in perceptual and motor skills. It is likely the students underutilize their bodies in learning. Knowing this, the teacher can gradually increase the use of gestures and movement in his or her lessons. Sarah may be called on to devise a way to solve a mathematics problem using a stepping-stone approach to logical problem solving. Sarah may also be teamed up with Jackson and Coen to develop an improvisational method of acting out a text or story. Tyler and Minh may also work on storyboarding the text and then present this to the class.

By identifying and building on the learning strengths of the students, the teacher has used his or her students' learning strengths to support the learning of everyone in the classroom. This is the power of neurodevelopmental differentiation.

Specialized Coaching

In addition to the actions outlined previously, this step best represents an entire school choosing to embrace the philosophy of "Here, everyone gets smart."

Once parent-teacher-student meetings are based on neurodevelopmental differentiation and prospective individualized learning plans are created for each forthcoming semester, specific teachers are asked to become specialists in one of the eight brain systems identified in this resource: (1) spatial reasoning,

(2) perceptual and motor skills, (3) concentration and memory, (4) planning and sequencing, (5) thinking and logic, (6) people smarts, (7) language and word smarts, and (8) number smarts.

If a student is not progressing as his or her teachers and parents hope, a support meeting is called with the student, his or her parents or guardians, a teacher who has specialized in the student's top learning strength, and a teacher who has specialized in an area that the student has yet to develop. The aim is to create strategies and a support network to help the student develop further learning strengths.

Some students who are progressing well in some areas but experiencing blockages in others will also benefit from this approach.

Schools that adopt neurodevelopmental differentiation provide a strong, positive message to all students—they can succeed.

Learning or Subject-Area Profile Tool

In the profile tool, note some common tasks in your learning area or subject area that rely on a specific learning strength.

Neurodevelopmental Profile	Spatial Reasoning	Perceptual and Motor Skills	Concentration and Memory
	Planning and Sequencing	Learning Area or Subject Names	Thinking and Logic
	People Smarts	Language and Word Smarts	Number Smarts

Neurodevelopmental Differentiation © 2024 Andrew Fuller & Lucy Fuller

Individual Learning Strength Student Tool

Think of a student who is currently not achieving well in your subject area. Note down his or her strengths and blockages in each of the eight areas.

Neurodevelopmental Profile			
	Spatial Reasoning	Perceptual and Motor Skills	Concentration and Memory
	Planning and Sequencing	Learning Area or Subject Names	Thinking and Logic
	People Smarts	Language and Word Smarts	Number Smarts

Neurodevelopmental Differentiation © 2024 Andrew Fuller & Lucy Fuller

The Neurodevelopmental Differentiation Individualized Learning Plan

Student's name:

Date: **Grade level:**

This information can be obtained from completing the learning-strengths analysis at My Learning Strengths (www.mylearningstrengths.com).

Issue	Rating
Spatial reasoning	
Perceptual and motor skills	
Concentration and memory	
Planning and sequencing	
Thinking and logic	
People smarts	
Language and word smarts	
Number smarts	

Inputs, processing, and outputs	Rating
Inputs	
Processing	
Outputs	

Blockages we will work on in the coming term		
Inputs	Processing	Outputs

Key strategies we will use:

Key people involved:

Review date:

REFERENCES AND RESOURCES

Ackerman, P. L., Beier, M. E., & Boyle, M. O. (2005). Working memory and intelligence: The same or different constructs? *Psychological Bulletin, 131*(1), 30–60. Accessed at https://doi.org/10.1037/0033-2909.131.1.30 on September 18, 2020.

Adams, J. L. (2019). *Conceptual blockbusting: A guide to better ideas* (5th ed.). New York: Basic Books.

Amen, D. G. (2015). *Change your brain, change your life: The breakthrough program for conquering anxiety, depression, obsessiveness, lack of focus, anger, and memory problems* (Rev. and updated 2nd ed.). New York: Harmony Books.

Barrett, L. F. (2017). *How emotions are made: The secret life of the brain*. Boston: Houghton Mifflin Harcourt.

Bauer, I., Crewther, D. P., Pipingas, A., Rowsell, R., Cockerell, R., & Crewther, S. G. (2011). Omega-3 fatty acids modify human cortical visual processing—a double-blind, crossover study. *PLoS ONE, 6*(12). Accessed at https://doi.org/10.1371/journal.pone.0028214 on September 18, 2020.

Bender, M. L. (1976). *The Bender-Purdue reflex test and training manual*. San Rafael, CA: Academic Therapy.

Benjafield, J. G. (2008). George Kelly: Cognitive psychologist, humanistic psychologist, or something else entirely? *History of Psychology, 11*(4), 239–262. Accessed at https://doi.org/10.1037/a0014108 on September 18, 2020.

Best, K. (2018, August 7). Know thyself: The philosophy of self-knowledge. *UConn Today*. Accessed at https://today.uconn.edu/2018/08/know-thyself-philosophy-self-knowledge/# on October 28, 2020.

Blythe, S. G. (2014). *Neuromotor immaturity in children and adults: The INPP screening test for clinicians and health practitioners*. Chichester, England: Wiley Blackwell.

Blythe, S. G. (2017). *Attention, balance and coordination: The A.B.C. of learning success* (2nd ed.). Hoboken, NJ: Wiley.

Booker, C. (2004). *The seven basic plots: Why we tell stories*. London: Continuum.

Brady, D. (2012, December 18). James Dyson on killing the contrarotator, his "educative failure." *Bloomberg*. Accessed at www.bloomberg.com/news/articles/2012-12-18/james-dyson-on-killing-the-contrarotator-his-educative-failure on September 18, 2020.

Butterworth, B. (2019). *Dyscalculia: From science to education*. New York: Routledge.

Buzsáki, G. (2019). *The brain from inside out*. New York: Oxford University Press.

Carnine, D. W., Silbert, J., Kame'enui, E. J., Slocum, T. A., & Travers, P. A. (2017). *Direct instruction reading* (6th ed.). Boston: Pearson.

Carnine, D. W., Silbert, J., Kame'enui, E. J., Tarver, S. G., & Jungjohann, K. (2006). *Teaching struggling and at-risk readers: A direct instruction approach*. Upper Saddle River, NJ: Pearson Merrill Prentice Hall.

Castel, A. D. (2008). Metacognition and learning about primacy and recency effects in free recall: The utilization of intrinsic and extrinsic cues when making judgments of learning. *Memory & Cognition, 36*(2), 429–437. Accessed at https://doi.org/10.3758/MC.36.2.429 on September 18, 2020.

Cherry, K. (2020, March 31). *The four stages of cognitive development: Background and key concepts of Piaget's theory*. Accessed at www.verywellmind.com/piagets-stages-of-cognitive-development-2795457 on September 18, 2020.

Chouake, T., Levy, T., Javitt, D. C., & Lavidor, M. (2012). Magnocellular training improves visual word recognition. *Frontiers in Human Neuroscience, 6*(14), 1–6. Accessed at https://doi.org/10.3389/fnhum.2012.00014 on September 18, 2020.

Clark, K. B., Naritoku, D. K., Smith, D. C., Browning, R. A., & Jensen, R. A. (1999). Enhanced recognition memory following vagus nerve stimulation in human subjects. *Nature Neuroscience, 2*(1), 94–98. Accessed at https://doi.org/10.1038/4600 on September 18, 2020.

Clark, R. C. (2008). *Building expertise: Cognitive methods for training and performance improvement*. San Francisco: Pfeiffer.

Clark, R. C., & Mayer, R. E. (2016). *E-learning and the science of instruction: Proven guidelines for consumers and designers of multimedia learning* (4th ed.). Hoboken, NJ: Wiley.

Clark, R. C., Nguyen, F., & Sweller, J. (2006). *Efficiency in learning: Evidence-based guidelines to manage cognitive load*. San Francisco: Jossey-Bass.

Claxton, G. (1999). *Hare brain, tortoise mind: Why intelligence increases when you think less*. Hopewell, NJ: Ecco Press.

Clement, G. F. (2017). *Exploring the influence of the Singapore modeling method on prospective elementary teachers in a university mathematics course*. Unpublished doctoral dissertation, Georgia State University, Atlanta, GA. Accessed at https://scholarworks.gsu.edu/cgi/viewcontent.cgi?article=1035&context=ece_diss on September 18, 2020.

Clement, R. (1991). *Counting on Frank*. Milwaukee, WI: Stevens Children's Books.

Collins, S. (2019). *Neuroscience for learning and development: How to apply neuroscience and psychology for improved learning and training* (2nd ed.). London: Kogan Page.

Colvin, G. (2018). *Talent is overrated: What really separates world-class performers from everybody else* (Rev. ed.). New York: Portfolio.

Day, L., & Lovitt, C. (2011). *Effectively teaching mathematics*. Accessed at https://andrewfuller.com.au/wp-content/uploads/2014/08/Effectively-teaching-mathematics.pdf on September 18, 2020.

de Bono, E. (1985). *Six hats of thinking*. New York: Little, Brown.

Dehaene, S. (2009). *Reading in the brain: The science and evolution of a human invention*. New York: Viking.

Dehaene, S. (2011). *The number sense: How the mind creates mathematics* (Rev. and updated ed.). New York: Oxford University Press.

Dehaene, S. (2014). *Consciousness and the brain: Deciphering how the brain codes our thoughts*. New York: Viking.

Diamond, A. (2012). Activities and programs that improve children's executive functions. *Current Directions in Psychological Science, 21*(5), 335–341. Accessed at https://doi.org/10.1177/0963721412453722 on September 18, 2020.

Diamond, A. (2013). Executive functions. *Annual Review of Psychology, 64*, 135–168. Accessed at https://doi.org/10.1146/annurev-psych-113011-143750 on September 18, 2020.

Diamond, A., Barnett, W. S., Thomas, J., & Munro, S. (2007). Preschool program improves cognitive control. *Science, 318*(5855), 1387–1388. Accessed at http://doi.org/10.1126/science.1151148 on September 18, 2020.

Diamond, A., & Lee, K. (2011). Interventions shown to aid executive function development in children four to twelve years old. *Science, 333*(6045), 959–964. Accessed at http://doi.org/10.1126/science.1204529 on September 18, 2020.

Doidge, N. (2007). *The brain that changes itself: Stories of personal triumph from the frontiers of brain science.* New York: Viking.

Doya, K. (2000). Complementary roles of basal ganglia and cerebellum in learning and motor control. *Current Opinions in Neurobiology, 10*(6), 732–739. Accessed at https://doi.org/10.1016/s0959-4388(00)00153-7 on September 18, 2020.

Dreary, I. J., Strand, S., Smith, P., & Fernandes, C. (2007). Intelligence and educational achievement. *Intelligence, 35*(1), 13–21. Accessed at https://doi.org/10.1016/j.intell.2006.02.001 on September 18, 2020.

Eccles, J. C. (1989). *Evolution of the brain: Creation of the self.* London: Routledge.

Ekman, P. (2012). *Emotions revealed: Understanding faces and feelings.* Sydney, Australia: Hachette.

Elmore, R. F. (Ed.). (2011). *I used to think—and now I think—: Twenty leading educators reflect on the work of school reform.* Cambridge, MA: Harvard Education Press.

Fergusson, D. M., & Horwood, J. L. (2001). The Christchurch Health and Development Study: Review of findings on child and adolescent mental health. *Australian and New Zealand Journal of Psychiatry, 35*(3), 287–296. Accessed at https://doi.org/10.1046/j.1440-1614.2001.00902.x on September 18, 2020.

Fleming, N., & Bonwell, C. (2019). *How do I learn best? A student's guide to improved learning* (2nd ed.). Christchurch, New Zealand: VARK Learn.

Flynn, J. R. (2012). *Are we getting smarter? Rising IQ in the twenty-first century.* New York: Cambridge University Press.

Freebody, P. (1992). A socio-cultural approach: Resourcing four roles as a literacy learner. In A. Watson & A. Badenhop (Eds.), *Prevention of reading failure* (pp. 48–60). Sydney, Australia: Scholastic Australia.

Freebody, P., & Luke, A. (1990). Literacies programs: Debates and demands in cultural context. *Prospect: An Australian Journal of Teaching/Teachers of English to Speakers of Other Languages (TESOL), 5*(3), 7–16.

Frey, N., & Fisher, D. (2010). Reading and the brain: What early childhood educators need to know. *Early Childhood Education Journal, 38*(2), 103–110. Accessed at https://doi.org/10.1007/s10643-010-0387-z on September 18, 2020.

Fuller, A. (2013a). *Tricky kids: Transforming conflict and freeing their potential.* New York: HarperCollins.

Fuller, A. (2013b). *Tricky people: How to deal with horrible types before they ruin your life.* New York: HarperCollins.

Fuller, A. (2014). *Tricky teens: How to create a great relationship with your teen . . . without going crazy!* Warriewood, Australia: Finch.

Fuller, A. (2015). *Unlocking your child's genius: How to discover and encourage your child's natural talents.* Warriewood, Australia: Finch.

Fuller, A. (2019a). *The revolutionary art of changing your heart: The essential guide to recharging your relationship.* Sydney, Australia: Hachette Australia.

Fuller, A. (2019b). *Your best life at any age: How to acknowledge your past, revive your present, and realise your future.* Arcadia, Australia: Bad Apple Press.

Fuller, A. (in press). *Feelings: How to stay sane in a crazy world.* Arcadia, Australia: Bad Apple Press.

Gable, S. L., & Algoe, S. B. (2010). Being there when things go right: Support processes for positive events. In K. T. Sullivan & J. Davila (Eds.), *Support processes in intimate relationships* (pp. 200–2016). Oxford, England: Oxford University Press.

Gable, S. L., Reis, H. T., Impett, E. A., & Asher, E. R. (2004). What to do when things go right? The intrapersonal and interpersonal benefits of sharing positive events. *Journal of Personality and Social Psychology, 87*(2), 228–245. Accessed at https://doi.org/10.1037/0022-3514.87.2.228 on September 18, 2020.

Gardner, H. (2011). *Frames of mind: The theory of multiple intelligences.* New York: Basic Books.

Giedd, J. N. (2015). Risky teen behavior is driven by an imbalance in brain development. *Scientific American, 312*(6), 32–37. Accessed at http://doi.org/10.1038/scientificamerican0615-32 on September 18, 2020.

Gogtay, N., Giedd, J. N., Lusk, L., Hayashi, K. M., Greenstein, D., Vaituzis, A. C., et al. (2004). Dynamic mapping of human cortical development during childhood through early adulthood. *Proceedings of the National Academy of Sciences, 101*(21), 8174–8179. Accessed at https://doi.org/10.1073/pnas.0402680101 on September 18, 2020.

Goleman, D. (2009). *Emotional intelligence: Why it can matter more than IQ*. London: Bloomsbury.

Gopnik, A., Meltzoff, A. N., & Kuhl, P. K. (1999). *How babies think: The science of childhood*. London: Weidenfeld & Nicolson.

Gottman, J. M. (2011). *The science of trust: Emotional attunement for couples*. New York: Norton.

Graham, L. (Ed.). (2009). *Proceedings of the narrowing the gap: Addressing Educational Disadvantage Conference*. Armidale, Australia: SiMERR National Research Centre, University of New England.

Graham, L., & Pegg, J. (2011). Evaluating the *QuickSmart* numeracy program: An effective Australian intervention that improves student achievement, responds to special educational needs, and fosters teacher collaboration. *Journal of Educational Administration, 29*(2), 87–102.

Greenleaf, C. L., Schoenbach, R., Cziko, C., & Mueller, F. L. (2001). Apprenticing adolescent readers to academic literacy. *Harvard Educational Review, 71*(1), 79–130. Accessed at https://doi.org/10.17763/haer.71.1.q811712577334038 on September 18, 2020.

Griffin, M. (2013). *Learning strategies for musical success*. Adelaide, Australia: Music Education World.

Hackett, W. (2016). *The best of Socrates: The founding philosophies of ethics, virtues and life* (3rd ed.). Scotts Valley, CA: CreateSpace.

Hallam, W. T., Olsson, C. A., O'Connor, M., Hawkins, M., Toumbourou, J. W., Bowes, G., et al. (2013). Association between adolescent eudaimonic behaviours and emotional competence in young adulthood. *Journal of Happiness Studies, 15*(5), 1165–1177. Accessed at https://doi.org/10.1007/s10902-013-9469-0 on September 18, 2020.

Hansen, N. (2019). Memory reinforcement and attenuation by activating the human locus coeruleus via transcutaneous vagus nerve stimulation. *Frontiers in Neuroscience, 12*. Accessed at https://doi.org/10.3389/fnins.2018.00955 on September 18, 2020.

Harris, D., & Lowrie, T. (2018). The distinction between mathematics and spatial reasoning in assessment: Do STEM educators and cognitive psychologists agree? In J. Hunter, L. Darragh, & P. Perger (Eds.), *Making waves, opening spaces: Proceedings of the 41st annual conference of the Mathematics Education Research Group of Australasia* (pp. 376–383). Adelaide, Australia: Mathematics Education Research Group of Australasia.

Hawkes, N., & Hawkes, J. (2018). *The inner curriculum: How to develop wellbeing, resilience and self-leadership*. Melton, Australia: Catt Educational.

Hawks, J. (2013, July 1). How has the human brain evolved? *Scientific American*. Accessed at www.scientificamerican.com/article/how-has-human-brain-evolved on October 23, 2020.

Herman, A. E. (2016). *Visual intelligence: Sharpen your perception, change your life*. Boston: Houghton Mifflin Harcourt.

Howard-Jones, P. A. (2014). *Neuroscience and education: A review of educational interventions and approaches informed by neuroscience—Full report and executive summary*. London: Education Endowment Foundation. Accessed at https://educationendowmentfoundation.org.uk/public/files/Presentations/Publications/EEF_Lit_Review_NeuroscienceAndEducation.pdf on September 18, 2020.

Howard-Jones, P. A., Ioannou, K., Bailey, R., Prior, J., Yau, S. H., & Jay, T. (2018). Applying the science of learning in the classroom. *Impact: Journal of the Chartered College of Teaching, 1*(2). Accessed at https://impact.chartered.college/article/howard-jones-applying-science-learning-classroom on September 18, 2020.

Hutton, J. S., Dudley, J., Horowitz-Kraus, T., DeWitt, T., & Holland, S. K. (2019). Associations between screen-based media use and brain white matter integrity in preschool-aged children. *JAMA Pediatrics, 174*(1). Accessed at https://doi.org/10.1001/jamapediatrics.2019.3869 on September 18, 2020.

Inhelder, B., & Piaget, J. (1999). *The growth of logical thinking from childhood to adolescence: An essay on the construction of formal operational structures.* London: Routledge.

Jaeggi, S. M., Buschkuehl, M., Jonides, J., & Perrig, W. J. (2008). Improving fluid intelligence with training on working memory. *Proceedings of the National Academy of Sciences of the United States of America, 105*(19), 6829–6833. Accessed at https://doi.org/10.1073/pnas.0801268105 on September 18, 2020.

Jairam, D., & Kiewra, K. A. (2009). An investigation of the SOAR study method. *Journal of Advanced Academics, 20*(4), 602–629. Accessed at https://doi.org/10.1177/1932202X0902000403 on September 18, 2020.

Johnson, D. W., Maruyama, G. M., Johnson, R., Nelson, D., & Skon, L. (1981). Effects of cooperative, competitive, and individualistic goal structures on achievement: A meta-analysis. *Psychological Bulletin, 89*(1), 47–62. Accessed at https://doi.org/10.1037/0033-2909.89.1.47 on October 21, 2020.

Just, M. A., & Varma, S. (2007). The organization of thinking: What functional brain imaging reveals about the neuroarchitecture of complex cognition. *Cognitive, Affective, and Behavioral Neuroscience, 7*(3), 153–191. Accessed at https://doi.org/10.3758/CABN.7.3.153 on September 18, 2020.

Kagan, S. (2013). *Kagan cooperative learning structures.* San Clemente, CA: Kagan.

Kahneman, D. (2013). *Thinking, fast and slow.* New York: Farrar, Straus and Giroux.

Karten, T. J. (2017). *Building on the strengths of students with special needs: How to move beyond disability labels in the classroom.* Alexandria, VA: Association for Supervision and Curriculum Development.

Keller, T. A., & Just, M. A. (2009). Altering cortical connectivity: Remediation-induced changes in the white matter of poor readers. *Neuron, 64*(5), 624–631. Accessed at https://doi.org/10.1016/j.neuron.2009.10.018 on September 18, 2020.

Konnikova, M. (2013). *Mastermind: How to think like Sherlock Holmes.* Edinburgh, Scotland: Canongate.

Konza, D. (2006). *Teaching children with reading difficulties* (2nd ed.). South Melbourne, Australia: Cengage Learning Australia.

Konza, D. (2011). *Phonics* (Research Into Practice Series 1, Paper 1.3). Adelaide: Government of South Australia Department of Education and Children's Services. Accessed at www.ecu.edu.au/__data/assets/pdf_file/0012/663699/SA-DECS-Phonics.pdf on September 18, 2020.

Levine, M. (2002). *A mind at a time.* New York: Simon & Schuster.

Linchevski, L., & Kutscher, B. (1998). Tell me with whom you're learning, and I'll tell you how much you've learned: Mixed-ability versus same-ability grouping in mathematics. *Journal for Research in Mathematics Education, 29*(5), 533–554. Accessed at https://doi.org/10.2307/749732 on September 18, 2020.

Lorayne, H. (1963). *How to develop a super-power memory* (2nd ed.). Preston, England: Thomas.

Lowrie, T., & Jorgensen, R. (2017). Equity and spatial reasoning: Reducing the mathematical achievement gap in gender and social disadvantage. *Mathematics Education Research Journal, 30*(1), 65–75. Accessed at https://doi.org/10.1007/s13394-017-0213-7 on September 18, 2020.

Marzano, R. J. (2007). *The art and science of teaching: A comprehensive framework for effective instruction.* Alexandria, VA: Association for Supervision and Curriculum Development.

Mason, C., Murphy, M. M. R., & Jackson, Y. (2019). *Mindfulness practices: Cultivating heart centered communities where students focus and flourish.* Bloomington, IN: Solution Tree Press.

Maths300. (n.d.). *About Maths300.* Accessed at www.maths300.com/about on October 28, 2020.

Maxwell, W. (2014). *The Accelerative Integrated Methodology.* Accessed at www.aimlanguagelearning.com/media on September 18, 2020.

May, K. E., & Elder, A. D. (2018). Efficient, helpful, or distracting? A literature review of media multitasking in relation to academic performance. *International Journal of Educational Technology in Higher Education, 15*. Accessed at https://doi.org/10.1186/s41239-018-0096-z on September 18, 2020.

McDowell, M. (2020). *Teaching for transfer: A guide for designing learning with real-world application*. Bloomington, IN: Solution Tree Press.

McGraw-Hill. (2006). *Spelling mastery*. New York: Author.

Mehrabian, A. (1971). *Silent messages*. Belmont, CA: Wadsworth.

Mighton, J. (2011). *The end of ignorance: Multiplying our human potential*. Toronto, Canada: Vintage Canada.

Miller, G. A. (1956). The magical number seven, plus or minus two: Some limits on our capacity for processing information. *Psychological Review, 63*(2), 81–97. Accessed at https://doi.org/10.1037/h0043158 on September 18, 2020.

Mischel, W. (2014). *The marshmallow test: Mastering self-control*. London: Bantam Press.

Mohanty, A., & Flint, R. W. (2001). Differential effects of glucose on modulation of emotional and nonemotional spatial memory tasks. *Cognitive, Affective, & Behavioral Neuroscience, 1*(1), 90–95. Accessed at https://doi.org/10.3758/CABN.1.1.90 on September 18, 2020.

Moss, M., Hewitt, S., Moss, L., & Wesnes, K. (2008). Modulation of cognitive performance and mood by aromas of peppermint and ylang-ylang. *International Journal of Neuroscience, 118*(1), 59–77. Accessed at https://doi.org/10.1080/00207450601042094 on September 18, 2020.

Mustard, J. F. (2010). *Early brain development and human development*. Accessed at www.child-encyclopedia.com/sites/default/files/textes-experts/en/669/early-brain-development-and-human-development.pdf on September 18, 2020.

My Learning Strengths. (n.d.). *Identifying learning strengths*. Accessed at https://mylearningstrengths.com/profile/ on February 22, 2021.

National Centre for Excellence in the Teaching of Mathematics. (n.d.). *Supporting research, evidence and argument*. Accessed at www.ncetm.org.uk/teaching-for-mastery/mastery-explained/supporting-research-evidence-and-argument on October 21, 2020.

Newcombe, N. S. (2010). Picture this: Increasing math and science learning by improving spatial thinking. *American Educator, 34*(2), 29–35.

Newcombe, N. S. (2017). *Harnessing spatial thinking to support STEM learning* (OECD Education Working Paper No. 161). Paris: Organisation for Economic Co-operation and Development. Accessed at https://doi.org/10.1787/7d5dcae6-en on October 21, 2020.

Newcombe, N. S., & Frick, A. (2010). Early education for spatial intelligence: Why, what, and how. *Mind, Brain, and Education, 4*(3), 102–111. Accessed at https://doi.org/10.1111/j.1751-228X.2010.01089.x on September 18, 2020.

Nilsson, J. (2010, March 20). Albert Einstein: "Imagination is more important than knowledge." *Saturday Evening Post*. Accessed at www.saturdayeveningpost.com/2010/03/imagination-important-knowledge on October 28, 2020.

Nørretranders, T. (1999). *The user illusion: Cutting consciousness down to size*. New York: Penguin.

O'Donnell, A., & Dansereau, D. F. (1993). Learning from lectures: Effects of cooperative review. *Journal of Experimental Education, 61*(2), 116–125. Accessed at https://doi.org/10.1080/00220973.1993.9943856 on September 18, 2020.

Pascale, R., Sternin, J., & Sternin, M. (2010). *The power of positive deviance: How unlikely innovators solve the world's toughest problems*. Boston: Harvard Business Press.

Pegg, J., & Graham, L. (2013). A three-level intervention pedagogy to enhance the academic achievement of Indigenous students: Evidence from *QuickSmart*. In R. Jorgensen, P. Sullivan, & P. Grootenboer (Eds.), *Pedagogies to enhance learning for indigenous students* (pp. 123–138). Singapore: Springer. Accessed at https://doi.org/10.1007/978-981-4021-84-5_8 on September 18, 2020.

Penner-Wilger, M., & Anderson, M. L. (2013). The relation between finger gnosis and mathematical ability: Why redeployment of neural circuits best explains the finding. *Frontiers in Psychology, 4*. Accessed at https://doi.org/10.3389/fpsyg.2013.00877 on September 18, 2020.

Peterson, C., & Seligman, M. E. (2004). *Character strengths and virtues: A handbook and classification*. New York: Oxford University Press.

Pithers, R. T., & Soden, R. (2000). Critical thinking in education: A review. *Educational Research, 42*(3), 237–249. Accessed at https://doi.org/10.1080/001318800440579 on September 18, 2020.

Pitler, H., Hubbell, E. R., & Kuhn, M. (2012). *Using technology with classroom instruction that works* (2nd ed.). Alexandria, VA: Association for Supervision and Curriculum Development.

Platas, L. M. (2017, November 8). Why spatial reasoning is important in early education. *Medium*. Accessed at https://medium.com/@DREMEmath/why-spatial-reasoning-is-important-in-early-education-ec88ef0f0e84 on October 27, 2020.

Pohl, M. (1997). *Teaching thinking skills in the primary years: A whole school approach*. Moorabbin, Australia: Hawker Brownlow Education.

Popova, M. (2012, September 4). Using pattern recognition to enhance memory and creativity. *Atlantic*. Accessed at www.theatlantic.com/health/archive/2012/09/using-pattern-recognition-to-enhance-memory-and-creativity/261925 on October 27, 2020.

Porges, S. W. (2017). *The pocket guide to the polyvagal theory: The transformative power of feeling safe*. New York: Norton.

Reif, F. (2008). *Applying cognitive science to education: Thinking and learning in scientific and other complex domains*. Cambridge, MA: MIT Press.

Restak, R. (2001). *The secret life of the brain*. Washington, DC: Henry Press.

Restak, R., & Kim, S. (2010). *The playful brain: The surprising science of how puzzles improve your mind*. New York: Riverhead Books.

Riby, L. M., Law, A. S., Mclaughlin, J., & Murray, J. (2011). Preliminary evidence that glucose ingestion facilitates prospective memory performance. *Nutrition Research, 31*(5), 370–377.

Ridderinkhof, K. R., & van der Stelt, O. (2000). Attention and selection in the growing child: Views derived from developmental psychophysiology. *Biological Psychology, 54*(1–3), 55–106. Accessed at http://doi.org/10.1016/S0301-0511(00)00053-3 on September 18, 2020.

Ritchhart, R., Church, M., & Morrison, K. (2011). *Making thinking visible: How to promote engagement, understanding, and independence for all learners*. San Francisco: Jossey-Bass.

Rosenbloom, M. H., Schmahmann, J. D., & Price, B. H. (2012). The functional neuroanatomy of decision-making. *Journal of Neuropsychiatry and Clinical Neurosciences, 24*(3), 266–277. Accessed at http://doi.org/10.1176/appi.neuropsych.11060139 on September 18, 2020.

Rowe, K., & National Inquiry Into the Teaching of Literacy (Australia). (2005). *Teaching reading: Report and recommendations*. Canberra, Australia: Department of Education, Science and Training. Accessed at https://research.acer.edu.au/tll_misc/5 on September 18, 2020.

Sapolsky, R. M. (2004). Stress and cognition. In M. S. Gazzaniga (Ed.), *The cognitive neurosciences* (3rd ed., pp. 1031–1042). Cambridge, MA: MIT Press.

Sapolsky, R. M. (2017a). *Behave: The biology of humans at our best and worst*. London: Bodley Head.

Sapolsky, R. M. (2017b, December 13–17). *The biology of humans at their best and worst* [Conference session]. Presented at the Evolution of Psychotherapy Conference, Anaheim, CA.

Searle, M. (2013). *Causes and cures in the classroom: Getting to the root of academic and behavior problems*. Alexandria, VA: Association for Supervision and Curriculum Development.

Sorby, S. A., Wysocki, A. F., & Baartmans, B. J. (2003). *Introduction to 3D spatial visualization: An active approach*. Clifton Park, NY: Delmar Cengage Learning.

Sousa, D. A. (2009). *How the brain influences behavior: Management strategies for every classroom*. Thousand Oaks, CA: Corwin Press.

Sousa, D. A., & Tomlinson, C. A. (2018). *Differentiation and the brain: How neuroscience supports the learner-friendly classroom* (2nd ed.). Bloomington, IN: Solution Tree Press.

Stein, J. (2001). The magnocellular theory of developmental dyslexia. *Dyslexia*, *7*(1), 12–36. Accessed at https://doi.org/10.1002/dys.186 on September 18, 2020.

Sterling, P., & Laughlin, S. (2015). *Principles of neural design*. Cambridge, MA: MIT Press.

Sternberg, R. J. (1996). *Successful intelligence: How practical and creative intelligence determine success in life*. New York: Simon & Schuster.

Tan, L. E. (1999). *Auditory processing at school*. Camberwell, Australia: Listening Works.

Taylor, M., Houghton, S., & Chapman, E. (2004). Primitive reflexes and attention-deficit/hyperactivity disorder: Developmental origins of classroom dysfunction. *International Journal of Special Education*, *19*(1), 23–37.

Thompson, P. M., Jahanshad, N., Ching, C. R. K., Salminen, L. E., Thomopoulos, S. I., Bright, J., et al. (2019). ENIGMA and global neuroscience: A decade of large-scale studies of the brain in health and disease across more than forty countries. *Translational Psychiatry*, *10*(1), 100. Accessed at https://doi.org/10.31234/osf.io/qnsh7 on September 18, 2020.

Tomlinson, C. A. (2017). *How to differentiate instruction in academically diverse classrooms* (3rd ed.). Alexandria, VA: Association for Supervision and Curriculum Development.

Tosto, M. G., Hanscombe, K. B., Haworth, C. M. A., Davis, O. S. P., Petrill, S. A., Dale, P. S., et al. (2014). Why do spatial abilities predict mathematical performance? *Developmental Science*, *17*(3), 462–470. Accessed at https://doi.org/10.1111/desc.12138 on September 18, 2020.

Treasure, J. (2011, July). *Julian Treasure: Five ways to listen better* [Video file]. Accessed at www.ted.com/talks/julian_treasure_5_ways_to_listen_better on September 18, 2020.

Wai, J., Lubinski, D., & Benbow, C. P. (2009). Spatial ability for STEM domains: Aligning over fifty years of cumulative psychological knowledge solidifies its importance. *Journal of Educational Psychology*, *101*(4), 817–835. Accessed at https://doi.org/10.1037/a0016127 on September 18, 2020.

Walker, M. P. (2017). *Why we sleep: Unlocking the power of sleep and dreams*. New York: Scribner.

Walker, M. P., & Stickgold, R. (2006). Sleep, memory, and plasticity. *Annual Review of Psychology*, *57*, 139–166. Accessed at https://doi.org/10.1146/annurev.psych.56.091103.070307 on September 18, 2020.

Walsh, C. (2020, February 27). What the nose knows. *Harvard Gazette*. Accessed at https://news.harvard.edu/gazette/story/2020/02/how-scent-emotion-and-memory-are-intertwined-and-exploited on October 27, 2020.

Wray, D., Medwell, J., Fox, R., & Poulson, L. (2000). The teaching practices of effective teachers of literacy. *Educational Review*, *52*(1), 75–84. Accessed at https://doi.org/10.1080/00131910097432 on September 18, 2020.

Yeo, B. T. T., Krienen, F. M., Sepulcre, J., Sabuncu, M. R., Lashkari, D., Hollinshead, M., et al. (2011). The organization of the human cerebral cortex estimated by intrinsic functional connectivity. *Journal of Neurophysiology*, *106*(3), 1125–1165. Accessed at https://doi.org/10.1152/jn.00338.2011 on September 18, 2020.

Zeliadt, N. (2014, October 7). Game tests theory of mind in autism, intellectual disability. *Spectrum News*. Accessed at www.spectrumnews.org/opinion/game-tests-theory-of-mind-in-autism-intellectual-disability on September 18, 2020.

INDEX

A

Accelerative Integrated Methodology (Maxwell), 78
accessing memory, 96
acetylcholine, 6
action estimation, 188
action plan assessment, 99
action potentials, 6
active learning, 176
adjusting task requirements, 3
aerobics, 52
ages of reading skill attainment, 152
alertness, 64
allostery, 6
amplifying positive emotions, 138
analysis assessment, 158
archer position, 47
aromas, 78
art, 15
    perceptual and motor skills, 42–43, 59
    planning and sequencing, 95
    spatial reasoning, 21–22, 25, 27, 36
assessing
    concentration and memory, 69–73
    language and word smarts, 157–161
    number smarts, 180
    people smarts, 133–136
    perceptual and motor skills, 42–46
    planning and sequencing, 98–100
    spatial reasoning, 26–28
    thinking and logic, 115–117
assessments
    action plan, 99
    auditory processing, 157
    clock-based, 180
    comprehension, 157–158
    decoding, 157
    implementation, 99
    self-monitoring, 100
    theory of the mind, 133–134
    vocabulary, 158
asymmetrical tonic neck reflex (ATNR), 47
attention deficit hyperactivity disorder (ADHD), 47
attentiveness, 15
attunement, 128, 130, 138
auditory attention, 160
auditory processing
    assessment, 157
    improving, 55–56
autism spectrum disorder, 47
avoidance, 54
axons, 6

B

balance, 41, 43, 48, 52, 58
BASE method, 78, 167
Battleship, 191
Bender, M. L., 48
best doozy, 175
blockages
    common causes in mathematics, 180
    common causes in reading, 159
    concentration and memory, 65
    language and word smarts, 153
    number smarts, 174
    people smarts, 130
    perceptual and motor skills, 41
    planning and sequencing, 90, 96
    spatial reasoning, 24
    thinking and logic, 112
Blythe, S. G., 50
body language
    people smarts, 145
    perceptual and motor skills, 43, 59
    thinking and logic, 124
Booker, C., 164

brain-based differentiation. *See* neurodevelopmental differentiation
brain density, 5
brain systems, 18
    concentration and memory, 64
    language and word smarts, 150–152
    number smarts, 173–174
    people smarts, 129–130
    perceptual and motor skills, 40–41
    planning and sequencing, 94–95
    spatial reasoning, 22–23
    thinking and logic, 109–111
breaking it down, 74–75
Brunelleschi, F., 21
Butterworth, B., 183, 185

C

calming ourselves and others, 127, 134–135, 139, 142
careers
    that use concentration and memory, 63
    that use language and word smarts, 149
    that use number smarts, 172
    that use people smarts, 127
    that use perceptual and motor skills, 39
    that use planning and sequencing, 91
    that use spatial reasoning, 22
    that use thinking and logic, 109
Carnine method, 154–155
changing problems, 181
character strengths, 3
chemical transmission, 6
chess, 122–123
Choose Your Own Adventure stories, 59, 105, 124, 167
chunking information, 78
clarity of thought, 117
Clement, G. F., 185
Clement, R., 193
clock-based assessment, 180
cloze-spelling method, 163
clumsiness, 41, 43
coaching, 3
    language, 138–139
    specialized, 200–201
COBRA (Herman), 31
Cody, R., xi
combining problems, 181
communication skills, 127
    language and word smarts, 150, 161–162
    number sense, 184
    people smarts, 135
comparison problems, 181–182
compassion, 15, 130
comprehension, 15
    assessment, 157–158
    language and word smarts, 163–164
computer games, 53–54
concentration and memory, 2, 11–12, 15, 63, 201
    additional glucose, 75
    BASE method, 79
    brain systems involved in, 64
    careers and use, 63
    chunking information, 78
    common blockages, 71–73
    cross-fertilization strategies, 85–89
    enhancing, 73
    evidence they can be improved, 73
    extending learning from language and word smarts, 167–168
    extending learning from number starts, 190, 194
    extending learning from people smarts, 145, 148
    extending learning from perceptual and motor skills, 55, 57, 60
    extending learning from spatial reasoning, 33, 36
    extending learning from thinking and logic, 111, 123, 125
    extending learning from, 86–89
    general memory assessment, 69
    helping students do better on tests, 82
    highlighting, 77
    improving inputs, 75
    improving outputs, 83
    improving processing, 77
    increasing repetition, 85
    inputs, 65–66
    journey method, 79–80
    links with other brain systems, 65
    long-term memory, 66–68
    making it visual, 76
    mapping memory across time, 76
    mnemonics, 80
    music and language training, 78
    note taking, 83–85
    other memory tests, 70
    paired associations, 70–73
    peg method, 80
    people smarts, 130
    planning and sequencing, 96
    power studying, 82–83
    practice, 79
    prioritizing, 74
    processing, 66
    reflection questions, 90
    short-term memory exercises, 81
    simplifying, 76–77
    sleep and, 77
    stimulation of the vagus nerve, 76
    sustain and selective attention, 81
    television and, 81
    unitasking, 78
    using aroma, 78
    ways to assess, 69
    what blockages look like, 65
    working memory assessment, 69–70
concrete operational stage of development, 110
confidence, 54
conflict resolution
    people smarts, 132, 135
    planning and sequencing, 105
conscious memories, 64

Index

consciousness, 4
consideration, 15
cooking, 190
coordinated activities, 15
coordination, 48
Counting on Frank (Clement), 193
creating a risk-taking classroom, 175
creativity, 15
    concentration and memory, 64
    language and word smarts, 150
    spatial reasoning, 21
Crick, F., 21
critical thinking skills, 150
cross-fertilization strategies, 4, 10–12, 17–18
    concentration and memory, 85–89
    language and word smarts, 165–168
    number smarts, 188–193
    people smarts, 143–147
    perceptual and motor skills, 56–60
    planning and sequencing, 104–106
    spatial reasoning, 32–36
    tables, 3
    thinking and logic, 121–126

D

dance
    language and word smarts, 166
    perceptual and motor skills, 39, 42, 52, 57
    planning and sequencing, 104
    spatial reasoning, 25, 29, 36
    thinking and logic, 122
da Vinci, L., 79
dealing with issues, 134
de Bono, 104
decoding, 15
    assessment, 157
deep breathing, 134
de-escalation methods, 127
deflating good news, 138
Dehaene, S., 154–155, 185
delayed gratification, 95
dendrites, 6
descriptive language, 166
design, 15
    spatial reasoning, 21–22
Diamond, A., 100
differentiated teaching, 200
digital tools, 3
distraction
    concentration and memory, 66, 72
    planning and sequencing, 96
dopamine, 6
dorsal caudal medial entorhinal cortex
    spatial reasoning, 23
drawing, 187, 189
dyscalculia, 158
    assessing, 182–183
Dyscalculia (Butterworth), 183
Dyscalculia Screener, 183

Dyscalculia Test, 183
dyslexia
    language and word smarts, 158–160
    perceptual and motor skills, 47
Dyson, J., 113
dysphasia, 160
dyspraxia, 47

E

Einstein, A., 21, 91–94
Ekman, P., 131
electrical signaling, 6
Elmore, R. F., 117
emotional intelligence, 15, 127
emotional regulation, 15
    people smarts, 127, 136
    planning and sequencing, 96
empathy, 130, 135–137
empowering, 139, 142
encoding, 15
engaging, 139–140
enhancing
    concentration and memory, 73–75
    language and word smarts, 162
    perceptual and motor skills, 51
    spatial reasoning, 29–30
Enhancing Neuro Imaging Genetics Through Meta-Analysis (ENIGMA) Consortium, 5
Escher, M. C., 122
essential fatty acids, 160
estimation activities, 181, 188
evaluating, 15
    language and word smarts, 150
    thinking and logic, 118
executive functioning, 95–96
explicit teaching, 8
    spelling, 162
expression, 15
extending learning
    from concentration and memory, 86–89
    from language and word smarts, 166–169
    from number smarts, 189–193
    from people smarts, 144–147
    from perceptual and motor skills, 57
    from planning and sequencing, 104, 106
    from spatial reasoning, 33–36
    from thinking and logic, 122–126
eye tracking. *See* visual tracking

F

false-belief tests, 133
fast and slow thinking, 91–94
feedback, 3
    constructive, 127
    perceptual and motor skills, 54
feelings barometer, 136
fencing position, 47
Fergusson, D. M., 95

Fermi questions, 123, 192
financial literacy, 174
finding your contribution, 142-142
fine motor function, 40
    improving, 53-54
    perceptual and motor skills, 44
finger gnosis, 176-177
fishbowl discussions, 121
flexible focus, 66
floppy muscle tone, 49
Flynn, J. R., 5
focus, 15
    concentration and memory, 72
    perceptual and motor skills, 54
fold-and-write method, 163
follow-through difficulties, 100
formal operational stage of development, 110
four corners, 121
Fox, R., 162
Franklin, R., 21
Frick, A., 30
Fuller, A., ix-xi, 9-11

G

Gardner, H., 4
Geelong Grammar School (Toorak, Victoria, Australia), xi
getting creative, 179
giving students time to work it out, 175-176
glucose, 75-76
glutamate, 6
goal setting, 15
    number smarts, 187
grapheme-phoneme correspondences, 155
graphemes, 154
GraphoGame, 164
graphomotor skills, 40
    improving, 54
greetings, 137
gross motor function, 40
    improving, 53
    perceptual and motor, 44
grouping students, 17
    perceptual and motor skills, 59
gullibility, 112

H

Hadid, Z., 21
hand-eye coordination
    perceptual and motor skills, 43, 48
    spatial reasoning, 24
Harris, D., 32
Hartley, V., 9-10
headlines, 121
hearing problems, 55
Herman, A. E., 31
highlighting, 77
Horwood, J. L., 95

I

identifying learning strengths, 9-10, 16-17
imagine forward and plan backward, 96
implementation
    of actions, 15
    assessment, 99
impulse control
    assessing, 98-99
    people smarts, 133
    perceptual and motor skills, 50
    planning and sequencing, 95
    thinking and logic, 112
increasing conceptual understanding, 178
individualized learning plans, x, 16
    implementing neurodevelopmental differentiation, 198, 204
    sample, 199
individual learning strength student tool, 196-197, 203
inductive and deductive reasoning, 124
influence-mapping template, 143
information processing methods
    allostery, 6
    chemical transmission, 6
    circuits of the brain
    concentration and memory, 2, 11-12, 15, 63-90
    electrical signaling, 6
    language and word smarts, 2, 11-12, 15, 149-170
    number smarts, 2, 11-12, 15, 171-194
    people smarts, 2, 11-12, 15, 127-148
    perceptual and motor skills, 2, 11-12, 15, 39-62
    planning and sequencing, 2, 11-12, 15, 91-107
    protein molecules, 6
    spatial reasoning, 2, 11-12, 15, 21-37
    thinking and logic, 2, 11-12, 15, 109-126
    understanding, 12
inputs, 10, 18
    concentration and memory, 64-68, 71-72
    defined, 13-15
    improving concentration and memory, 75-77
    improving language and word smarts, 162-164
    improving number smarts, 185-186
    improving people smarts, 136-137
    improving perceptual and motor skills, 51
    improving planning and sequencing, 102
    improving spatial reasoning, 30
    improving thinking and logic, 117-118
    language and word smarts, 154-155, 161
    number smarts, 174-177, 179-180, 184
    people smarts, 130-131, 133, 135
    perceptual and motor skills, 41, 46, 54
    planning and sequencing, 96-97, 101
    spatial reasoning, 24, 26, 28
    thinking and logic, 112, 114, 116
intelligence
    memory and, 63
    scores rising, 5-7
intentionality, 91
I Used to Think—and Now I Think— (Elmore), 117

Index

J
journey method, 77–79, 190

K
Kahneman, D., 92
Karten, T., 155
Kelly, G., 118
Kennedy, J. F., 113
knowledge of others, 134
knowledge of self, 134
Konza, D., 155
KWL charts, 178

L
labeling, 9
lack of transfer, 15
language and word smarts, 2, 11–12, 15, 149–150, 201
    brain systems involved in, 150–152
    careers that use, 149
    common causes of reading blockages, 158
    cross-fertilization strategies, 165–168
    evidence it can be improved, 162
    extending learning from, 166–168
    extending learning from concentration and memory, 88–90
    extending learning from number starts, 193–194
    extending learning from people smarts, 30, 146, 148
    extending learning from perceptual and motor skills, 40, 50, 61
    extending learning from planning and sequencing, 105, 107
    extending learning from spatial reasoning, 35–36
    extending learning from thinking and logic, 124
    how the literate brain develops, 152
    how to enhance, 162
    improving inputs, 162–164
    improving outputs, 164–165
    improving processing, 164
    inputs, 154–156, 161
    language telescopes, 153
    links with other brain systems, 153
    outputs, 156–157, 161
    processing, 156, 161
    reflection questions, 169
    ways to assess, 157–161
    what blockages look like, 153
language coaching, 138–139
language telescopes, 153
language training, 78
learning disabilities, 9
learning or subject-area profile tool, 196–197, 202
learning strengths, 1, 3, 7–8
    analysis, 198
    building on, 3
    determining, 16
    how brains process information, 4–5
    identifying, 9–10, 16–17
    leveraging, 10–12
    people smarts, 147–148
    perceptual and motor skills, 60–61
    sample grid, 17
    what they are not, 4
letter-sound combinations, 15
linking
    images, 15
    with other learning, 3, 21
    perceptual and motor skills, 54
links
    between concentration and memory and other systems, 65
    between language and word smarts and other brain systems, 153
    between number smarts and other brain systems, 174
    between people smarts and other brain systems, 130
    between perceptual and motor skills and other brain systems, 40
    between planning and sequencing and other systems, 95–96
    between spatial and other brain systems, 23
    between thinking and logic and other systems, 111
listening skills, 15
    perceptual and motor skills, 52
listening teams, 165
long-term memory, 66–68
Lovitt, C., 179
lowering the tone, 139, 142
Lowrie, T., 32

M
magnocellular cells, 159–160
making mistakes, 113
manipulating numbers, 15
many routes, same destination, 175
mapping skills
    number smarts, 191
    perceptual and motor skills, 58
    spatial reasoning, 25, 27–28
mathematics. *See also* number smarts
    concentration and memory, 64
    language and word smarts, 167, 169
    number smarts, 147
    perceptual and motor skills, 48, 60
    planning and sequencing, 95
    Shanghai mastery method, 175–176
    spatial reasoning, 22, 24, 36
    thinking and logic, 122, 125
Maths300 (Lovitt), 179
Maxwell, W., 78
Medwell, J., 162
Mehrabian, A., 140
memory. *See also* concentration and memory
    accessing, 96
    conscious, 64

intelligence and, 63
long-term, 66–68
muscle, 15, 53, 57
short-term exercises, 81
skills, 57
thinking and logic, 111
unconscious, 64
mental rotation, 29, 32
Michelangelo, 21
Mighton, J., 185
Minecraft, 122
mirror neurons, 129–130
Mischel, W., 95
mnemonics, 80
modeling
culture of learning, 175
language and word smarts, 164
number smarts, 178
spatial reasoning, 26
Monopoly, 189
Monument Valley, 122
motivation, 8
people smarts, 135
multicultural classrooms, 136
multiple intelligences (Gardner), 4
muscle memory, 15
improving, 53, 57
music
concentration and memory, 78
language and word smarts, 166
number smarts, 190
perceptual and motor skills, 42, 58, 60
planning and sequencing, 95, 102, 104, 106
myelination, 4
My Learning Strengths, 3, 10, 16, 195–196, 198, 200

N

NASA, 113
navigation skills, 22
neurodevelopmental differentiation, x, 1, 3, 8–9
approach, 12–13, 197–198
differentiated teaching, 200
implementing, 195
individualized learning plans, 198–199, 204
individual learning strength student tool, 196–197, 203
introducing to teachers, 195–196
learning or subject-area profile tool, 196–197, 202
learning-strengths analysis, 198
leveraging learning strengths, 10–12
purpose of, 16
specialized coaching, 200–201
ten things teachers need to know, 7–8
neurodiversity, 7
Neuromotor Immaturity in Children and Adults (Blythe), 50
neurons, 6
neuroplasticity, 6, 50–52

neurotransmitters, 6
Newcombe, N. S., 30
norepinephrine, 6
North Eastern Education and Library Board, 47
note taking
concentration and memory, 83–85
language and word smarts, 165
number sense, 172, 176, 179
number smarts, 2, 11–12, 15, 171–172, 201
brain systems involved in, 173–174
careers that use, 172
common causes of mathematics blockages, 180
cross-fertilization strategies, 188–193
evidence they can be improved, 185
extending learning from, 189–193
extending learning from concentration and memory, 89, 90
extending learning from people smarts, 130, 147
extending learning from perceptual and motor skills, 60–61
extending learning from planning and sequencing, 106–107
extending learning from spatial reasoning, 36
extending learning from thinking and logic, 125–126
extending learning through language and word smarts, 167, 169
improving inputs, 185–186
improving outputs, 187–188
improving processing, 186
inputs, 174–177, 179, 184
links with other brain systems, 174
outputs, 179, 184
processing, 177–179, 184
reflection questions, 194
ways to assess, 180–185
what blockages look like, 174
numeracy, 187
Numeracy Screener, 183

O

observing feelings, 139, 141
optimizing information processing, 177
oral language, 150
Organisation for Economic Co-operation and Development, 32
organizing
information, 15
planning and sequencing, 96
spatial reasoning, 26
orienteering
perceptual and motor skills, 58
spatial reasoning, 25
origami
perceptual and motor skills, 52, 57
planning and sequencing, 104
spatial reasoning, 29, 32

Index

oromotor skills, 40
    improving, 56
    perceptual and motor, 44–45
orthographic stage of reading, 155
outputs, 10, 18
    concentration and memory, 64, 67–68, 71–73
    defined, 13–15
    improving concentration and memory, 83–85
    improving language and word smarts, 164–165
    improving number smarts, 187–188
    improving people smarts, 139–143
    improving perceptual and motor skills, 53–56
    improving planning and sequencing, 102–103
    improving spatial reasoning, 31
    improving thinking and logic, 120–121
    language and word smarts, 156–157, 161
    number smarts, 179–180, 184
    people smarts, 132–133, 135
    perceptual and motor skills, 42–43, 46, 54
    planning and sequencing, 97, 101
    sequential, 103
    spatial reasoning, 25–26, 28
    thinking and logic, 114, 116
oxytocin, 129

P

pack-up time, 188
paired associations, 70–73
Panamath, 183
parent-teacher-student meetings, 1, 200–201
parvocellular cells, 159
pattern detection/matching
    concentration and memory, 63, 66, 72
    language and word smarts, 159
    number smarts, 172
    perceptual and motor skills, 54
    spatial reasoning, 22, 24–25
Pegg, J., 164
peg method, 80
people smarts, 2, 11–12, 15, 127, 201
    attunement, 128
    blockages, 130
    brain systems involved in, 129–130
    careers that use, 127
    concentration and memory, 65
    cross-fertilization strategies, 143–147
    elements of advanced, 128
    extending learning from, 144–147
    extending learning from concentration and memory, 88–89
    extending learning from language and word smarts. 167
    extending learning from number starts, 193–194
    extending learning from perceptual and motor skills, 59, 61
    extending learning from planning and sequencing, 105–106
    extending learning from spatial reasoning, 35, 36
    extending learning from thinking and logic, 124, 126
    how to assess, 133–136
    improving inputs, 136–137
    improving output, 139–143
    improving processing, 137–139
    inputs, 130–131
    links with other brain systems, 130
    outputs, 132
    processing, 131–132
    reflection questions, 148
    security, 128
    theory of mind, 128
perceptual and motor skills, 2, 11–12, 15, 39–40, 117, 201
    addressing primitive reflexes, 50
    assessing, 42–43
    asymmetrical tonic neck reflex, 47
    brain systems involved, 40–41
    careers that use, 39
    cross-fertilization strategies, 56–60
    enhancing, 52
    evidence they can be improved, 50–52
    extending learning from concentration and memory, 86, 89
    extending learning from language and word smarts, 166, 168
    extending learning from number starts, 190, 194
    extending learning from people smarts, 130, 144, 148
    extending learning from planning and sequencing, 104, 106
    extending learning from spatial reasoning, 33, 36
    extending learning from thinking and logic, 122, 125
    fine motor skills, 44
    general, 45
    gross motor skills, 44
    how to improve auditory processing, 55–56
    how to improve eye tracking, 54–55
    how to improve fine motor functioning, 53–54
    how to improve graphomotor skills, 54
    how to improve gross motor functioning, 53
    how to improve muscle memory, 53
    how to improve oromotor functioning, 56
    improving inputs, 52
    improving outputs, 53
    improving processing, 52–53
    inputs, 41
    links with other brain systems, 41
    list of, 46
    oromotor skills, 44–45
    outputs, 42
    primitive reflexes, 45–50
    processing, 42
    reflection questions, 61
    symmetrical tonic neck reflex, 48
    tonic labyrinthine reflex, 48
    visual tracking, 43–44
    what blockages look like, 41
perceptual sensitivity, 15
persistence, 96

personal space, 133, 135, 140
phonemes, 154
phonemic awareness, 150
phonological games, 154
phonological stage of reading, 154
phonology, 154
Piaget, J., 110
Pictionary, 166
pictorial stage of reading, 153, 156
planning and sequencing, 2, 11–12, 15, 91, 201
    assessing, 98–100
    brain systems involved in, 94–95
    careers that use, 91
    cross-fertilization strategies, 104
    different types of thinking, 92–94
    evidence they can be improved, 100–101
    extending learning from, 104–106
    extending learning from concentration and memory, 87, 89
    extending learning from language and word smarts, 168
    extending learning from number starts, 191, 194
    extending learning from people smarts, 130, 145, 148
    extending learning from perceptual and motor skills, 48, 58, 60
    extending learning from spatial reasoning, 25–26, 28, 34, 36
    extending learning from thinking and logic, 123, 125
    improving inputs, 102
    improving outputs, 102
    improving processing, 102
    inputs, 96–79, 101
    links with other brain systems, 95–96
    outputs, 97, 101
    processing, 97, 101
    reflection questions, 107
    sequencing, 103
    sequential ordering, 103
    sequential outputs, 103
    what blockages look like, 96
planning a virtual trip, 188
Poulson, L., 162
power studying, 82–83
practical intelligence projects, 84–85
practice, 5–7, 53, 57
    concentration and memory, 78
    deliberate, 29
    language and word smarts, 162
    number smarts, 177, 190
preoperational stage of development, 110
primacy and recency effect, 75
primitive reflexes, 45–47
    addressing, 50
    ATNR, 47
    list of issues with, 51
    signs of, 49–50
    STNR, 48
    TLR, 48

prioritization, 15, 74
processing, 10, 18
    concentration and memory, 64, 66–68, 71–73
    defined, 13–15
    improving concentration and memory, 77–81
    improving language and word smarts, 164
    improving number smarts, 186
    improving people skills, 137–139
    improving perceptual and motor skills, 52–53
    improving planning and sequencing, 102
    improving spatial reasoning, 30–31
    improving thinking and logic, 118–119
    language and word smarts, 156, 161
    number smarts, 177–180, 184
    people smarts, 131–133, 135
    perceptual and motor skills, 42–43, 46, 54
    planning and sequencing, 97, 101
    spatial reasoning, 24–26, 28
    thinking and logic, 113–114, 116
puzzles
    perceptual and motor skills, 54
    spatial reasoning, 25, 27–28, 32
    thinking and logic, 122

Q

questioning yourself, 113
QuickSmart Literacy (Pegg et al.), 164

R

reading, 15 (*see also* language and word smarts)
    ages of skill attainment, 152
    auditory processing, 56
    brain systems involved, 150–151
    concentration and memory, 64
    people, 127
    perceptual and motor skills, 48–49, 59
    planning and sequencing, 95
    stages of learning, 153–154
    whole-word vs. phonics education, 155–156
Reading in the Brain (Dehaene), 154
reflection, 187
reflection questions
    concentration and memory, 90
    language and word smarts, 169
    number smarts, 194
    people smarts, 148
    perceptual and motor skills, 61
    planning and sequencing, 107
    spatial reasoning, 37
    thinking and logic, 126
repetition
    increasing, 85
    number smarts, 177–178
RESOLVE method, 139
responding
    to good news, 138
    with respect, 139
retrieval, 15

Index

retrosplenial cortex, 23
rhythm games
    number smarts, 190
    perceptual and motor skills, 50, 52
    planning and sequencing, 102
rock climbing, 52, 58
Rowe, K., 155
Rube Goldberg machines, 104
rubrics, 3

S

same, same but different, 118–119
Sapolsky, R. M., 100
science skills
    planning and sequencing, 95
    spatial reasoning, 22
Searle, M., 100
security, 128
see, think, wonder, 120
seeking understanding, 139–141
self-awareness, 133, 135
self-denigration, 2, 9
self-monitoring assessment, 100
sensitivity toward others, 131–132
sensorimotor stage of development, 110
sensory awareness, 41
sequencing. *See also* planning and sequencing
    assessment, 100
    language and word smarts, 164
    number sense, 184
sequential ordering, 103
sequential outputs, 103, 191
serotonin, 6
Shanghai mastery method of mathematics, 175–176
Short-Term Auditory Memory (STAM) test, 55
short-term memory exercises, 81
sight words, 156
similarities and differences, 15
simplifying, 76–77
Singapore bar method, 176–177
sitting straight, 49
sleep
    concentration and memory, 77
    deprivation, 111
slumping, 49
social cues, 133
social skills, 15
Sorby, S. A., 32
spatial reasoning, 2, 11–12, 15, 21, 200
    brain systems involved, 22–23
    careers that use, 22
    cross-fertilization strategies, 32
    enhancing, 29–30
    evidence it can be improved, 29
    extending learning from, 33–36
    extending learning from concentration and memory, 86, 89
    extending learning from language and word smarts, 166, 168
    extending learning from number smarts, 176, 187, 189, 194
    extending learning from people smarts, 130, 144, 148
    extending learning from perceptual and motor skills, 57, 60–61
    extending learning from planning and sequencing, 104, 106
    extending learning from thinking and logic, 122, 125
    improving inputs, 30
    improving outputs, 31
    improving processing, 30–31
    inputs, 24
    key signs, 26
    links with other brain systems, 23
    outputs, 25–26
    processing, 24–25
    reflection questions, 37
    STEM and, 32
    ways to assess, 26–28
    what blockages look like, 24
specialized coaching, 200–201
Speech Perception in Noise (SPIN) test, 55
speech therapy, 56
spelling, 162–163
splaying, 49
sports, 15
    perceptual and motor skills, 41–42, 58
    spatial reasoning, 21
    thinking and logic, 122
stages of developing thinking and logic, 110
stalling conversations, 138
statements and the fears behind them, 141
stealing the limelight, 138
STEAM, 176
Stein, J., 160
STEM
    perceptual and motor skills, 58
    spatial reasoning, 32
stress, 130
    managing, 127
Students Create the Future, 142–143
sustained and selective attention exercise, 81
sustained learning, 15
syllabification, 163
symbolic language
    spatial reasoning, 23
symmetrical tonic neck reflex (STNR), 48
synapses, 6

T

table tennis, 52
tactile learning, 24
take-a-picture method, 163
Tan, L. E., 55
team poetry, 165

television
    concentration and memory, 81
    language and word smarts, 167
test taking
    concentration and memory, 64
    helping students, 81
    power studying, 82–83
Tetris
    spatial reasoning, 29
    thinking and logic, 122
theory of the mind, 128
    assessment, 133–134
think, puzzle, explore, 120
thinking and logic, 2, 11–12, 15, 201, 109–110
    brain systems involved in, 110–111
    careers that use, 109
    cross-fertilization strategies, 121–122
    evidence they can be improved, 117
    extending learning from, 122–125
    extending learning from concentration and memory, 87, 89
    extending learning from language and word smarts, 167, 169
    extending learning from number starts, 192, 194
    extending learning from people smarts, 130, 146, 148
    extending learning from perceptual and motor skills, 58, 61
    extending learning from planning and sequencing, 105–106
    extending learning from spatial reasoning, 34, 36
    improving inputs, 117–118
    improving outputs, 120–121
    improving processing, 118–119
    inputs, 112, 116
    links with other brain systems, 111
    outputs, 114, 116
    processing, 113, 116
    reflection questions, 126
    stages of development, 110
    ways to assess, 115–117
    what blockages look like, 112
thinking twice, 146
time sense
    perceptual and motor skills, 48
    planning and sequencing, 95
tonic labyrinthine reflex (TLR), 48
Tools to Grow, 50
trail-making tests
    planning and sequencing, 105
    spatial reasoning, 27–28
trigonometry, 21

U

unconscious memories, 64
understanding simple ideas, 112
unitasking, 78
universal emotions, 131
Unlocking Your Child's Genius (Fuller), 10
upper, dorsal stream, 159

V

vagus nerve, 5
    stimulation, 76
value adding, 139, 142
vestibular system, 42–43
vision problems, 47
visual awareness, 15
visualization
    number sense, 184
    number smarts, 176
    spatial reasoning, 21–22, 31, 36
visual processing, 159–160
visuals, 3
    concentration and memory, 76, 83
    planning and sequencing, 104, 106
    symbols, 150
visual tracking, 43–44
    improving, 54–55
vocabulary
    assessment, 158
    language and word smarts, 153–154, 162
    perceptual and motor skills, 54

W

Watson, J., 21
whole-word vs. phonics education, 155–156
within yourself, 131–132
word finds, 165
working together, 175
Wray, D., 162
writing
    common blockages, 54
    language and word smarts, 150, 161, 164
    perceptual and motor skills, 40, 43, 59

Y

yoga, 52

Z

zoom in, 120

www.ingramcontent.com/pod-product-compliance
Lightning Source LLC
Chambersburg PA
CBHW081719100526
44591CB00016B/2431